Applied Linguistics and Language Study

General Editor: C. N. Candlin

Bilingualism in Education:

Aspects of theory, research and practice

Jim Cummins and Merrill Swain

Longman

London and New York

Longman Group UK Limited
Longman House, Burnt Mill, Harlow,
Essex CM20 2JE, England
and Associated Companies throughout the world.

© Longman Group Limited 1986

Published in the United States of America by
Longman Inc., New York

First published 1986

BRITISH LIBRARY CATALOGUING IN PUBLICATION DATA
Cummins, Jim, *1949–*
  Bilingualism in education: aspects of theory,
  research and practice. – (Applied linguistics
  and language study)
  1. Education, Bilingual
  I. Title   II. Swain, Merrill   III. Series
  371.97   LC3715

LIBRARY OF CONGRESS CATALOGING IN PUBLICATION DATA
Cummins, Jim, 1949–
  Bilingualism in education.
  (Applied linguistics and language study)
  Bibliography: p.
  Includes index.
  1. Education, Bilingual – Canada. 2. Bilingualism in
  children – Canada. 3. Bilingualism in children – Canada –
  Evaluation. 4. Students – Canada – Language – Evaluation.
  5. Linguistic minorities – Education – Canada. I. Swain,
  Merrill. II. Title. III. Series.
  LC3734.C853   1986   371.97'00971   85-23149

Set in 10/12pt Erhardt Roman, Linotron 202
Printed in Great Britain
by Mackay's of Chatham, Kent

ISBN 0 582 55380 6

Acknowledgements

There are a number of people who have had input in so many ways to the ideas in this book. We would particularly like to thank those who have taken the time from their busy schedules to read and comment on one or more drafts of one or more chapters which appear in this volume: Patrick Allen, Christina Bratt Paulston, Michael Canale, Alister Cumming, Sonia Fiorucci, Daina Green, Birgit Harley, R. Keith Johnson, Jill Kamin, Lilly Katsaiti, Eric Kellerman, Richard Kidd, Sharon Lapkin, Francis Mangubhai, David Olson, Sandra Savignon, Jacquelyn Schachter, Tove Skutnabb-Kangas, Nina Spada, Peter Tung, Mari Wesche and Lily Wong Fillmore. We also wish to express thanks to Mary Lou King, Jud Burtis and Gila Hanna who have been invaluable in keeping data files organized and systematic and in providing statistical advice and interpretation in our recent research.

We are indebted to the following for permission to reproduce articles written by the authors:

Cambridge University Press for 'Bilingualism, cognitive functioning and education' from pp. 4–18 *Language Teaching and Linguistics: Abstracts* (1979); Newbury House Publishers Inc. for 'Language proficiency and academic achievement' from pp. 108–126 *Issues in Language Testing Research* ed. J W Oller Jr, Copyright 1983 Newbury House Publishers Inc., Rowley, Mass. 01969 and 'Communicative competence: some roles of comprehensible input and comprehensible output in its development' from pp. 235–253 *Input and Second Language Acquisition* eds. S Gass and C Madden, Copyright 1985 Newbury House Publishers Inc.; Pergamon Press Ltd for 'A review of immersion education in Canada: research and evaluation studies' from pp. 35–51 *ELT Documents 119* (1984); Sage Publications Inc. for 'Bilingualism and the development of metalinguistic awareness' from pp. 131–149 *Journal of Cross-Cultural Psychology* Vol. 9 No. 2 (June 1978); M Swain, S Lapkin and C M Andrew for their article 'Early French immersion later on' from pp. 1–23 *Journal of*

Multilingual and Multicultural Development Vol. 2 No. 1 (1981); Swets Publishing Service for 'Minority students and learning difficulties: issues in assessment and placement' from pp. 47–68 *Early Bilingualism and Child Development* eds. Y Lebrun and M Paradis (1984); Teachers of English to Speakers of Other Languages for 'Bilingualism without tears' from pp. 35–46 *On TESOL '82: Pacific Perspectives on Language Learning and Teaching* eds. M Clarke and J Handscombe (1983): John Wiley and Sons Inc., Addison-Wesley Publishing Company and Pergamon Press Ltd for 'Large scale communicative language testing: a case study' from pp. 133–147 *Language Learning and Communication* Vol. 2 No. 2 (1983) reprinted by Addison-Wesley Publishing Co. in *Initiatives in Communicative Language Teaching: A Book of Readings* eds. S Savignon and M Berns (1984) and in *New Directions in Language Testing* eds. A Fok and G Low (1985) by Pergamon Press Ltd.

Contents

	page
Preface	ix
Introduction	xiii
Part One: The educational development of bilingual children	1
Section 1 Metalinguistic and cognitive development	3
1 Bilingualism, cognitive functioning and education	7
2 Bilingualism and the development of metalinguistic awareness	20
Section 2 Bilingual education	33
3 A review of immersion education in Canada: research and evaluation studies	37
4 Early French immersion later on	57
5 Linguistic interdependence: a central principle of bilingual education	80
Section 3 Programme planning for bilingualism	97
6 Bilingualism without tears	99

Part Two: Bilingual proficiency   111

Section 4 The construct of bilingual proficiency   113

7 Communicative competence: some roles of comprehensible
   input and comprehensible output in its development   116

8 Language proficiency and academic achievement   138

Section 5 The assessment of language proficiency   163

9 Large-scale communicative language testing: a case study   165

10 Minority students and learning difficulties: issues in
    assessment and placement   183

Section 6 A synthesis   205

11 Towards a theory of bilingual proficiency development   207

Bibliography   215

Index   231

Preface

For researchers and practitioners engaged in bilingual education, the Canadian experience has long been an area of central interest. Until recently, however, there has been a lack of a convenient guide to this applied research, in a form which could speak to teachers and policy-makers as well as to academic researchers. In this latest contribution to the *Applied Linguistics and Language Study* series, Jim Cummins and Merrill Swain offer a coherent synthesis of recent theoretical and empirical work relating to the educational development of bilingual children from both majority and minority language backgrounds. Issues that have long been controversial, such as the consequences of bilingualism for cognitive development, or the impact of maintaining and developing the minority child's mother tongue on the acquisition of the majority language, receive critical attention and analysis in this edited collection of papers. Furthermore, the book gives focus to the importance of defining the nature of language proficiency in a cross-lingual context, and to the modes of its assessment. In so doing, the arguments of the authors have considerable implications for language planning and educational policy in a wide variety of countries and educational systems, not merely in the Canadian and North American context.

Implicit in these arguments is a triangular interdependence between research, policy and practice. This is not merely characteristic of bilingualism and education, but of applied linguistics more generally. Indeed, this book is an admirable defence of the subject matter of the series as a whole of which it forms a part. The papers see issues in human communication as problems to be explored and responded to; they demonstrate experimental procedures in action and are admirably explicit about their execution in the work and study places of their subjects; they make a contribution to theory and do not merely draw upon it; most particularly, they concentrate on raising problems and suggesting practical solutions. The collection thus serves those who research, those who make policy and those whose practice ought, desirably, to contribute to both. Despite this general relevance, however, Jim Cummins' and Merrill Swain's volume has a particular topic and message.

For the practitioners, we hope that the evidence and experience marshalled here will not only confirm what many believe, that there is a major advantage to be won in developing to the full proficiency in both the languages of bilinguals. It will also help to satisfy a need to provide practitioners with arguments to make cases for resource allocation and for flexibility within the organization of teaching in their schools. More than that, however, the explicitness of the research documentation will provide for some at least, the opportunity and the occasion for their own action research within their schools.

For researchers, there is evidence here to be corroborated and challenged in different circumstances than those of the authors' original studies, as well as agenda for future investigations: into universals in language acquisition, into explanatory hypotheses upon which performance predictions can be based, into the appropriate mix of research methods. Beyond these, however, is the challenge posed by the papers to make research available to those who have not only contributed to their data but deserve their results. That has always been an unsung maxim of the research tradition of the current authors and ought to be recognized as a major principle of applied linguistics research more generally.

For policy-makers, bi- and multilingualism is a critical and tendentious issue, fraught with social, personal and political problems for educational planning. This is everywhere to be seen, not merely in Canada or in the U.K. A glance at the reception of recent policy documents (*inter alia* the 1985 Swann Report *Education for All* in the U.K.) only serves to underline the need for such public statements to be based on the broadest possible research and evidence, especially if they are intent upon curriculum change. There would be less fudging of the issues, and a clearer link between hopes and fulfilment if consistent research findings were consistently followed through into practice. There is little defence against prejudiced publicity if even educational policy documents are under-informed. Not that the authors are proclaiming the direct transferability of research from one system, one set of linguistic, social and educational factors, to any other. What is being argued for is an awareness of the underlying theory, empirically supported, on the basis of which predictive statements can be made with the expectation of general applicability. At very least, given the theoretical position outlined in this book, policy-makers should now be encouraged to promote local initiatives aimed at testing out the theory.

It would, however, be misleading to suggest in this General Editor's Preface, that all aspects of this expansive topic were touched upon, let alone given adequate treatment. Two such aspects spring to mind, both of which are honestly acknowledged in the papers and the useful Introduction which follows. First is the need for clear, classroom and school-based models for bi- and multilingual educational practice, aimed at the heart of the roles of teachers and learners and the social climate of the institution. Second, to augment the quantitative measures of educational research with equally relevant qualitative accounts of participants' reactions to the process of bilingual education, sensitive to the ethnic and social variation characteristic of the domain. These two aspects are, of course, crucially related, and neither can be separated from those political, social, ethnic and ideological pressures to which we have earlier referred. It ought not to be a pious hope to advocate a consortial approach between the three contributors to applied linguistics – research, policy and practice: it ought to be indispensable, as this book makes plain.

Christopher N. Candlin *Lancaster*
General Editor *1985*

Introduction

This book is about one facet of the relationship between schools and children. That facet is bilingualism. It is a facet which is enormously rich and diverse in its complexity. Bilingual children, for example, may go to school and face a unilingual or a bilingual environment, just as unilingual children may go to school and face a bilingual or a second unilingual environment. A child's ability in each language may vary from none to fluent proficiency in both oral and literacy skills on entry to school. Each language may have associated with it a particular ethnicity, a particular religion or a particular nationality that will give it its own social, economic and political status in the community.

This book is about one small part of the bilingual interface between school and child. It is an attempt to come to terms with the meaning of 'bilingual proficiency'[1] in an *educational* setting. Is the best way to develop second language skills to immerse a child in that language? Why have bilingual education at all if the point of the educational system is to foster growth and development in only one language? When is a child ready to be instructed in his or her second language? How does one interpret test scores of children tested in their second language? Questions such as these can be answered only with an adequate conceptualization of 'bilingual proficiency'. In this book, through an analysis of relevant theoretical and empirical literature, two concepts of bilingual proficiency are defined and reconciled, and questions such as those above are considered.

The book addresses several audiences. Researchers are one audience. This book is intended to indicate useful directions for future research. For example, our synthesis of current research concerned with bilingual proficiency raises questions about which specific aspects of language are cross-lingual and which are not (Wald 1984). The research discussed also serves to remind us that our theory is only as good as the operationalizations of our constructs. If these are weak, then so are the generalizations drawn from them. Finally, the research illustrates the need to use a variety of analytical procedures: regression analyses, correlational analyses and analyses of variance, each provides a different window through which to observe one's data. Not considered in this volume, but equally important, is the need to use ethnographic tools to complement the sort of quantitative data found in this book.

We particularly hope that policy-makers and educational practitioners read this book because practice in schools can change only as a result of decisions based on their understanding of the issues. This book should help to provide policy-makers and teachers with a research and theory-based rationale for bilingual education and suggestions for its programmatic structure and implementation. The bilingual education research reported in the present volume is focused primarily on programmatic rather than instructional variables. This focus reflects the concern of many policy-makers and educators in the evolution of bilingual programmes for both majority and minority students to assess the consequences of less instructional time through the majority language.

The polarization that is evident among press commentators and educators regarding the effects of bilingual education on the academic progress of minority language students is sobering when one considers that bilingualism and bilingual education are phenomena which have been studied since ancient times (Lewis 1976) and which exist in a large majority of nations. Systematic empirical research on these issues has been carried out since the early 1900s, and yet the general impression, at least in the United States, appears to be that the research basis for bilingual education policy is minimal or nonexistent.

In fact, there is a considerable amount of policy-relevant research on bilingual education whose findings are consistent and unambiguous (e.g. Egan and Goldsmith 1981; Rosier and Holm, 1980; Troike 1978). This research has been ignored in the policy debate for several interrelated reasons: first, policy-makers and researchers have tended to ask simplistic, unanswerable questions (e.g. 'Is bilingual education effective?') rather than carefully examining and attempting to understand the patterns that exist in the research data. Second, the political polarization of the issue has resulted in each side clinging to conventional wisdoms and selectively screening out or dismissing any incompatible data. Although some advocates and opponents of bilingual education may realize that their assumptions are inadequate to account for all the data, they fear the political consequences of admitting this. The result is that, to policy-makers, the research data invoked to support opposing conventional wisdoms appears contradictory.

The third, and most fundamental reason why there appears to be little research basis for policy, is that commentators and policy-makers have failed to realize that data or 'facts' from bilingual programmes become interpretable only in the context of a coherent theory from which predictions about programme outcomes under different conditions can be generated. Policy-makers and educators have not realized that although research findings cannot be *directly* applied across contexts (e.g. French immersion findings cannot be applied directly to the minority language situations in the United States), theories are almost by definition applicable across contexts in that the validity of any theoretical principle is assessed precisely by how well it can account for the research findings in a variety of contexts. If a theory cannot account for a particular set of research findings, then it is an inadequate or incomplete theory.

The two conventional wisdoms which constitute the most frequently invoked arguments for and against bilingual education in the United States are examples of patently inadequate theoretical principles. The 'linguistic mismatch' hypothesis that a home-school language switch results in academic retardation is refuted by the French immersion data as well as by the success of a considerable number of minority students under language switch conditions. The opposing argument is that if minority students are deficient in English then they need as much exposure to English as possible. This 'maximum exposure' hypothesis is similarly refuted by the results of virtually every bilingual programme that has ever been evaluated (including French immersion programmes), all of which show that students instructed through a minority language for all or part of the school day perform over time as well or better in the majority language (e.g. English) as students instructed exclusively through the majority language.

In examining what the research on bilingual programmes tells us about second language acquisition and pedagogy, it is useful to distinguish two types of explanatory hypotheses or variables. The first involves variables such as 'exposure to the second language (L2)' and 'linguistic mismatch' which are likely to play some role in accounting for learning outcomes but whose effects are mediated or even offset by other variables. Thus, it is certainly more difficult to learn initial academic skills through the second language than through the first (L1), but under some conditions this difficulty is mitigated such that no long-term academic problems are encountered. These types of variables can be termed interactive predictor variables in that their effects in any particular context are dependent upon how they interact with other predictor variables. Educational policy based exclusively on one of these variables in isolation with no account taken of its interactions with other predictor variables is unlikely to achieve the desired policy objectives. This is a major reason why bilingual education policy in the United States, which is based on the linguistic mismatch hypothesis, has had such mixed results.

The second type of explanatory hypotheses involves what can be termed universal predictor variables in that consistent effects are observed across a wide variety of contexts. For example, if it were shown that children's L1 conceptual proficiency on school entry reliably predicted the development of L2 academic proficiency in a large number of socio-educational contexts, then L1 conceptual proficiency might be regarded as a universal predictor variable. Educational policy can be reliably based on these explanatory principles since their effects are not significantly mediated or reduced through interaction with other variables. Two candidates for this status will be suggested in Part One of this book: the 'threshold hypothesis' and the 'interdependence hypothesis'.

In discussing theory in bilingual education we refer to both 'hypotheses' and 'principles'. Our use of these terms can be distinguished with reference to the probability of predictions based on the hypothesis or principle being borne out. Specifically, we use the term 'hypotheses' in a neutral sense with respect to the probable correctness of predictions whereas 'principles' strongly imply that associated predictions will be borne out. Thus, the same prediction may initially be referred to as a 'hypothesis' but later, as a result of cumulative supportive evidence, warrant the status of 'principle'.

Outline of book

This book is divided into two parts, each with three sections. Part One is concerned with the linguistic, cognitive and academic consequences of bilingual education for both minority and majority language children. In its totality, it provides evidence to support two explanatory hypotheses.

The first hypothesis is that linguistic, cognitive and academic advantages are associated with high levels of proficiency in *both* languages. In other words, in order for positive consequences of bilingualism to manifest themselves, 'threshold' levels of proficiency in both languages must be attained. Different educational treatments for minority and majority language children will be needed to achieve this goal. For majority children large doses of education in their *second* language will be required, whereas for minority language children large doses of education in their *first* language will be required. That is to say, the way to achieve high levels of bilingual proficiency is to promote the development of the minority language – the non-dominant, non-prestige language – in school. Section 1, in particular, makes this point.

The second hypothesis is that some aspects of linguistic proficiency are cross-lingual. This means that for those aspects of language proficiency which are interdependent across languages, instruction in one language will benefit both languages. This point is developed in Section 2 through reference to the outcomes of research associated with bilingual education for majority and minority language children. Also research examining the relationships between age and second language learning and between patterns of language use in the home and academic achievement is reviewed to provide evidence to support the 'interdependence hypothesis'.

In Section 3, the concluding section of Part One, several peda-gogical proposals for planning programmes aimed at achieving bilingualism are outlined. The proposals made are consistent with the threshold and interdependence hypotheses.

Part Two presents two different ways of conceptualizing bilingual proficiency, illustrating in Section 4 how theory and research interact in developing a particular view, and illustrating in Section 5 how each view provides a rationale for the development and interpretation of assessment procedures.

Section 4 reinforces the fact that any concept of bilingual pro-ficiency must be a dynamic one: one whose internal relationships are seen to change with the social, cultural and educational contexts of learning. Research should be directed at uncovering how the internal dimensions of bilingual proficiency change with changing conditions rather than trying to demonstrate the existence of any 'absolute' model. In this way our understanding of the complexities of bilingualism will be enhanced.

Section 5 demonstrates the very direct way in which theory and practice interact. Chapter 9 shows how one particular model of language proficiency determined the form that test construction took and the scoring procedures used. Chapter 10 illustrates how a particular view of bilingual language proficiency can influence the ways in which test scores are interpreted. Without an adequate conceptualization of bilingual proficiency, the very real danger of misinterpretation is present. Misinterpretation of test scores can lead to inappropriate diagnosis and treatment, and serious underrating of students' academic potential.

We have always considered the two views of bilingual proficiency presented in this book as complementary, each appropriate for the use it was developed. In Section 6, the concluding section, we attempt to synthesize the two frameworks. The synthesis is an empirically-based one. That is to say, it is a synthesis based on the research data we have presented throughout the book. The conclusion reached is that while all aspects of language proficiency are dependent both on variables associated with attributes of the learner and with use of the target languages, some aspects of language proficiency are relatively more dependent on one set of variables than the other. Those aspects which are relatively more related to attributes of the learner are those aspects which are cross-lingual and hence are supported by development in either of the bilingual's languages. Those aspects which are relatively more related to language use variables – in particular, grammatical proficiency – rely on interaction with target language speakers and texts in each language for their development.

Notes

1. We use the terms 'proficiency', 'performance' and 'competence' interchangeably throughout the text for stylistic variation. Similarly, 'learning' and 'acquisition' are used interchangeably. Theoretical distinctions made elsewhere with respect to these terms are not intended.

Part One

The educational development of bilingual children

Section 1
Metalinguistic and cognitive development

This section is concerned with the cognitive and metalinguistic development of bilingual children. Both in the research and public-media literature, controversy about the relationship between bilingualism and cognitive functioning exists. Some have argued that bilingualism will necessarily have a negative effect on cognitive development because having, for example, two labels for each concept will be confusing and result in retarded conceptual development. Others have argued that this very same phenomenon will enhance cognitive growth: having two labels will force an early separation of word from its referent. This early separation of linguistic form from meaning, it is argued, will lead to a more analytic orientation to language and to the substance it conveys, thus enriching conceptual development. From this viewpoint, one would predict, for example, that a bilingual individual would be better able to detect linguistic ambiguities than would a unilingual individual, or be better able to restructure conceptual schemata.

In summarizing the research literature addressing this question, McLaughlin (1984) states that: 'It seems clear that the child who has mastered two languages has a linguistic advantage over the monolingual child. Bilingual children become aware that there are two ways of saying the same thing.' (p. 214). However, he goes on to raise the issue of whether this sensitivity to the lexical and formal aspects of language generalizes to cognitive functioning.

As Chapter 1 indicates, there is evidence to support both the position that bilingualism is negatively associated with metalinguistic and cognitive development and the position that it is positively associated with them. Chapter 2 provides a concrete example of a study which examines the relationship between bilingualism and metalinguistic development. The study is included in order that readers can see first-hand the nature of the studies which underlie the summary statements found in Chapter 1. This study, like many others discussed in Chapter 1, has its methodological weaknesses.

Indeed, one likely reason for the contradictory findings – of discovering both positive and negative associations between bilingualism and metalinguistic and cognitive development – lies in the methodology of the research. For example, the dependent variables which have been used in the studies, all of which purport to measure an aspect of metalinguistic or cognitive functioning, are themselves quite diverse. Measures have ranged from detection of structural ambiguities in isolated sentences to performance on Piagetian tasks and standardized tests of intelligence. It is not at all clear what the variety of dependent measures which have been used have in common. An understanding of task commonalities awaits theoretical advances (see, for example, Bialystok and Ryan (in press)).

Similarly, the independent measure – bilingualism – has been variously measured. Measurement of bilingualism has ranged from an examination of the surnames of the students tested to a comparison of performance on language proficiency tasks in both languages. Recent studies have tended to select as participants in the experimental (bilingual) group 'balanced bilinguals', that is, those bilingual individuals who perform at similar levels of proficiency on language tasks in both their languages. This also, however, has problems associated with it. It may be, as Macnamara (1970) and MacNab (1979) have argued, that balanced bilinguals are a unique class of bilinguals, who, because they are cognitively more able in the first place are more likely to become highly proficient bilinguals. In other words, the question of the direction of the relationship between bilingualism and cognitive and metalinguistic development is left begging. Is it that bilingualism affects cognitive development or conversely, that cognitive development affects bilingualism?

Research can play a significant role in addressing this issue. To address the question directly, it will need to have several characteristics. It will need to be longitudinal in design. In Chapter 1 there is only one study with this characteristic (Barik and Swain 1976a). In this study, it was found that aspects of the cognitive development of primary level immersion students with a relatively high level of second language proficiency increased significantly more over a period of several years than they did for students with a lower level of second language proficiency. This finding has subsequently been replicated by Harley and Lapkin (1984) in a study spanning six years of bilingual and cognitive growth.

Hakuta and Diaz (1984) carried out a study using a similar research design and longitudinally collected data. Using a non-verbal measure of cognitive development and Spanish and English vocabulary measures to determine degree of bilingualism, their results indicated that degree of bilingualism and cognitive ability were related at two points in time. Furthermore, when two alternative models testing for the direction of causality between bilingualism and cognitive ability were examined using the longitudinal data, 'the model claiming degree of bilingualism to be the causal link was more consistent with the obtained data than the model claiming cognitive ability to be the causal variable' (p. 340).

Since Chapter 1 was written, only a handful of studies employing a longitudinal design have appeared in the literature. One such study is that carried out by Bain and Yu (1980) who examined the cognitive consequences of raising children unilingually and bilingually. Their measures of cognitive development followed from the theoretical/empirical research paradigm of Vygotsky (1962) and Luria (1961) who suggest that the development of children's ability to control their own cognitive processes is contingent upon their mastery of language. In the Bain and Yu study, bilingual and unilingual children living in Alsace, in Alberta or in Hong Kong were tested at ages 22 to 24 months, and again at ages 46 to 48 months. No differences were initially found between the bilingual and unilingual children. However, at the time of the second testing some two years later, significant differences were found in favour of the bilingual children.

From a methodological viewpoint, the Bain and Yu study still suffers from one problem: the children were not randomly assigned to experimental and control groups. Essentially they ended up in the particular group they did because their parents had 'volunteered' them: the parents had answered an advertisement asking for their participation in a study of speech acquisition. In order to participate in the study of bilingual speech acquisition, one but preferably both of the parents had to be bilingual. As MacNab (1979) points out, there may be differences between the families of these children that will be more powerful in explaining differences than is bilingualism itself: 'To learn a second language is a commitment to a second culture, and people who learn to speak two languages are, therefore, very likely to be quite different from those who stay unilingual.' (p. 243).

Achieving random assignment of children to bilingual and unilingual groups, however, is a difficult, if not impossible, methodological demand given the reality of bilingual development. One solution to this problem is to look at effects within a bilingual sample: 'If *degree* of bilingualism can be reliably measured within a sample of children becoming bilingual and if this measure of degree can be shown to be related to cognitive flexibility, then one would have come one step closer to finding a pure relationship between bilingualism and cognitive flexibility.' (Hakuta and Diaz 1984, p. 330). This is essentially the research design used by Barik and Swain (1976a), Harley and Lapkin (1984) and Hakuta and Diaz (1984) to reach their conclusions noted above.

We have gone to some pains to indicate some of the methodological problems associated with research concerned with the association between bilingualism and cognitive growth in order to suggest that some of the contradictory findings can be accounted for by them. However, having said this, we suggest that finding both negative and positive cognitive consequences associated with bilingualism is not necessarily contradictory. As will be seen again in Section 2, an underlying theoretical principle can link together the disparate findings. In this section, the key theoretical hypothesis to be advanced is the 'threshold hypothesis'.

The threshold hypothesis proposes that there may be threshold levels of linguistic competence which bilingual children must attain in their first and second languages both in order to avoid cognitive disadvantages and to allow the potentially beneficial aspects of becoming bilingual to influence cognitive functioning. In other words, two thresholds are hypothesized: one below which cognitive growth would suffer without further linguistic development: and one above which cognitive growth would be enhanced. As we point out in Chapter 1, one implication of the threshold hypothesis is that educational programmes should aim to foster high levels of proficiency in both languages. In societal situations where there is likely to be serious erosion of the first language, it is particularly crucial that school programmes aim toward its development and maintenance. As we will argue in Section 2, such an educational programme will support second language development as well.

The threshold hypothesis has proved a useful heuristic device for making sense of seemingly contradictory evidence. It has provided a useful framework for interpreting the results. Obviously, however, what actually constitutes threshold levels needs to be further specified. Diaz (in press) notes that when first language proficiency is high, enhanced cognitive effects are associated with relatively low levels of second language proficiency. Diaz suggests that the positive effects of bilingualism may be related 'to the initial efforts required to understand and produce a second language rather than to increasingly higher levels of bilingual proficiency'. This presents an intriguing new perspective on the notion of a threshold level.

1 Bilingualism, cognitive functioning and education*

The purposes of this chapter are to review recent studies which have investigated the relationships between bilingualism and cognitive functioning, and to outline the implications of these research findings for educational settings.

Terminology

The term 'bilingualism' has not been used in a consistent way among researchers and theoreticians. Definitions vary considerably. Macnamara (1967), for example, defines bilinguals as those who possess at least one of the language skills (listening, speaking, reading and writing) even to a minimal degree in their second language. At the other end of the scale, bilinguals have been defined as those who demonstrate complete mastery of two different languages without interference between the two linguistic processes (Oestreicher 1974) or who have native-like control of two or more languages (Bloomfield 1933). The tendency has been to focus on speaking and listening skills (e.g. Haugen 1953; Pohl 1965; Weinreich 1953).

Other definitions of bilingualism have considered the age at which the second language is learned (*simultaneous* versus *sequential; early* versus *late*); the contexts in which the two languages have been learned (*compound* versus *coordinate* (Osgood and Sebeok 1965), *artificial* versus *natural* (Stern 1973)); or the domains in which each language is used (e.g. Fishman 1968; Oksaar 1971).

It is clear, then, that there is little consensus as to the exact meaning of the term bilingualism, and that it has been used to refer

* This chapter first appeared as an article of the same title by M. Swain and J. Cummins in *Language Teaching and Linguistics: Abstracts*. Cambridge: Cambridge University Press, 1979: 4–18, and was reprinted in V. Kinsella (ed.) *Surveys 1: Eight State-of-the-Art Articles of Key Areas in Language Teaching*. Cambridge: Cambridge University Press, 1982: 23–37. Permission to reprint this article has been granted by Cambridge University Press.

to a wide variety of phenomena. Research associated with bilingualism reflects this semantic confusion. It is essential, therefore, in reconciling contradictory results associated with bilingualism, to be aware of the levels of bilingualism attained by the experimental students, and the social and psychological factors which lie behind the particular 'bilingualism' attained.

This review is specifically concerned with the association between bilingualism and cognitive functioning. Cognitive functioning is used in this chapter to refer to measures involving general intellectual and linguistic skills such as verbal and non-verbal IQ, divergent thinking, academic performance and metalinguistic awareness.

For the purposes of this review it is also important to introduce two terms associated with educational programmes. Both terms – 'immersion' and 'submersion' – relate to situations where the child is required to use in school a language that is different from that used in the home. Immersion refers to a situation in which children from the *same* linguistic and cultural background who have had *no* prior contact with the school language are put *together* in a classroom setting in which the second language is used as the medium of instruction. Submersion, on the other hand, refers to the situation encountered by *some* children wherein they must make a home–school language switch, while others can already function in the school language. Within the same classroom, then, one might find children who have no knowledge of the school language, varying degrees of facility in the school language through contact with the wider community, and native speakers of the school language (Swain 1978c).

In the next two sections, studies which report a negative association between bilingualism and cognitive functioning and studies which report a positive association between bilingualism and cognitive functioning will be reviewed. Following that, several of the factors which appear to differentiate the positive and negative studies will be reviewed, and the resultant implications for educational programmes will be summarized.

Studies reporting negative associations

Several comprehensive reviews exist of studies conducted prior to 1960 (see Darcy 1953; Macnamara 1966; Peal and Lambert 1962) and consequently these studies will not be considered here. Although the majority of these early studies had serious methodological defects, taken together they seemed to indicate that bilinguals suffered from a language handicap when measured by verbal tests of intelligence or academic achievement.

The general findings of earlier studies are supported by those of Skutnabb-Kangas and Toukomaa (1976) who reported that children of Finnish migrant workers in Sweden tended to be characterized by 'semilingualism', i.e. their skills in both Finnish and Swedish (as measured by standardized tests) were considerably below Finnish and Swedish norms. The extent to which the mother tongue had been developed prior to contact with Swedish was strongly related to how well Swedish was learned. Children who migrated at the age of ten maintained a level of Finnish close to Finnish students in Finland and achieved Swedish language skills comparable to those of Swedes. However, children who were seven to eight years of age when they moved to Sweden or who moved before starting school were most likely to achieve low levels of literacy skills in both languages. Skutnabb-Kangas and Toukomaa argue on the basis of these results that the minority child's first language (L1) has functional significance in the developmental process and should be reinforced by the school.

Vernacular education is also supported by Macnamara's (1966) study of bilingualism in Irish primary education. Macnamara reported that Irish primary school children, whose home language was English but who were instructed through the medium of Irish, were eleven months behind in problem arithmetic relative to other Irish children taught through the medium of English. No differences were found between the Irish immersion group and comparison groups in either mechanical arithmetic or English achievement. Macnamara's study has been criticized (Cummins 1977b, c) on the grounds that the Irish immersion group was administered the problem arithmetic test through their weaker language (Irish) whereas comparison groups took the test in their stronger language (English). Thus, according to Cummins, Macnamara's study confounds the immersion children's competence in arithmetic with their ability to demonstrate this competence when tested through their weaker language.

Tsushima and Hogan (1975) report that grade 4 and 5 Japanese–English bilinguals performed at a significantly lower level on measures of verbal and academic skills than a unilingual group matched on nonverbal IQ. The bilingual group was comprised of children whose mothers were Japanese and whose fathers were born and raised in the United States. All the parents of children in the unilingual group were born and raised in the United States. Tsushima and Hogan report that the bilingual children had been exposed to both English and Japanese in the home from infancy. However, they give no details of the present pattern of bilingual usage in the home nor of the bilinguals' relative competence in both languages. Thus, while this study provides evidence of an increasing deficit in verbal skills among bilingual children between grades 3 and 5, it fails to provide any information about the bilingual learning conditions under which such a deficit might occur.

The same criticism can be made of a study conducted in Singapore by Torrance, Gowan, Wu and Aliotti (1970) who report that grades 3, 4 and 5 children attending English (L2) medium schools performed at a significantly lower level than unilingual children on the fluency and flexibility scales of the Torrance Tests of Creative Thinking, a measure of divergent thinking. Although the study involves more than a thousand subjects little detail is given regarding the comparability of the groups in terms of IQ or SES nor about the level of bilingualism of the bilingual subjects.

In studies involving middle-class Hebrew–English and Spanish–English lower-class children, Ben-Zeev (1977a, b) reported lower vocabulary scores for bilinguals in comparison to unilinguals when matched for IQ. A similar finding has been reported with pre-school French–English bilinguals (Doyle, Champagne and Segalowitz 1977).

Studies reporting positive associations

A variety of cognitive advantages have been reported in association with bilingualism. Some studies have reported higher levels of linguistic skills. A positive association has also been reported between bilingualism and both general intellectual skills and divergent thinking. In addition, several studies have reported evidence that bilingualism promotes an analytic orientation to linguistic and perceptual structures and increases sensitivity to feedback cues.

Linguistic skills

Several studies conducted within the context of primary immersion programmes have reported that the immersion students performed better than children in regular programmes on measures of L1 skills despite considerably less instruction through the medium of L1. Barik and Swain (1978a), for example, report that by grade 5 children in the Ottawa early total French immersion programme were performing better than control students on some aspects of English skills. Swain (1975a) has also reported that French immersion students used more complex syntactic structures in written English composition than regular programme students. Tremaine (1975) compared the syntactical development of grades 1, 2 and 3 children in a total French immersion programme with that of children who were given 75 minutes of French instruction per day. As would be expected there were large differences between the groups in French syntactical development; however, differences in favour of the immersion group in English syntactical development were also significant even when the level of Piagetian operations was controlled. Tremaine concludes that intensive exposure to French facilitated the comprehension of certain English syntactic structures.

Ekstrand (1978) also reports preliminary results of an experimental project in Sweden in which elementary school children with an early start in learning English (L2) did significantly better in Swedish (L1) than control children. Enhancement of linguistic skills as a function of intensity of bilingual learning experiences is also suggested in a longitudinal study conducted by Genesee, Tucker and Lambert (1978). Grades 3 and 5 children in a trilingual English–Hebrew–French programme in Montreal performed at the same level in English and significantly better in Hebrew when compared to children in a bilingual English–Hebrew programme. Genesee *et al.* point out that the Hebrew curriculum in experimental and control schools was essentially the same.

Where the development of both languages is promoted by the school programme, there is also evidence of positive linguistic effects. Dubé and Hébert (1975), for example, report that minority francophone children in a French–English bilingual education project in Maine developed higher levels of English skills than a control group of children in an English-only programme.

Orientation to linguistic and perceptual structures

Several studies have reported evidence that bilingualism can promote an analytic orientation to language and increase aspects of metalinguistic awareness. Feldman and Shen (1971), for example, reported that five-year-old bilingual 'head start' children were superior to unilinguals in their ability to switch labels, and in their use of common names and nonsense names in relational statements.

Ianco-Worrall (1972), in a study conducted in South Africa, reported that bilingual children, brought up in a one-person, one-language home environment, were significantly more sensitive than unilingual children, matched on IQ, to semantic relations between words and were also more advanced in realizing the arbitrary assignment of names to referents. Unilingual children were more likely to interpret similarity between words in terms of an acoustic rather than a semantic dimension (e.g. *cap–can* rather than *cap–hat*) and felt that the names of objects could not be interchanged.

Ianco-Worrall's finding that bilinguals were more aware of the arbitrary assignment of words to referents was supported by Cummins (1978b) in a study involving grades 3 and 6 Irish–English bilinguals matched on IQ with a unilingual group. However, a subsequent study (Cummins and Mulcahy, 1978a) involving grades 1 and 3 Ukrainian–English bilinguals found no differences between bilingual and unilingual groups on this task. Cummins and Mulcahy suggest that the equivocal nature of the findings may be a reflection of the relative crudeness of the measures used to assess aspects of children's metalinguistic awareness.

The results of several studies are consistent with the hypothesis that bilingualism can increase children's ability to analyse linguistic input. Cummins (1978b) reported that both grade 3 and grade 6 bilingual children were significantly better able than unilingual children to evaluate nonempirical contradictory statements (e.g. 'The poker chip (hidden) in my hand is blue and it is not blue.' – 'True, False or Can't tell?'). Cummins and Mulcahy (1978a) reported that grades 1 and 3 Ukrainian–English bilingual children were significantly better able to analyse ambiguities in sentence structure than a control group of unilingual children matched for IQ, SES and school.

In two studies involving middle-class Hebrew–English bilinguals and lower-class Spanish–English bilinguals, Ben-Zeev (1977a, b) reported that in comparison to unilingual children matched on IQ, bilingual children were better able to treat sentence structure analytically and also performed better on several nonverbal tasks which required perceptual analysis. She suggested that bilingual children develop an analytic strategy of linguistic processing in order to overcome interlingual interference. Bilingual–unilingual differences on the perceptual tasks were interpreted as evidence for the generalization of bilinguals' analytic strategy towards language to other kinds of structures.

Ben-Zeev (1977a) also reports higher latency of paradigmatic responses by bilingual children on a word association task. Cummins and Mulcahy (1978b) have also reported that Ukrainian–English bilingual children took significantly longer than unilingual children to respond on a word association task. The longer latency of the word association responses may be a result of the increased semantic processing necessary to overcome interlingual interference.

Superior performance by bilinguals on tasks involving an ability to restructure linguistic and perceptual schemata has also been reported by Balkan (1970). In a study conducted in Switzerland, Balkan matched bilinguals and unilinguals on nonverbal intelligence and found that the bilingual group performed significantly better on two variables which he claims measure cognitive flexibility. One of these tests was similar to the Embedded Figures Test, and involved an ability to restructure a perceptual situation. The other test required a sensitivity to the different meanings of words. Bruck, Lambert and Tucker (1976) also found large differences between experimental and control groups on the Embedded Figures Test at the grade 6 level in the St Lambert French immersion programme.

A possible neuropsychological basis for findings of a more analytic orientation to linguistic and perceptual structures among bilingual children is provided in the results of a study carried out by Starck, Genesee, Lambert and Seitz (1977). Starck *et al.* demonstrated more reliable ear asymmetry effects on a dichotic listening task among children attending a trilingual Hebrew–French–English programme as compared to a control group of children whose instruction was totally in English. The significance of this finding is that right ear advantage on dichotic listening tasks reflects greater development of the more analytic left hemisphere functions in comparison to right hemisphere functions.

The findings that bilingual children display a more analytic orientation to language than unilingual children are consistent with the views of Vygotsky (1962) who argued that being able to express the same thought in different languages will enable the child to 'see his language as one particular system among many, to view its phenomena under more general categories, and this leads to awareness of his linguistic operations' (p. 110). Lambert and Tucker (1972) argued that a similar process was likely to operate among children in immersion programmes. They suggested that as children develop high level bilingual skills they are likely to practise a form of 'incipient contrastive linguistics' by comparing the syntax and vocabulary of their two languages.

Sensitivity to feedback cues

Several studies provide evidence of both greater social sensitivity and greater ability to react more flexibly to cognitive feedback among bilinguals. Ben-Zeev (1977b) suggests that increased attention to feedback cues has adaptive significance for bilingual children in that it might help them understand the communication of others, make them aware of mistakes in their own speech and provide them with information regarding the appropriate times for switching languages. In both Spanish–English and Hebrew–English studies, Ben-Zeev (1977a, b) reports that bilinguals were significantly more susceptible to the verbal transformation illusion (Warren and Warren 1966). In this task a nonsense word is repeated continuously by means of a tape loop and adults typically perceive the verbal stimulus as repeatedly changing. Ben-Zeev interprets the fact that bilinguals perceived a higher number of auditory changes as indicating increased processing effort on their part and increased attention to cues from linguistic input in order to achieve satisfactory closure. However, this interpretation is questioned by Cummins and Mulcahy (1978b) who found no differences between bilinguals and unilinguals on the verbal transformation illusion.

Ben-Zeev also reports that the Spanish–English bilinguals were significantly better able to use hints as cues to successful restructuring on classification tasks. Cummins and Mulcahy (1978a) similarly report that bilingual children made significantly better use of prompts in interpreting ambiguous sentences. However, differences between bilinguals and unilinguals on the ambiguities task remained significant even when the prompting data were eliminated.

The findings of several investigations suggest that bilinguals may be more sensitive to interpersonal feedback and more adept at certain kinds of communication tasks. Genesee, Tucker and Lambert (1975), for example, asked children in immersion classes and regular programme classes to explain how to play a game to two different listeners, one blindfolded and the other not blindfolded. The immersion group was found to be the most sensitive to the needs of listeners and responded most differentially, showing the largest difference between sighted and blindfolded conditions. The authors suggest that the immersion children's school experiences may have made them more aware of possible difficulties in communicating as well as provided them with some experience in coping with such difficulties.

Bain (1975) and Bain and Yu (1978) have undertaken several studies which examined bilingual–unilingual differences in sensitivity to facial expressions. Bain (1975) found significant differences between bilingual and unilingual children at grades 1 and 6 on the Portrait Sensitivity Test in which children were required to identify the facial expressions on a series of twenty-four portraits painted by famous artists. This finding was replicated cross-culturally by Bain and Yu (1978).

General intellectual development

Peal and Lambert (1962) reported that ten-year-old French–English bilingual children showed a higher level of both verbal and nonverbal intelligence than a comparison group of unilingual children matched on SES and sex. In addition, factor analysis of the cognitive measures revealed a more differentiated subtest profile in the bilingual group. Cummins and Gulutsan (1974) also reported significantly higher levels of verbal and nonverbal ability among bilingual children.

Two further studies involving French–English bilinguals attending bilingual schools in western Canada have reported that bilingual children performed better than unilinguals on measures of concept formation. Liedke and Nelson (1968) found that bilingual grade 1 children performed significantly better on a Piagetian concept formation task than a unilingual group matched for age, SES, sex and IQ. The authors hypothesized that the bilingual child is exposed to a wider range of experiences due to the greater amount of social interaction involved in learning two languages as compared to one. Bain (1975) reported significant differences between grade 1 bilinguals and unilinguals on a rule discovery task at the grade 1 level. Bilingual and unilingual groups were matched for SES, sex, IQ and developmental level of operations. Although in the same direction, differences at the grade 6 level did not reach significance.

Using longitudinal data from the Ottawa and Toronto French immersion programmes, Barik and Swain (1976a) investigated the hypothesis that cognitive advantages are associated with the attainment of high levels of bilingual skills. It was found that children who had attained high levels of French skills performed significantly better than low French achievers on two of the three Otis-Lennon IQ subtests when scores were adjusted for initial IQ and age differences between the two groups. The IQ scores of the low French achievers remained unchanged over the three-year period whereas the IQ scores of the high French achievers increased, suggesting that the attainment of high levels of L2 skills is associated with greater cognitive growth.

Divergent thinking

Cummins and Gulutsan (1974) reported significant differences

between bilingual and unilingual grade 6 children on a verbal originality measure. When intelligence was partialled out the level of
significance was reduced but the difference was still significant.
However, no differences were found on four other measures of
divergent thinking. Further analysis of the data (Cummins 1977a)
suggested that only those bilinguals who had attained a relatively high
level of second language competence performed at a higher level on
the verbal originality task (administered in L1) while children who
remained dominant in their home language were at a disadvantage in
relation to unilingual children on verbal fluency and flexibility skills.
Torrance *et al.* (1970) have also reported that bilingual children in
Singapore performed at a higher level than unilingual children on
originality and elaboration scales of the Torrance Tests of Creative
Thinking. Landry (1974) reported that grade 6 children attending
schools where a FLES programme (i.e. between 20 and 45 minutes
of second language instruction per day) was operative, scored significantly higher than a unilingual control group on both the verbal and
figural parts of the Torrance Tests of Creative Thinking. Differences
between FLES and non-FLES schools at the grade 1 and grade 4
levels were non-significant.

Scott (1973) reported significant differences in divergent thinking
between the experimental children in the St Lambert bilingual
programme in Montreal and unilingual comparison groups. She also
reports that the French speaking skills of the experimental children
at the grade 6 level were significantly predicted by earlier (grade 3)
divergent thinking abilities. Scott concludes that higher levels of
divergent thinking may be either an effect or a causal element in the
attainment of functional bilingualism.

A study conducted in Mexico by Carringer (1974) reported that
twenty-four Spanish–English bilinguals performed at a significantly
higher level than twenty-four Spanish-speaking unilinguals on several
measures of divergent thinking.

Although, in general, these recent studies are better controlled
than the earlier studies which reported negative findings, few are
without methodological limitations. A problem in many of these studies
(Bain and Yu 1978; Carringer 1974; Cummins and Gulutsan 1974;
Feldman and Shen 1971; Landry 1974; Peal and Lambert 1962) is
lack of adequate controls for possible background differences
between bilingual and unilingual groups. An index of SES based on
parental occupation provides inadequate protection against bias. Also,
matching only on overall stage of cognitive development (e.g. pre-
operational, concrete operational, etc.) is insufficient since there can

be extremely large individual differences on cognitive variables within stages. Although the remaining studies have matched bilingual and unilingual groups on IQ in addition to SES, the validity of some of the dependent measures used to assess constructs such as 'analytic orientation to language' or 'sensitivity to feedback cues' is open to question. Also, some studies are difficult to evaluate because of inadequate descriptions either of the bilingual learning situation or of the levels of L1 and L2 competence attained by the bilingual students.

Factors differentiating positive and negative results

Several factors may be extracted from the studies cited above which in part account for the contradictory results.

For the most part, positive findings are associated with children from majority language groups whereas negative findings are associated with minority language groups (Lambert 1977; Burnaby 1976). One exception to this generalization as it relates to majority group children is Macnamara's (1966) study of English–Irish bilinguals. This study, however, has been criticized on methodological grounds (Cummins 1977b). Other exceptions, but which relate to minority language children (e.g. Dubé and Hébert 1975), indicate that the minority group factor can be overcome through the reinforcement and development of high levels of L1 proficiency.

Another factor, related in part to the first, is the perceived value and prestige of the L1 and L2 in the home and community (Fishman 1976; Tucker 1977; Swain 1978c). Positive results tend to be associated with situations where both the L1 and L2 have perceived social and economic value.

A third factor, again in part related to the first, is socio-economic status. Higher SES children tend to perform well (Paulston 1975). Lower SES bilingual children tend not to perform as well as higher SES children, although they do perform as well or better than unilingual groups of a similar SES level (e.g. Bruck, Jakimik and Tucker 1976).

Finally, school programme variables play an important role. Positive results tend to be associated with immersion programmes while negative results tend to be associated with submersion programmes. The nature of the programme differences are outlined in Cohen and Swain 1976; Burnaby 1976; Swain 1978c.

Research in this area will continue to uncover additional factors, and examine the effects of their interaction. Currently, however, the factors mentioned above have been summarized by the notions of additive and subtractive forms of bilingualism (Lambert 1977).

Lambert points out that the majority of positive studies have involved bilingual students whose L1 was dominant and prestigious and in no danger of replacement by L2. The resulting form of bilingualism is termed 'additive' in that the bilingual is adding another socially relevant language to his repertoire of skills at no cost to his L1 competence. Thus the bilingual students in studies which have reported cognitive advantages associated with bilingualism have generally attained a high level of competence in both languages.

In contrast, many of the negative studies involved bilingual students from minority language groups whose L1 was gradually being replaced by a more prestigious L2. Lambert (1977) terms the resulting form of bilingualism 'subtractive' since the bilingual's competence in his two languages at any point in time is likely to reflect some stage in the 'subtraction' of L1 and its replacement by L2. Consequently, many of the bilingual students in these studies may be characterized by less than native-like competence in both languages.

On the basis of this analysis it has been suggested (Cummins 1976, 1978a, 1979a; Toukomaa and Skutnabb-Kangas 1977) that there may be threshold levels of linguistic competence which a bilingual child must attain both in order to avoid cognitive disadvantages and allow the potentially beneficial aspects of becoming bilingual to influence his cognitive functioning. In other words, the level of competence bilingual children achieve in their two languages may act as an intervening variable in mediating the effects of bilingual learning experiences on cognitive functioning.

Educational implications

One major educational implication of the threshold hypothesis is that if *optimal* development of minority language children's academic and cognitive potential is a goal, then the school programme must aim to promote an additive form of bilingualism (Cummins 1979a). Attainment of this goal will necessarily involve a home–school language switch at some stage in the educational process, but when and how must be determined in relation to the linguistic and socio-economic characteristics of the learner and of the learning environment (Swain 1978c). Specifically when the home language is different from the school language and the home language tends to be denigrated by others and selves, and where the children come from socioeconomically deprived homes, it would appear appropriate to begin initial instruction in the child's first language, switching at a later stage to instruction in the school language. On the other hand, where the home language is a majority language valued by the community, and where literacy is encouraged in the home, then the most efficient means of promoting an additive form of bilingualism is to provide initial instruction in the second language (Tucker 1977; Swain and Bruck 1976).

2 Bilingualism and the development of metalinguistic awareness*

A considerable number of studies conducted since the early 1960s have reported that bilingual children performed at a significantly higher level than unilingual children on various measures of cognitive abilities (e.g. Bain 1975; Balkan 1970; Ben-Zeev 1977a, 1977b; Feldman and Shen 1971; Ianco-Worrall 1972; Liedke and Nelson 1968; Peal and Lambert 1962). Several of these studies have investigated aspects of bilingual children's orientation to language. Feldman and Shen (1971), for example, reported that bilingual 'head start' children were superior to unilinguals in their ability to switch names and in the use of common names and nonsense names in relational statements. Ianco-Worrall (1972), in a study conducted in South Africa, reported that bilingual children brought up in a one-person, one-language home environment were more oriented to the semantic rather than the acoustic properties of words and were more aware of the arbitrary assignment of words to referents than were unilingual children. In studies conducted with middle-class Hebrew–English and lower-class Spanish–English bilinguals, Ben-Zeev (1977a, 1977b) has reported findings which suggest that bilinguals develop a more analytic orientation to language and more sensitivity to feedback cues. Ben-Zeev (1977b) hypothesized that bilinguals develop this analytic strategy towards language as a means of overcoming interlingual interference.

The results of these studies are consistent with observations of the linguistic development of individual bilingual children (Imedadze 1960; Leopold 1949). These investigators have suggested that early bilingualism can accelerate the separation of sound and meaning and focus the child's attention on certain aspects of language. Vygotsky

* This chapter first appeared as an article of the same title by J. Cummins in *Journal of Cross-Cultural Psychology* 9[2]: 131–149, 1978. Copyright 1978 by Western Washington University. Permission to reprint this article has been granted by Sage Publications Inc.

(1962, p. 110) too has argued that being able to express the same thought in different languages will enable the child to 'see his language as one particular system among many, to view its phenomena under more general categories, and this leads to awareness of his linguistic operations'.

The present study further investigated the effects of bilingualism on the development of children's awareness of certain properties of language and on their ability to analyse linguistic input. Methodological aspects of previous studies suggested the necessity for replication and extension of .their findings. For example, the findings of the Feldman and Shen (1971) study must be considered tentative because there were no controls for possible intellectual differences between bilingual and unilingual groups. Ianco-Worrall (1972) and Ben-Zeev (1977a, 1977b) did control for IQ but the interpretation of some of the dependent measures used in these studies can be questioned. In assessing children's awareness of the arbitrary nature of word-referent relationships, for example, Ianco-Worrall did not require children to justify their responses to questions such as: 'Suppose you were making up names for things, could you then call a cow "dog" and a dog "cow"?' An answer of 'yes' to this question does not necessarily demonstrate understanding of the arbitrary assignment of words to referents.

Similarly, Ben-Zeev (1977a, 1977b) interprets the finding that both Hebrew–English and Spanish–English bilinguals perceived significantly more changes in the verbal transformation illusion (Warren and Warren 1966) than their unilingual controls as indicating increased processing effort on their part in an attempt to make sense out of the stimulus. While this interpretation is certainly plausible, considerably more research is needed on the nature of the verbal transformation illusion before it can be unequivocally accepted.

This discussion highlights a problem to which the present study is by no means immune. In investigating the effects of bilingualism on phenomena as little understood as children's metalinguistic awareness and orientation to language the dependent variables are necessarily exploratory in nature. Thus, caution is required in interpreting results and it is only on the basis of cumulated evidence from different bilingual learning contexts that generalizations can be attempted.

METHOD
Subjects

The subjects were eighty grade 3 children and twenty-six grade 6 children selected from four middle-class schools in Dublin, Ireland. In two of the schools all subjects were taught through Irish (a second language for the majority of pupils) while in the other two schools subjects were taught through English (pupils' home language). Two criteria were used to select the bilingual sample from the Irish medium schools:

a) that at least some Irish be spoken in the children's homes;
b) that teachers rated children at least three on a five-point scale of Irish expressive skills. A rating of three signified that a child was able to express himself through Irish with little hesitation, though not always with grammatical correctness.

Forty grade 3 children from the two Irish medium schools met these criteria and these children were matched on IQ, SES, sex, and age with forty grade 3 children from the English medium schools. Although pupils in the English medium schools were taught Irish as a school subject, their fluency in Irish was negligible. There were twenty boys and twenty girls in each group. The mean age of the unilingual group was 8 years 11 months and that of the bilingual group 8 years 9 months. The mean IQ of the bilingual group on the Otis-Lennon IQ test (Irish version) was 113.79 (S.D. 9.67) and that of the unilingual group 113.54 (S.D. 9.57).

Grade 6 children in one of the schools were unavailable for testing and consequently grade 6 children from just one of the Irish medium and one of the English medium schools were tested. Thirteen children from the Irish medium school who met the selection criteria outlined above were matched on IQ, SES, sex, and age with thirteen English medium pupils. There were seven girls and six boys in each group. The mean age of the unilingual group was 11 years 9 months and that of the bilingual group 11 years 11 months. The mean IQ of the bilingual group on the Drumcondra Verbal Reasoning Test was 120.54 (S.D. 10.74) and that of the unilingual group 120.85 (S.D. 11.22).

Dependent variables and procedure

Osherson and Markman (1975) developed a series of tasks designed to assess children's ability to examine language in an objective manner, apart from objects and events to which it refers, and also

children's ability to evaluate nonempirical contradictory and tautological statements. With slight modifications as a result of pilot testing
these tasks were used as dependent measures in the present study.

Language objectivity tests

1. Meaning and reference

This task assessed the child's belief in the stability of the meaning
of words in the face of destruction of the world's empirical referent.
The subject was asked if he knew what the word *flimp* meant and was
told that it means a fairy-tale creature like a bird which has four wings
and several different colours. A felt toy fitting this description was
shown to the child and he was asked how he would describe a flimp
to a boy or girl in grade 1 who asked what the word flimp meant.
After the child responded correctly ihe experimenter said: 'Now
suppose that this flimp is the last flimp left in the world and it gets
sick and dies [experimenter removes flimp]. If that happened and there
were no more flimps left in the world, what would you say to a boy
or girl in grade 1 who asked you what the word flimp meant?
[The child responds.] Suppose someone said that flimps have four
wings, would he be right? [The child responds.] Has the meaning of
the word flimp changed now that they are all dead? [The child
responds.] Does the word flimp have any meaning now that they are
all dead?'

After the questions concerning flimps, the child was asked to
imagine that all giraffes in the world had been killed and essentially
the same questions were asked about the meaning of the word *giraffe*.
The procedure in the *meaning and reference* task was basically the same
as that used by Osherson and Markman (1975) (although the content
of the flimp item was different) and the same scoring criteria were
used. A subject was scored correct only if he claimed that the word
(*flimp* or *giraffe*) had essentially the same meaning as before its
referent disappeared. Only the giraffe item was administered to the
grade 6 children since the flimp item was considered inappropriate
for this age level.

2. Arbitrariness of language

The procedure in this task differed somewhat from that used by
Osherson and Markman (1975). The initial question was similar to
those used by Ianco-Worrall (1972) to investigate bilingual-unilingual
differences in the child's realization of the arbitrary nature of word-
referent relationships. Children were asked: 'Suppose you were

making up names for things, could you then call the sun "the moon" and the moon "the sun"? [The child responds.] Why could you change/not change the names?' After this, the same procedure used by Osherson and Markman was followed. Children who claimed that the names could not be changed were persuaded that they could be changed if everybody in the world agreed to it and all we were going to do was change the *names*. After the child acquiesced the experimenter continued: 'Now suppose that that happened and everybody decided to call the sun "the moon" and the moon "the sun" what would you call the thing in the sky when you go to bed at night?' Almost all children responded correctly; the few who did not were coached. Then the child was asked to describe what the sky would look like when he was going to bed. The correct answer was to describe a night sky.

After the sun-moon item, the child was asked to imagine that the names of cats and dogs had been interchanged. He was shown a picture of a cat and asked what this animal's new name would be. He was then asked what sound this animal would make. The same procedure was repeated with a picture of a dog.

3. Nonphysical nature of words
Subjects were asked the following questions:

1. Is the *word* 'book' made of paper?
2. Does the *word* 'bird' have feathers?
3. Can you buy sweets with the *word* 'penny'?

The questions are essentially the same as those used by Osherson and Markman, although slight changes were introduced to make the content more appropriate for the Irish context. Also, the word 'word' was emphasized in order to minimize the possibility of misunderstanding the questions.

Empirical and nonempirical questions

The materials were small plastic counters or poker chips of assorted colours which, at the start of the session, were placed on a table between the experimenter (E) and subject. The subject was instructed to listen carefully to what E said and say whether the statement was true, false or whether it was not possible to know. He was also instructed *not* to guess if he was not sure whether the statement was true or false. The counters were then placed in a box which was put under the table out of the subject's sight.

After the subject had given his response to each item he was asked why he thought so and all justifications were recorded by the experimenter. The seven nonempirical items consisted of four contradictions and three tautologies. For three of the contradictory statements and two of the tautologies the counter was hidden from the child's view in the experimenter's hand. The seven nonempirical items were followed by four empirical items which were included in order to assess the relationship between empirical and nonempirical items. The items, together with the colour of the counter, if visible, and the correct answer, are shown in Table 2.3, p. 30. The items were presented to all subjects in the order shown in that table.

Unlike Osherson and Markman's procedure children's justifications for their responses to the nonempirical questions rather than the responses themselves (true, false, can't tell) were scored correct or incorrect. Thus, children who gave a 'correct' response but inappropriate justification were scored incorrect, while children who gave an 'incorrect' response but appropriate justification were scored correct. Appropriate justifications were those that indicated an awareness of the contradictory or tautological nature of the sentence. These justifications invariably involved an emphatic rehearsal of the item (e.g., 'Can't tell, because you said the counter *was* blue and *was not* blue') and were clearly distinguishable from justifications which treated the statement as an empirical statement (e.g., 'Can't tell, because I can't see it'; 'True, because I think it is blue'). The awareness of the contradictory or tautological nature of the nonempirical statements assessed in the present study is clearly a necessary, but not a sufficient, condition for correct evaluation of the statement's truth or falsity.

Justifications were scored rather than actual responses because it was apparent that on the hidden nonempirical items (1-5, Table 2.3) many 'correct' responses were given with no understanding of the contradictory or tautological nature of the statement. For example, on item 1, 32.5% of the grade 3 sample gave the 'correct' 'true' response but none of their justifications indicated an awareness of the tautological nature of the statement. Another indication of the error associated with the actual responses is that these responses revealed no improvement between grades 3 and 6 whereas considerable improvement was evidenced when justifications were scored. However, it is possible that error may also be involved in scoring justifications since some children may have intuitively understood the principle (and given the correct answer) but were unable to verbalize this understanding in their justifications. It is clearly preferable, however, to risk the possibility of this source of error rather than the certainty of error associated with scoring actual responses.

The order of presentation of language objectivity tasks and empirical and nonempirical questions was counterbalanced within each linguistic group.

RESULTS
Meaning and reference

Responses on the *meaning and reference* task revealed a development from the belief that the meaning of a word is totally dependent upon the physical existence of its referent ('incorrect') to the realization that the meaning of a word is independent of its referent's physical existence ('correct'). Intermediate between these two categories were responses in which children gave inconsistent justifications to successive questions ('inconsistent'). For example, one child maintained that the meaning of the word *giraffe* would change 'because if giraffes were all dead the word would have no meaning', yet in response to the next question she said that the word would have some meaning 'because we'd know that it was like a horse with a long neck'.

Table 2.1 shows the percentage of bilingual and unilingual children at both grade levels who fell into each of these three response categories. The actual numbers are presented in brackets after the percentages.

Chi-square (X^2) analyses of the distribution of bilingual and unilingual children in each cell revealed no significant differences at

TABLE 2.1   Bilingual and unilingual responses on the meaning and reference task

	Grade 3			Grade 6		
	Bilingual	*Unilingual*	*Average %*	*Bilingual*	*Unilingual*	*Average %*
Flimp						
Incorrect	47.5 (19)	45.0 (18)	46.3			
Inconsistent	20.0 (8)	37.5 (15)	28.7			
Correct	32.5 (13)	17.5 (7)	25.0			
Giraffe						
Incorrect	27.5 (11)	27.5 (11)	27.5	7.7 (1)	15.4 (2)	11.5
Inconsistent	40.0 (16)	47.5 (19)	43.8	7.7 (1)	46.2 (6)	26.9
Correct	32.5 (13)	25.0 (10)	28.7	84.6 (11)	38.5 (5)	61.5

the grade 3 level, although there was a trend towards bilingual superiority on the 'flimp' item ($X^2(2) = 3.96$, p = .14). In order to meet the assumptions of the Chi-square test (Siegel 1956, p. 110) in the grade 6 analysis, 'incorrect' and 'inconsistent' response categories were combined. The analysis revealed significant differences between bilingual and unilingual groups ($X^2(1) = 5.85$, p < .02).

Arbitrariness of language

Responses to the first question of this task ('Suppose you were making up names for things, could you then call the sun "the moon" and the moon "the sun"?') revealed marked differences between bilingual and unilingual groups at the grade 3 level. Almost 70% of bilingual children compared to only 27.5% of unilingual children asserted that the names could be interchanged. However, analysis of justifications given by children showed less marked, but still significant, differences between the groups. Three categories of response justification were distinguished. The most primitive of these were 'empirical' justifications in which the subject invoked empirical attributes of the objects to justify his response ('You could change the names because both the sun and the moon shine'). The second consisted of 'rigid conventional' justifications such as 'They are their right names so you couldn't change them' or 'God gave things their names and people can't change them'. The third category of justifications were those that recognized the arbitrary assignment of names to referents ('You could change the names because it doesn't matter what things are called'). Also included in this third category in the present analysis were responses which held that the names could not be interchanged 'because people would get confused'. This response was considered legitimate (and scored correct) even though it does not explicitly recognize the arbitrary assignment of names to referents. One bilingual and two unilingual children at the grade 3 level and two bilingual grade 6 children gave this response. When questioned further these children invariably stated that in principle the names could be interchanged if everyone agreed. Six children at the grade 3 level, three from each group, were unable to justify their response. For purposes of analysis, these children were classified in the 'empirical' category.

The distribution of bilingual and unilingual responses to the items in the *arbitrariness of language* task is shown in Table 2.2. On the first question, differences in the distribution of bilingual and unilingual responses are significant at both grade levels (grade 3, $X^2(2) = 7.40$,

TABLE 2.2   Bilingual and unilingual responses on the arbitrariness of language task

| | Grade 3 | | | Grade 6 | | |
	Bilingual	Unilingual	Average %	Bilingual	Unilingual	Average %
Q1.						
Empirical	57.5 (23)	57.5 (23)	57.5	7.7 (1)	46.2 (6)	26.9
Rigid Conventional	2.5 (1)	20.0 (8)	11.3	7.7 (1)	15.4 (2)	11.6
Arbitrary	40.0 (16)	22.5 (9)	31.2	84.6 (11)	38.5 (5)	61.5
Q2.						
(Sun – Moon)	45.0 (18)	32.5 (13)	38.7	69.2 (9)	46.2 (6)	57.7
Q3.						
(Cat – Dog)	47.5 (19)	40.0 (16)	43.8	61.5 (8)	46.2 (6)	53.8
Q4.						
(Dog – Cat)	50.0 (20)	40.0 (16)	45.0	61.5 (8)	46.2 (6)	53.8

p = .02); grade 6 (empirical and rigid conventional categories collapsed): $X^2(1) = 5.85$, p < .02). However, despite the fact that the bilingual children were better able to state the principle that words and things are arbitrarily related (Q2), they were almost as likely as unilingual children to assert that an exchange of names (*sun* and *moon*, Q2; *cat* and *dog*, Q3 and Q4) implied an exchange of empirical characteristics. About half the children at both grade levels asserted that if cats were called 'dogs' they would bark (and vice versa) despite the fact that pictures of a cat and a dog were in full view. Thus, bilinguals were better able to state the principle but were no different from unilinguals in their application of it. This discrepancy suggests that the results should be interpreted cautiously until the cognitive processes underlying performance of this type of task are better understood. It would be a mistake to assume that application of the principle was more indicative of cognitive skills than ability to state it since, at the grade 3 level, the latter was significantly related to IQ (r = .41, p < .001) whereas the correlation of the former with IQ was nonsignificant.

Nonphysical nature of words

There were no significant differences between bilingual and unilingual groups at either grade level either in the number of items correctly answered (grade 3: bilingual x̄ = 1.60, unilingual x̄ = 1.25; grade 6:

bilingual $\bar{x}$ = 2.69; unilingual $\bar{x}$ = 2.08) or in the proportion of bilingual and unilingual subjects who articulated the principle that words did not share the physical properties of their referents (grade 3: bilingual, 57.5%, unilingual, 47.5%; grade 6: bilingual 92.3%, unilingual, 84.6%).

Empirical and nonempirical questions

The empirical (items 8–11) and nonempirical (items 1–7) questions and the percentages of bilingual and unilingual children correct at each grade level are shown in Table 2.3. Scoring justifications rather than actual responses revealed that the nonempirical items were considerably more difficult than Osherson and Markman's (1975) data had suggested.

At the grade 3 level there are significant differences between bilingual and unilingual groups on contradictory items 3 and 6 ($X^2(1)$ = 4.02, p < .05) and differences between the groups on the two other contradictory items (2 and 6) show a trend towards bilingual superiority (item 2: $X^2(1)$ = 3.66, p < .06; item 6: $X^2(1)$ = 2.58, p < .11). At least twice as many bilingual children as unilingual children were correct on each of the four contradictory items. Differences between bilingual and unilingual groups in the total number of nonempirical items correct were significant (F(1,78) = 4.62, p < .05).

On the empirical questions, differences between the groups are nonsignificant on items 8, 9, and 10 but the unilingual group performs significantly better on item 11 ($X^2(1)$ = 4.71, p < .05). The inferior performance of the bilingual group on items 10 and 11 can be attributed to failure to shift strategies between the 'hidden' nonempirical items and the 'hidden' empirical items (10 and 11). Many of the bilingual children were just beginning to grapple with the reasoning processes involved in solving the nonempirical items and their application of this strategy was still relatively inflexible. A larger number of the unilingual group did not have the problem of shifting strategies since they had applied an inappropriate empirical strategy to the nonempirical items.

At the grade 6 level, there is also evidence of bilingual superiority on the 'hidden' nonempirical items. Between group differences are significant on item 2 ($X^2(1)$ = 4.25, p < .05) and show a trend towards bilingual superiority on items 1 and 5 (item 1: $X^2(1)$ = 3.39, p < .07; item 5: $X^2(1)$ = 2.60, p < .11). There were no differences between the groups on the 'visible' items 6 and 7. The fact that the

TABLE 2.3   Performance of bilingual and unilingual groups on nonempirical and empirical questions

	Grade 3			Grade 6		
	Bilingual	Unilingual	Average %	Bilingual	Unilingual	Average %
Nonempirical:						
1. Either the counter in my hand is not white or it is white (H, T)*	0.0	0.0	0.0	23.1 (3)	0.0	11.5
2. The counter in my hand is blue and it is not blue (H, F)	30.0 (12)	12.5 (5)	21.2	53.8 (7)	15.4 (2)	34.6
3. The counter in my hand is not white and it is white (H, F)	27.5 (11)	10.0 (4)	18.8	53.8 (7)	30.8 (4)	42.3
4. Either the counter in my hand is yellow or it is not yellow (H, T)	0.0	0.0	0.0	23.1 (3)	15.4 (2)	19.2
5. The counter in my hand is both blue and it is not blue (H, F)	30.0 (12)	15.0 (6)	22.5	53.8 (7)	23.1 (3)	38.5
6. The counter in my hand is green and it is not green (V, F, green)	27.5 (11)	10.0 (4)	18.8	46.2 (6)	38.5 (5)	42.3
7. Either the counter in my hand is red or it is not red (V, T, blue)	10.0 (4)	7.5 (3)	8.7	38.5 (5)	23.1 (3)	30.8
Mean number correct nonempirical	1.25	.55	.90	2.9	1.5	2.2
Empirical:						
8. The counter in my hand is either not yellow or it is blue (V, T, blue)	85.0 (34)	80.0 (32)	82.5	100 (13)	61.5 (8)	80.8
9. The counter in my hand is yellow and it is not green (V, F, green)	87.5 (35)	77.5 (31)	82.5	100 (13)	92.3 (12)	96.2
10. The counter in my hand is blue and it is not yellow (H, CT)	27.5 (11)	37.5 (15)	32.5	92.3 (12)	53.8 (7)	73.1
11. The counter in my hand is either red or it is not green (H, CT)	20.0 (8)	42.5 (17)	31.3	92.3 (12)	53.8 (7)	73.1
Mean number correct empirical	2.38	2.20	2.29	3.80	2.70	3.25

* The first letter in brackets after each item signifies the status of the counter, whether hidden (H) or visible (V). The second letter signifies the correct answer, either true (T), false (F) or can't tell (CT). For the visible items the colour of the counter is also shown.

counter was visible (thereby ruling out a 'can't tell' response) and the practice effect of items 1–5 seems to have improved the performance of the unilingual children on these items. This suggests that the unilingual children are as capable of the appropriate reasoning as the bilingual children (which they are, since groups are matched on verbal reasoning scores) but they analyse linguistic input less closely, being more content to give the obvious 'can't tell' response to the 'hidden' nonempirical items 1 to 5. Differences between bilingual and unilingual groups in the total number of nonempirical items correct did not attain statistical significance (F (1, 24) = 2.33, p < .14).

The performance of the bilingual and unilingual grade 6 children on the empirical items is quite revealing. There are significant differences between the groups on three of the four items (item 8: $X^2(1)$ = 6.19, p < .01; items 10 and 11: $X^2(1)$ = 4.89, p < .05) and the difference in total number of empirical items correct is significant (F (1, 24) = 11.25, p < .01). It is clear that the unilingual children have difficulty in switching strategy between the nonempirical and empirical items. Only 61.5% of this group are correct on the first empirical question, considerably less than the grade 3 unilinguals. They recover on the second empirical question but may again fail to shift strategy on items 10 and 11. There is little doubt that the vast majority of the grade 6 unilingual children would have solved the empirical problems had these problems been presented on their own. Their relative inferiority on these problems under the conditions of the present study is attributable, therefore, not to lack of reasoning ability, but to a less flexible and analytic orientation to linguistic input.

CONCLUSIONS

The bilingual children at both grade levels showed a significantly greater awareness of the arbitrary nature of word-referent relationships and were also better able to evaluate nonempirical contradictory statements. These results support the findings of Ianco-Worrall (1972) and Ben-Zeev (1977a, 1977b) and are consistent with Vygotsky's (1962) hypothesis that bilingualism can promote awareness of linguistic operations.

However, the study is subject to the limitations of other studies in this area in that the construct validity of the dependent measures has not been adequately demonstrated. For example, the *meaning and reference, arbitrariness of language,* and *nonphysical nature of words* tasks were devised by Osherson and Markman as measures of an 'objective' orientation to language. However, the correlations between these tasks in the present study (reported in Cummins 1978c) suggest that although they do have elements in common, they do not represent a single unitary dimension. Thus, considerably more research is needed to elucidate the nature of children's metalinguistic awareness and the development of an analytic orientation to language. The present findings suggest that it may be worthwhile to include bilingualism as an independent variable in this research and that the study of bilingual development may contribute substantially to our understanding of these phenomena.

Section 2
Bilingual education

This section includes three chapters which have bilingual education as their common theme. Chapter 3 summarizes the rather considerable data that have been collected with respect to the outcomes of French immersion programmes in Canada. Chapter 4 provides an example of the evaluation of a specific immersion programme. The focus of Chapter 5 is on bilingual programmes for minority language children.

French immersion programmes are an example of bilingual education for majority language children. That is to say, the students who enrol in the programme are members of the dominant sociocultural group in the Canadian/North American context. As a result, their participation and possible assimilation into another linguistic and/or cultural group is likely to be by choice rather than because of political or economic necessity as is frequently the case for minority language speakers. Furthermore, because of the dominant position of their language in society, majority language children's first language continues to develop and be maintained even while a second language is being learned. Lambert (1977) has, as we saw in Chapter 1, referred to this situation as one of additive bilingualism where a second language is added to the individual's linguistic repertoire with no loss to the first language. This is in sharp contrast to the situation of subtractive bilingualism often faced by minority speakers where because of the weaker role their first language plays in the broader societal context, learning the majority language is often accompanied by first language loss.

The results from French immersion programmes have been used by policy-makers to argue that bilingual education for minority children is not needed. After all, French immersion children are educated in a second language and they succeed academically. In an argument such as this, a multitude of factors are overlooked (Burnaby 1980; Cohen and Swain 1976; Swain 1978c). For example, in French immersion programmes, the teachers are bilingual in the child's home language and the target language. Although teachers address their students only in the target language, they understand and respond appropriately to their students' use of their mother tongue. In non-bilingual programmes for minority students, it is rare that teachers are proficient in the students' home language, let alone comprehend the cultural context in which their students' language is embedded.

Another extremely important factor that is overlooked is the fact that the French immersion programme is a *bilingual* one. In the case of early total immersion programmes, it is true that there is not mother tongue instruction in the first several years of education. However, by grades 2 or 3 French immersion students have at least a first language arts programme taught to them in their mother tongue. Education in their mother tongue increases in subsequent years, continues throughout the remainder of their education and occurs in a variety of content areas. A bilingual education which lasts throughout a student's academic career is a relatively rare occurrence for a minority language speaker.

Such factors are important in accounting for differences in research findings between French immersion programmes and minority 'immersion' programmes, or even between French immersion programmes and bilingual education programmes for minority language children. The consequence of looking only at the facts that emerge from different evaluations, however, is that the claim is made that the results are not generalizable beyond the particular programme. For research to provide a basis for making policy, it must be realized that data or 'facts' from bilingual programmes become interpretable only in the context of a coherent theory from which predictions about programme outcomes under different conditions can be generated. Policy-makers and educators need to realize that although research findings cannot be *directly* applied across contexts, theories are almost by definition applicable across contexts in that the validity of any theoretical principle is assessed precisely by how well it can account for the research findings in a variety of contexts.

In Chapter 5 we present just such a theoretical principle – that there are aspects of language proficiency that are common to both first and second languages. In other words, there are aspects of first and second language proficiency that are interdependent. This 'interde-pendence principle' permits us, for example, to understand why *less* instruction in the second language often results in higher second language proficiency scores for minority students, while for majority language students *more* instruction in the second language results in higher second language proficiency scores. It also is consistent with the research evidence that exists and which denies conventional folk wisdom: with respect to some aspects of second language learning, older learners are more efficient learners. Inevitably the question of just what the common underlying proficiency consists of is an empirical one. It is the issue with which much of Part Two of this book is concerned. It is an issue we have addressed at the macro level, and are beginning in this book to address at the micro level. However, a great deal more research needs to be done.

Just as in Section 1 we thought that it would be useful to have an example of the sort of study being summarized in Chapter 1, so too in this section we felt that a chapter which illustrated the type of programme evaluation on which so much of Chapters 3 and 5 are based would similarly be of value. Chapter 4, therefore, describes an evaluation of early French immersion students at grades 6 and 8. The results show that in English language skills and work-study skills, the immersion students perform as well as, or better than, English programme comparison groups; that in mathematics and science, the immersion students perform as well as their comparison groups; and that in French language skills, the immersion students' performance is approaching or equivalent to that of native speakers of French in some tests of French.

Chapter 4 illustrates how review papers like that of Chapter 3 can neglect certain aspects detailed in a particular evaluation. For example, in Chapter 4 one can follow the progress of individual groups (cohorts) of students from grade to grade. Although Chapter 3 documents the general progress made by students over time, it smooths out the untidy ups and downs of progress that may occur from year to year. Additionally, such findings as those reported in Chapter 4 with respect to achievement in science and mathematics depending on the language of instruction, rarely reach a general review article if they remain, as these have, isolated and unreplicated findings. However, these isolated findings provide additional evidence supporting the interdependence principle: content learned in one language is interdependent across languages, given, of course, sufficient proficiency (threshold levels) in both languages.

Many studies like that illustrated in Chapter 4 suffer from the same design problems as those outlined in Section 1. For example, the children in the Chapter 4 study were not randomly assigned to educational programmes: parents chose in which programme their children would enrol. This situation leaves open the possibility that the students in the immersion programme may have characteristics that differentiate them from their comparison groups, such as generally having a greater motivation to learn French. Under these conditions the only reasonable approach to evaluating immersion programmes is to recognize that students possessing these characteristics constitute part of the very nature of the programme itself. The question which the evaluation results can answer, therefore, is how do students in the immersion programme perform relative to students receiving the usual educational programme rather than the more rigorous question of how students in the immersion programme perform relative to how they would perform if they were in the regular English programme (Swain 1978d). From this point of view, it is particularly interesting to see in Chapter 5 the results of the Punjabi–English bilingual project undertaken in Britain where students were randomly assigned to educational treatments.

3 A review of immersion education in Canada: research and evaluation studies*

Introduction

From the time it began in 1965 in St Lambert, Quebec, up to and including the present, immersion education has been viewed as a somewhat radical means of teaching French to anglophone students. Not only was it uncertain how well students would learn French under conditions where it was used as a medium of communication to teach curriculum content areas, but also it was uncertain whether the curriculum content would be adequately learned and the first language adequately maintained and developed. These concerns were expressed by parents and educators alike, and formed the basis of the many research and evaluation studies which have been undertaken across Canada. The extensive bibliography in Swain and Lapkin (1982) listing reports, published articles and books concerned with immersion education, attests to these concerns.

This chapter will review the results of the research and evaluation studies associated with immersion education in Canada. The results will be reviewed in line with the goals of immersion programmes, first with respect to the achievement attained by participating students in academic subjects such as mathematics and science. Secondly, the promotion and maintenance of first language development will be examined. Thirdly, the results pertaining to second language proficiency will be discussed. Fourthly, the effectiveness of immersion education for children with below average IQ or with learning disabilities will be examined. Finally, the social and psychological

* This chapter is a slightly revised version of an article of the same title by M. Swain appearing in *Studies on Immersion Education: A Collection for US Educators*. Sacramento: California State Department of Education, 1984. Without the support of California State Department's Office of Bilingual Bicultural Education and its staff, this chapter would not have been written. Permission to reprint the revised version has been granted by Pergamon Press which published it under the same title in *ELT Documents* 119: 35–51, 1984.

impact of immersion education on the participating students and on the communities involved will be considered.

Academic achievement

One principle of immersion education is that the same academic content will be covered as in the regular English programme, the only difference between the two programmes being the language of instruction. In the immersion programme where the language of instruction is the students' second language, the concern that the immersion students will be able to keep up in their academic achievement with students taught in their first language is of considerable importance. This concern has largely been allayed as a result of the research evidence.

Immersion students have been tested using standardized tests of mathematics (at all grade levels) and science (from about grade 5 on), and their performance has been compared to that of students in the English-only programme. The tests were typically administered in English even though students were taught the subjects in French. The reason for this was straightforward: although parents wanted their children to learn French, they wanted to be assured that their children would be able to deal with mathematical and scientific concepts in English, the dominant language in North American society. Testing the students in English seemed the best way to gauge their ability to do so. It was thought at the time, however, that not testing the students in the language of instruction might seriously handicap their performance.

The results associated with early total immersion programmes consistently show that, both in science and mathematics, the immersion students perform as well as their English-instructed comparison groups. For example, in summarizing the results of nine years of testing early total immersion students in Ontario, Swain and Lapkin (1982) report that in thirty-eight separate administrations of standardized mathematics achievement tests from grades 1 to 8, the immersion students performed as well as, or better than, their English-taught comparison groups in thirty-five instances. In three instances, an English-instructed group scored significantly higher than an immersion group on one or two of the subtests, but never on the test as a whole. The results with respect to science achievement are similar in that the average scores of the immersion and comparison groups were equivalent in fourteen separate administrations from grades 5 to 8.

The results associated with early partial and late immersion programmes do not consistently provide evidence for the equivalence of performance between the immersion and comparison groups. In mathematics, inferior performance has occasionally been measured among some groups of early partial immersion students from grade 3 on (Barik and Swain 1977a; Barik, Swain and Nwanunobi 1977; Edmonton Public Schools 1980b), and in science, from grade 5 on (Barik and Swain 1978b).

In the late immersion programmes, when French as a second language (FSL) instruction has been limited to one or two grades prior to entry into the immersion programme, the immersion group's performance is occasionally inferior to that of its comparison group in science and mathematics (Barik, Swain and Gaudino 1976). However, when late immersion students have had FSL instruction each year through to the immersion year, the level of mastery of content taught in French is comparable to that attained by their English-instructed comparison groups (Genesee, Polich and Stanley 1977; Stern *et al.* 1976). The results from the early partial and late immersion programmes suggest that the second language skills of the students may at times be insufficient to deal with the complexities of the subject material taught to them in French. In general and over the long run, however, the results suggest that immersion students are able to maintain standards of academic achievement comparable with those of their English-educated peers (see also Tucker 1975).

The issue of the language of testing is relevant here. As has been noted, the students were usually tested in their first language although they were taught mathematics and science in their second language. This does not seem to have handicapped the students as was suspected. This adds credence to Cummins' (1981b) 'interdependence hypothesis' which suggests that cognitive academic knowledge is held in common storage and underlies the ability to understand or express it in either language given adequate levels of linguistic proficiency in both languages. In this case, the immersion students gained the knowledge in one language but made full use of it in the other language context, both activities being dependent upon a threshold level of linguistic competence in each language.

Would the results have been different had the language of the tests been French? The existing evidence suggests they would not have been different for the early total immersion students (e.g. Barik and Swain 1975) or for the late immersion students who had had sufficient prior FSL instruction (Genesee 1976a).

The impact of second language proficiency level on test performance is a serious issue, and one which has not been well attended to in the testing of academic achievement among minority students. An example from the immersion data speaks to this point: the performance on a social studies test of grade 4 early immersion students and students studying only social studies in French (60 minutes a day of instruction in French since beginning school) were compared. Two different versions of the same test were given: one in English and one in French. Results from the English version of the test revealed no differences in social studies achievement between the groups. Results from the French version of the test, however, revealed a significant difference between the two groups in favour of the immersion students. Furthermore, the immersion group performed in French as it had in English, whereas the other group's score when tested in French was much lower than when tested in English, even though they had been taught social studies in French. These results indicate quite clearly that testing students in a second language in which they are not highly proficient may not accurately reflect their level of knowledge related to the content of the test. In other words, testing in a second language is a risky business if one wishes to measure accurately subject content knowledge.

First language development

Because the immersion programmes place so much emphasis on curricular instruction in French, there was naturally a concern that the development of first language skills might be negatively affected. This was thought to be potentially most serious at the primary level when literacy skills in the first language would normally be taught. Indeed, one of the reasons early partial immersion programmes exist is because of the fear on the part of some parents and educators that the negative consequences of the early total immersion programme on the development of first language literacy skills in the formative years would be irreparable, and rather than run this risk, it was felt that English literacy training should be introduced right from the beginning.

To what extent were these fears well-founded? The research evidence on this issue suggests that for these children, such fears have no basis in fact. In part, this is because these children are members of the dominant linguistic and cultural majority of Canada and as a consequence, English pervades all of their out-of-school life.

On the one hand, the results for students in the early total immersion programme indicate that, although initially behind students in unilingual English programmes in literacy skills, within a year of the introduction of an English Language Arts component into the curriculum, the immersion students perform equivalently on standardized tests of English achievement to that of students in the English-only programme (Genesee 1978a; Swain 1978b). This is the case even if English is not introduced until grade 3 (Edwards and Casserly 1976) or grade 4 (Protestant School Board of Greater Montreal 1972; Genesee and Lambert 1983). Furthermore, in some instances, the initial gap is not only closed but the immersion students end up out-performing their English-only programme peers in some aspects of measured English language skills (Swain, Lapkin and Andrew 1981).

On the other hand, the results for the early partial immersion students who have approximately half their programme devoted to instruction in, and about, English indicate that they do not perform as well on some aspects of measured English language skills as either their own comparison group in grades 2 or 3, or as well as immersion students at the same grade levels who began to be taught to read in English only in grades 2 or 3 (Barik, Swain and Nwanunobi 1977; Swain 1974). One interpretation of these results is that by teaching literacy skills in both languages at the same time, the interfering and competing surface linguistic features cause confusion, and it takes a period of time for this confusion to sort itself out.

The implication for bilingual education is that it is preferable initially to teach literacy-related skills directly in only one language, whether it be the first or second language. Once literacy-related skills are well-established in one language, they will transfer readily and rapidly to the other language (provided it is mastered), even possibly without explicit instruction. That this is so is strongly indicated by the results of immersion programmes which begin at later grade levels. For example, Cziko (1976) compared the performance on tests of reading comprehension in English and French of a group of early total immersion students with that of a group of children who began their immersion programme at the grade 4 level. The scores of the two groups were equivalent in English. The students who had begun their immersion experience at grade 4 had apparently reached the same outcome as the early partial immersion students, but without the intervening confusion. The results from immersion programmes which begin at the grade 7 or 8 level, and discussed below with respect to second language skills, also support this view (e.g. Genesee 1981; Lapkin, Swain, Kamin and Hanna 1983). However, in a community or social context where the first language may be less strongly supported as is the case for many language minority children, teaching initially in the first language is likely to compensate for the possibly limited use of the language in its full range of functions and skills. Teaching in the first language first is more likely to lead to full bilingualism among minority language students than leaving the first language in second place (Cummins 1981b; Swain 1983).

Results from other studies of early total French immersion students' English language skills are in line with those from standardized achievement tests, indicating an initial discrepancy in literacy-based skills between immersion and English programme students in favour of the latter group, followed in later grades with equivalent perform-ance being noted. For example, the writing skills of grade 3, 4 and 5 immersion students have been examined. Short stories written by grade 3 children were analysed for, among other things, vocabulary use, technical skills (punctuation, spelling and capitalization), gram-matical skills, and the ability to write in logical chronological sequence. There were small differences noted between immersion and non-immersion students in each of these areas (Swain 1975a). Genesee (1974) reports on a study of the writing skills of grade 4 immersion students. Based on teacher ratings, the immersion group lagged behind English programme students in spelling, but their stories were considered more original. Ratings were similar for sentence accuracy, vocabulary choice, sentence complexity and variety, and overall organization.

Lapkin (1982) had elementary teachers globally assess compositions written by grade 5 students from both programmes. The teachers did not know which programme the students were in (also the case in Genesee 1974 above); they only knew that the compositions were written by grade 5 students. The compositions of the two groups were judged to be equivalent. A further analysis of variety in vocabulary use and length of composition revealed no differences between the groups.

The type of tasks involved in these studies of English writing and achievement represent the context-reduced, cognitively demanding quadrant of Cummins' (1981b) language proficiency model (see Chapter 8). But what about tasks that are at the context-embedded end of the contextual support continuum? One group of people to ask this question of are the children's own parents. In a parent survey conducted in British Columbia, McEachern (1980) asked whether they thought children in primary French immersion programmes suffer in their English language development. Of parents who had a child in a French immersion programme, an overwhelming 80% answered with an unqualified 'No'. Interestingly, of parents who did not have a child in the immersion programme, only 40% responded in this way. In Ontario, a questionnaire distributed to immersion parents included a question about their children's ability to express their thoughts in English. Over 90% of the parents indicated that they perceived no negative effects.

With the same question in mind, Genesee, Tucker and Lambert (1975) undertook a study which examined the communicative effectiveness of total immersion students in kindergarten, grades 1 and 2. They found that the immersion children were more communicatively effective and suggested that this was because their experience in the second language classroom had made the children more sensitive to the communication needs of the listener (see also Lambert and Tucker 1972).

Thus, there is substantial evidence that children in early total immersion programmes, although initially behind their English-educated comparison groups in literacy-related skills, catch up and even surpass their comparison groups once English is introduced into the curriculum. However, the evidence also suggests that no benefit derives from introducing English and French literacy training at the same time. It would appear preferable to learn these skills in one language first. The choice of language must be sensitive to community and societal factors external to the school programme. As has been shown, the immersion children at no time show retardation in their oral communicative skills, a fact due in large part to the overwhelming use of English in their environment, including school.

Second language development

In this section, the results from studies which have examined the second language development of students in immersion programmes will be reviewed. The section begins with a discussion of the results associated with students in early total immersion programmes and, within this context, a discussion of the 'double standard' that seems apparent according to whether second language learners come from majority or minority language situations. This is followed by a brief review of the early partial and late immersion results. The section concludes with a comparison of the second language abilities of early and late immersion students.

When early immersion programmes began, it was believed that by using the second language to communicate with the children, they would pick up the language much as children learning a first language do. Although the theoretical rationales seemed sound and were strongly reinforced by commonly held intuitions that second language learning is relatively easy for children, there was no guarantee that the programme would work. Indeed, some educators were sceptical that learning through a language could be more effective than being taught a language. But the desire to experiment with finding ways to improve students' second language skills prevailed. And with good reason, as the research evidence has demonstrated.

Each and every study that has compared the second language performance of students in early total immersion programmes with that of students in core FSL programmes (20–40 minutes of daily FSL instruction which focuses on teaching specified vocabulary and grammatical structures) has revealed a significant difference in favour of the immersion student (e.g. Barik and Swain 1975; Edwards and Casserly 1976). In fact, it soon became clear that giving the same test to immersion and core FSL students was ill-advised. If the level of difficulty was appropriate for immersion students, then the core FSL students would become frustrated, some even to the point of tears, at being unable to do any part of the test. If the level of difficulty of the test was appropriate for the core FSL students, then the immersion students became bored and quickly lost interest in the task. It can safely be concluded, therefore, that the combination of the increased time in French and the communicative methodology employed in immersion programmes vastly improves the second language proficiency of the students.

But what about the second language performance of the early total immersion students relative to native speakers of French? To answer this question we will look first at their receptive (listening and reading) skills and then at their productive (speaking and writing) skills.

The receptive skills of the immersion students have been measured over the years using a variety of listening and reading comprehension tests. The tests have included standardized tests of French achievement, as well as more communicatively-oriented tests. In the latter category, for example, are such tests as the *Test de Compréhension Aurale* (TCA) and the *Test de Compréhension Écrit* (TCE) developed by the Bilingual Education Project (1978, 1979) in the Modern Language Centre. In these tests, authentic texts from a variety of communicative domains are heard or read, and the students respond to questions about them. In the TCA students listen, for example, to a news report over the radio, a portion of a soap opera, an advertisement, and an interview. In the TCE students read, for example, a comic strip, a clipping from a newspaper, a recipe, and a poem.

On the standardized tests of French achievement, the results from Ontario (Swain and Lapkin 1982) show that after six or seven years in a primary immersion programme (that is, by grade 5 or 6) students perform on the average at about the 50th percentile. It is worthy of note that it took these children of middle-class background, with parents supportive of their programme and with positive attitudes towards learning French, until grade 5 or 6 to attain an average level of performance. It is appropriate to ask, given these data (see also Cummins 1981c), whether the expectations that children in bilingual education programmes from minority language backgrounds in the United States reach grade norms after a year or two in the programme are not somewhat unrealistic!

On some of the locally-developed comprehension tests, equivalence between immersion and francophone students has been noted as early as grade 2 (Lambert and Tucker 1972). In Ontario, comparisons with francophones were not made until the grade 5 level. When comparisons have been made, immersion students compare favourably to francophones (e.g. Swain, Lapkin and Andrew 1981). From these data, therefore, it appears that early immersion students develop native-like skills in their ability to understand spoken and written texts.

The productive skills of the early immersion students have also been examined over the years using a variety of techniques. It is clear from the results that the immersion students do not attain native-like proficiency in their spoken or written French (e.g. Adiv 1981; Genesee 1978a; Harley 1979, 1982; Harley and Swain 1977, 1978; Spilka 1976).

For example, in a study designed to provide a description of the verb system as used in the speech of grade 5 immersion children compared to bilingual and monolingual francophones, Harley and Swain (1977) concluded that, in general, the immersion children may be said to be operating with simpler and grammatically less redundant verb systems. They tend to lack forms for which grammatically less complex alternative means of conveying the appropriate meaning exist. The forms and rules that they have mastered appear to be those that are the most generalized in the target verb system (for example, the first conjugation *-er* verb pattern). In the area of verb syntax, it appears that where French has a more complex system than English, as in the placement of object pronouns, the immersion children tend to opt for a simpler pattern that approximates the one they are already familiar with in their first language.

Numerous other examples could be given of differences between the immersion and francophone students. However, the point here is that the immersion students' communicative abilities (Adiv 1981; Szamosi, Swain and Lapkin 1979) outstrip their abilities to express themselves in grammatically accurate ways. One might ask to what extent this affects native-speaker judgements about immersion students, or why their productive capacity is grammatically limited. These questions are dealt with elsewhere (Harley 1982; Lepicq 1980; Swain 1978c) and will not be considered further here. What is of importance to consider is the comparison between the second language productive performance of the immersion students in Canada and that of minority students in the United States. Such a comparison provides an excellent example of what might be labelled the 'linguistic double standard'.

The linguistic double standard is simply that majority language children are praised for learning a second language even if the result is non-native-like in its characteristics, whereas minority language children must demonstrate full native-like competence in the second language to receive the same praise. The reasons for the double standard may be clear, but that does not make it any less of a double standard. Recognition of the double standard should surely make us reappraise our expectations for one, if not both groups.

The results from early partial immersion programmes with respect to second language development are as might be expected given the usual relationship between time and level of performance that holds for majority language students studying a second (or foreign) language (Carroll 1975). The scores of the early partial immersion students tend to fall between those of early total immersion students and core FSL students (e.g. Barik and Swain 1976b; Edwards *et al.* 1980). Although partial immersion students do not perform as well as total immersion students at the same grade level, they tend to perform as well as total immersion students at lower grade levels who have had similar amounts of contact time with French. For example, a grade 5 partial immersion student and a grade 2 total immersion student who have each accumulated two and a half years of French instruction time, tend to demonstrate equivalent performance levels. By grade 8, the partial immersion students tend to perform as well as total immersion students one grade level below them (Andrew, Lapkin and Swain 1979c). The lower level of linguistic proficiency exhibited by the partial immersion students in the earlier grades may account for their poorer academic achievement in some of the instances noted above.

For example, the grade 6 partial immersion students in one study

(Barik and Swain 1978b) did not perform as well as their English-educated peers in science or mathematics. It was also the case that their level of French performance most closely approximated grade 3 and 4 total immersion students. It may therefore be the case that their level of French was not adequate to deal with the more sophisticated level of mathematical and scientific concepts being presented to them in French.

As with the early total and partial immersion students, the late immersion students' second language performance is superior to that of core FSL students at the same grade level. However, it has been noted that unless there is a strong follow-up programme to the one or two years of immersion that constitute the programme, the advantages gained by students entering an immersion programme at the later grade levels with respect to second language skills may dissipate (Lapkin, Swain, Kamin and Hanna 1983). Indeed the question of the maintenance of second language skills of both early and late immersion students in their follow-up programmes at the secondary school level is one that needs to be investigated.

Now that early immersion students are entering and beginning to graduate from high school in the Ontario and Quebec programmes, it is possible to compare the performance of early and late immersion students. The results of these comparisons emanating from Quebec differ somewhat from those in Ontario. It would appear that the differences can in part be accounted for in terms of programme variations, most obviously with respect to the overall amount of time students have been studying in French. These differences in programme structures, their associated second language outcomes, and the implications for second language immersion programmes will be discussed below.

In Ontario, the lead groups of early total immersion students were tested at the grade 8 level and their performance has been compared with late immersion students also in grade 8 who had been in a one, two or three year immersion programme (beginning at the grade 8, 7 or 6 level respectively). The results indicate that the early immersion students outperform the late immersion groups on tests of French listening comprehension, reading comprehension, general French achievement and proficiency (Lapkin, Swain, Kamin and Hanna 1983; Morrison 1979).

In Montreal, comparisons of the early and late immersion programme students from grades 7 to 11 have been made (Adiv 1980; Adiv and Morcos 1979; Genesee 1981). The results indicate that the early total immersion students outperform the late immersion students after one year (grade 7) of immersion education. However, in general, from the end of the second year of the late immersion experience, the performance of early and late immersion students on a variety of second language tests including all four skills of reading, writing, listening and speaking appears to be equivalent. This finding is somewhat unexpected given the results from Ontario, and the presumed advantage of early second language learning.

The differences in results between the Ontario and Montreal programmes are an indication of the impact that programme design can have on the second language performance of majority language students. In the case of the Ontario programmes, the early immersion programme maintained a French to English ratio of 80:20 in grades 3 to 5 and 50:50 in grades 6 to 8, whereas the corresponding figures for the Montreal programme was 60:40 in grade 3 and 40:60 in grades 4 to 8. This means that the Ontario early immersion students had considerably more in-school contact time in French than did the Montreal students, which could account for their superior second language performance relative to late immersion students. These results argue for the maximum allotment of time to the second language for majority students in order to maintain and further develop their second language skills. This is essential for majority language children because of the limited use they may make of the second language in out-of-school contexts. (Genesee 1978b; Swain and Lapkin 1982).

The comparison of early and late immersion students raises the issue of the relative ease of second language learning by younger and older learners. Even in the case of the Ontario students where the late immersion students remain behind the early immersion students, it is clear that they have made considerable progress towards the proficiency levels exhibited by the early immersion students. The issue of age and second language learning is a much debated topic (see for example Cummins 1980a; Genesee 1978c; Krashen, Long and Scarcella 1979 for reviews), and will not be dealt with in this chapter. Suffice it to say that the immersion results suggest that older learners may be more effective than younger ones in some aspects of second language learning, most notably in those aspects associated with literacy-related and literacy-supported language skills. It may be, however, that early immersion students feel more comfortable and at ease in the second language and maintain their facility in the second language to a greater extent over the long run. Furthermore, in the case of late immersion programmes for majority children, some students will choose not to learn a second language, since it is only one of many competing interests and since it is recognized that a language takes a great deal of time and energy to learn. Finally, early immersion programmes seem to be able to accommodate a wider range of personality types and cognitive styles than late immersion programmes (Swain and Burnaby 1976; Tucker, Hamayan and Genesee 1976).

In summary, the second language results of the immersion research and evaluation studies indicate that immersion students attain levels of performance that far exceed that of students in core FSL programmes, and they develop receptive skills in the second language comparable to francophones of the same age. However, for early immersion students, the attainment of average performance on standardized tests of French achievement can take up to six or seven years, raising the issue that unrealistic expectations are being held for minority language children in bilingual education programmes in the United States.

Although immersion students appear to attain native-like receptive skills, their productive skills continue to remain non-native-like. They are, however, quite capable of communicating their ideas in spite of their grammatical weaknesses. It was suggested that this same level of productive skills in the second language among minority students would not be considered acceptable by the educational system. That it is praised within the majority culture when attained by majority language students and denigrated when attained by minority language students, is indicative of a linguistic double standard.

Finally, comparisons between early and late immersion students suggest that late immersion programmes can be as effective in developing some aspects of students' second language skills as early immersion programmes. However, the advantages in second language performance of the early immersion students can be maintained with an adequate allotment of instruction time in French. The apparently more rapid second language learning exhibited by the late immersion students should not be taken as an indication that it is, therefore, the best option. As an option it must be balanced against potential long-term advantages of early bilingualism, and the very likely possibility that early immersion education makes bilingualism a viable goal for a wider spectrum of the population.

IQ, learning disabilities and immersion

Many students enrolled in primary immersion education are anglophone students of middle to upper-middle socio-economic backgrounds. However, students with other background characteristics have enrolled in immersion programmes, and some studies have been undertaken to determine whether they benefit as much from immersion education as their classmates in immersion programmes and/or as much as their peers (children with similar characteristics) in the regular English programme. In this section, the results of these studies will be summarized for two groups of children: those with below average IQ, and those with learning disabilities.

A commonly held view is that immersion education is only for children of above average intelligence. The research evidence contradicts this view. There are several ways this issue might be examined. One way is to determine how immersion students who obtain above average IQ scores perform relative to immersion students who obtain below average IQ scores. It would be expected that above average students would obtain higher scores on second language measures than below average students, given the usual relationship between IQ and academic performance. In one study (Genesee 1976b), grade 4 early immersion and grade 7 late immersion students who were below average, average and above average IQ were administered a battery of French language tests which included measures of literacy-related language skills such as reading and language use, as well as measures of interpersonal communicative skills such as speaking and listening comprehension. It was found that, as expected, the above average students scored better than the average students who, in turn, scored better than the below average students on the tests of literacy-related language skills. However, there was no similar stratification by IQ of performance on the measures of interpersonal communication skills. In other words, the below average students understood as much spoken French as did the above average students, and they were rated as highly as the above average students on all measures of oral production: grammar, pronunciation, vocabulary and fluency of communication. Thus, it seems that the below average students were able to benefit from French immersion as much as the average and above average students in terms of acquiring interpersonal communication skills in the second language. Furthermore, from the English language and academic achievement testing that was carried out with the same samples of students, there was no evidence that the below average students in French immersion were farther behind in English skills development or academic achievement than were the below average students in the regular English programme.

There is another way of looking at this issue. If IQ is more important to success in school in an immersion programme than it is in a regular English programme, then it would be expected that a student's IQ would be more highly related to performance on achievement tests in the immersion programme than it is in the regular programme. Swain (1975b) found, however, that this was not the case; that is, the relationship between IQ and achievement scores was the same for early immersion children and children in the regular English programme. The relationship between IQ and tests of French listening comprehension and French reading and language usage was also examined. The same pattern was found as in Genesee's study cited above; that is, that the acquisition of comprehension skills was not related to IQ level, but the acquisition of second language literacy-related skills was.

These studies, then, suggest that IQ does not play a more significant role in the immersion programme than in the regular English programme as far as success in school is concerned. Furthermore, acquiring interpersonal communicative skills in a second language would appear in this context to be unrelated to IQ. Thus, although there will be differences in performance among students, the below average IQ students are not at any more of a disadvantage in an immersion programme than they would be if they were in a regular English programme, plus they have an equal opportunity of learning second language communicative skills.

Basically the same conclusion has been reached about children with language learning disabilities. The child with a language learning disability is one who has normal intelligence and no primary emotional, motivational, or physical difficulties, and yet has difficulty acquiring specific basic skills such as reading, spelling, and oral or written language (Bruck 1979). It has been found in an ongoing research project designed to investigate the suitability of early French immersion for children with language learning disabilities that, 'when compared to a carefully selected group of language disabled children in English programmes, the learning disabled children continue to develop facility in their first language; they learn their basic academic skills at the predicted rate; they exhibit no severe behavioural problems, and, perhaps of most importance, they acquire greater competency in French' (Bruck 1979, p. 43). In her report of this study, Bruck (1978) points out that many learning disabled children who have followed the core FSL programme leave school with almost no knowledge of French because the nature of the teaching method seems to exploit their areas of weakness (memory work, repetition of language out of context, explicit teaching of abstract rules). Thus, if learning disabled children are to learn French in school, immersion is the best method for doing this.

In summary, as with children with below average IQ, there is no evidence which suggests that expectations for learning disabled children in immersion programmes, should be any different from those of similar children in regular English programmes.

Social and psychological effects

In this final section the social and psychological effects of immersion education will be reviewed. First, the immersion students' perceptions of themselves, English-Canadians, French-Canadians and the broader sociocultural aspects of Canada will be discussed. This will be followed by a brief section on satisfaction with the programme as expressed by student participants and members of the community.

A number of studies have been undertaken in Montreal which examine the immersion students' perception of their own ethnolinguistic group, themselves, and the French-Canadian ethnolinguistic group. In one study, early immersion and English-educated children were asked to rate themselves, English-Canadians and French-Canadians on 13 bipolar adjectives such as strong–weak, friendly–unfriendly (Lambert and Tucker 1972). The immersion and English comparison groups both made favourable assessments of themselves and of English-Canadians. In the earlier grades, the immersion students made more favourable assessments of French-Canadians than did their English comparison groups. Although this difference in their assessments of French-Canadians had disappeared by grade 5, nevertheless when they were asked *directly* about their feelings and attitudes, the immersion students were clearly more positive. For example, when asked: 'Suppose you happened to be born into a French-Canadian family, would you be just as happy to be a French-Canadian person as an English-Canadian person?', 84% of the grade 5 immersion children responded with 'just as happy to be French-Canadian', whereas only 48% of the English-educated group responded in this way.

In another study (Cziko, Lambert and Gutter 1979), grade 5 and 6 immersion and English-educated students were asked to make judgements about the similarity/dissimilarity of pairs of concepts such as 'myself' compared with monolingual English-Canadians, monolingual French-Canadians, bilingual French-Canadians, and bilingual English-Canadians. The results indicated that the early immersion students perceived themselves as more similar to bilingual English-Canadians and bilingual French-Canadians than did the late immersion or English programme students. The authors conclude that 'the early immersion experience seems to have reduced the social distance perceived between self and French-Canadians, especially French-Canadians who are bilingual' (p. 26).

It is possible that the educational experience of the immersion students might lead to a more sophisticated understanding of the social and cultural aspects of Canadian life. To investigate this question, grade 5 and 6 immersion students were asked to write a composition on the topic of 'Why I like (or do not like) being Canadian' (Swain 1980). Each composition was subjected to a content analysis and the substantive comments were identified and tabulated. Several interesting findings emerged. First, the immersion students' commentary spanned a much broader perspective in that they gave on the average two to three times as many reasons as did the English comparison groups. Secondly, three times as many immersion students as English programme students commented specifically on the rich and varied cultural and/or linguistic composition of Canada. Thirdly, over 20% of the immersion children, but none of the English-educated children, commented on the possibility in Canada of being able to speak more than one language. In general most of the compositions written by the English students focused on the natural beauty of Canada as opposed to the beauty of linguistic and cultural diversity which was more likely to be mentioned in the compositions of the immersion students.

Whether the immersion students' views are the result of their schooling experience, the influence of their parents, or their experience in the wider community cannot be determined from the studies undertaken. Probably their views reflect the interaction of all three influences. Practically speaking, the source of their views is probably less important than their existence.

Immersion and core FSL students have been asked their views about the French programmes in which they are enrolled. Lambert and Tucker (1972) found that relative to core FSL students, grade 4 and 5 immersion students were much more likely to say that they enjoy studying French the way they do, they think their programme has just about the right amount of time spent on French – core FSL tended to say that too much time was spent on French – and that they wanted to continue learning French. This study suggests a general endorsement by immersion students of their programme and way of learning French.

In a study in which these same immersion children in grade 11 and their parents were interviewed, Cziko *et al.* (1978) concluded that 'there is a very clear appreciation for the early immersion experience on the part of the early immersion students and their parents who, in the vast majority, say they would choose the immersion option if they had to do it all over' (p. 23).

In a comparison of the early and late immersion students in Ontario at the grade 8 level (Lapkin, Swain, Kamin and Hanna 1983), it was found that the early immersion students were more likely to respond that they would prefer a bilingual high school programme than late immersion students. Early immersion students also were likely to say that the amount of time they were currently spending in French was 'about right' or 'a bit too short', whereas the late immersion students were more likely to respond that they would prefer a programme with less French in it, and that the amount of time spent in French was 'a bit too long'. Thus, in general, immersion students express satisfaction with their programme, with early immersion students being most positive and core FSL students being least positive.

Although parents who have children enrolled in an immersion programme express satisfaction with it, the growth of immersion programmes has not been without its tensions. As immersion programmes grow in size and number, certain sectors of the community feel threatened (Burns and Olson 1981). One sector is the English-speaking parents who want their children to attend, or continue to attend, the regular English programme in their neighbourhood school. They see the space in their neighbourhood school being swallowed up by increasing numbers of immersion students, and have formed 'concerned parents' organizations to argue against the growth of immersion programmes. The tensions created by the pro-immersion and anti-immersion parents have surfaced in communities across Canada, and have recently received nationwide press coverage (e.g. Toronto *Globe and Mail* 9th January, 1982).

The problem would probably not be so serious were it not for the current period of declining enrolment being felt by schools across Canada. During this period of declining enrolment, the only area of growth is in the French immersion programmes, thus exacerbating the problems in English schools. The most threatened group, and therefore, predictably, the most loudly outspoken group against French immersion programmes are monolingual English-speaking teachers (Burns and Olson 1981). They consider their own job security to be threatened by immersion programmes, and recognize that they themselves could never, even if they wanted to, make the transition to teaching in an immersion programme where native-speaking proficiency in French is essential. Thus the current rapid expansion of immersion programmes has brought with it concern on the part of English-speaking teachers which is supported by parents of their students in the local community. The resolution of these tensions is yet to come.

To summarize, the psychological and social impact of immersion programmes has in no way negatively affected the immersion students' views of themselves or of their own ethnolinguistic group, while at the same time it has closed somewhat the social gap between the perceptions of themselves and French-Canadians. Immersion students and their parents express satisfaction with their programme. However, conditions of declining enrolment in the wider society have resulted in a threat to job security for teachers, and a threat of school closings in their neighbourhood for parents, leading to inevitable tensions in the school and in the community. Immersion education may become a scapegoat for these groups as a result of its unqualified success within the Canadian context in improving the second language proficiency of English-speaking students.

Conclusions

The results of the research and evaluation studies associated with immersion education for majority language children in Canada indicate that the goals of the programme have been met. The students have achieved high levels of proficiency in the second language while developing and maintaining normal levels of first language development. This degree of bilingualism has been attained with no long-term deficit observed in achievement in academic subjects. The immersion students appreciate the programme in which they have participated, and express positive attitudes toward the target language group while maintaining a healthy self-identity and appreciation for their own linguistic and cultural membership.

The results also highlight several important principles related to the schooling of majority and minority children:

1. The language of tests is an important consideration when testing for knowledge of subject content. Students' knowledge may be underrated if their proficiency in the language of the test has not reached a 'threshold' level. Even though students may have been taught the subject content in one language, this does not necessarily imply that testing should occur in that language.

2. Teaching initial literacy in two languages at the same time may lead to slower rates of progress than first developing literacy-related skills in one language.
3. Communicative effectiveness in the first or second language does not imply grade level performance on literacy-based academic tasks. It is, however, an important precursor.
4. The ability to function in context-reduced cognitively demanding tasks in the second language is a gradual learning process extending over a number of years indicated by the fact that immersion students take up to six or seven years to demonstrate average levels of achievement in the second language relative to native speakers of the language.
5. Developing the ability to function in context-reduced cognitively demanding tasks in the first language underlies the ability to do the same in the second language. Thus, students, who begin their immersion programme at a later age than early immersion students make more rapid progress in literacy-related aspects of the second language.

The results of immersion education for English-speaking Canadians are impressive. In order to achieve similar goals for minority language children, their first language will need to play as strong a role cognitively, psychologically, and culturally as it does for immersion students.

4 Early French immersion later on*

In many parts of the world, bilingualism is a fact of life. In North America, however, bilingualism on a wide-scale tends to be limited to minority language groups who must learn English in order to function within the dominant English-speaking majority. Second or foreign languages have been taught to English-speaking students, but, in general, such teaching has had little success in developing a bilingual citizenry. This lack of success has concerned many an English-Canadian who, over the last decade, has become acutely aware of the French 'fact' in Canadian life. And among some parents and educators in Canada, the situation has led to a concerted effort to improve the outcomes of French as a second language (FSL) instruction (see, for example, Lambert and Tucker 1972; Stern *et al.* 1976; Swain 1978a).

Early French immersion (EFI) programmes are one manifestation of the attempt to improve FSL instruction. One assumption underlying the development of EFI programmes is that an environment in which language is used for real communication in meaningful, contextually-rich settings will be more conducive to second language learning than one in which it is not (as is the case in many traditional FSL classes). A second assumption is that more exposure to the second language will lead to greater proficiency in that language (see Cummins 1980b; Swain 1981 and this volume, chapter 5 for a refinement of this assumption).

A typical EFI programme then is one in which unilingual English-speaking children receive *all* of their instruction in the second language for the first several years of their schooling. In the third or fourth year of schooling (grades 2 or 3), a programme of English Language Arts is introduced and taught in English. With each successive year, other subjects may also be taught in English

* This chapter originally appeared as an article of the same title by M. Swain, S. Lapkin and C. M. Andrew in the *Journal of Multilingual and Multicultural Development* 2: 1–23, 1981. Permission to reprint this article has been granted by the authors.

such that by grade 6 approximately half of their instruction is in English and half in French. (For more detailed descriptions of EFI programmes, see Cohen and Swain 1976; Lambert and Tucker 1972; Swain 1978b, Swain and Bruck 1976).

The EFI programme was a radical departure from other FSL programmes, and it was not implemented without considerable concern for the possible detrimental effects the programme might have on the children's academic achievement and their continued development of first language skills. For this reason, many of the programmes incorporated an evaluation component into their implementation plans.

This chapter presents the results of an ongoing evaluation of two of the first EFI programmes to be initiated in the public school system of Ontario (province of Canada), by the Carleton Board of Education (CBE) and the Ottawa Board of Education (OBE). Their programmes have been evaluated each year since their inception in 1970–71 by the Bilingual Education Project of the Ontario Institute for Studies in Education (Andrew, Lapkin and Swain 1979a; Barik and Swain 1975, 1977b, 1978a; Swain and Barik 1976a, 1977; see also Swain and Barik 1976b). The students who enrolled in the EFI programme in Autumn 1970 (Cohort I) were completing grade 8 in Spring 1979, and those who enrolled in Autumn 1972 (Cohort III) were completing grade 6 in Spring 1979 when the testing for the current evaluation took place.

Purposes of the testing

In the early years of the EFI programme in OBE and CBE, testing was carried out to compare the progress of EFI programme and English programme pupils in four main areas: cognitive ability, French language skills, English language skills and other academic skills such as mathematics. The purpose was to determine whether the French language skills of the French immersion pupils were superior to those of the English programme pupils (receiving 20 to 30 minutes of French per day), and to monitor for possible detrimental effects of studying in French on the immersion pupils' cognitive ability, English and other academic skills. Because of the great differences in French skills between the immersion and English programme groups even at the earliest grade levels, it became clear that a more appropriate comparison group for the immersion pupils would be native French-speaking pupils of the same age and grade level. Such comparisons have been made when it was feasible to collect such data.

English language development and other academic skills, as well as cognitive ability, have continued to be monitored for both the immersion and English programme groups, as they progress through their school career. In addition, differences among groups of immersion students are now of interest since programme differences between the boards or among the schools within a board (e.g. different amounts of time allocated to instruction in French and English; different subjects taught in English, different amounts of French in the school environment) may possibly result in differences in achievement among groups of EFI students.

Previous findings

Table 4.1 (p. 60) summarizes the findings of previous evaluations as well as those of the 1979 testing programme. For each area tested, any significant differences between the immersion students and their comparison group are indicated. In the area of French skills, the immersion students' results are presented for the *Test de rendement en français*, the only French measure administered in all annual evaluations. Table 4.1 provides a longitudinal summary, in that the annual results for each cohort can be seen from kindergarten to the present grade level. In addition, it provides a replicational summary, since the results obtained at each grade level are shown for all three cohorts.

These results have been discussed in previous papers. However, some general trends are worth noting again. First, with respect to cognitive ability, there have been no detrimental effects of the immersion programme on IQ. In fact, since grade 4, the mean IQ score of the Cohort I immersion group has been significantly higher than that of the comparison group. Similar differences in favour of the Cohort II and III immersion groups have occurred at the grade 6 level. While it is not clear that the immersion students' superior IQ scores are due to the immersion programme, it is clear that the programme has not had any ill effects on cognitive ability as measured by the CCAT (see also Barik and Swain 1976a). Secondly, the immersion students experienced initial lags in some aspects of English and mathematics up to the grade 3 level. However, from grade 4 onwards, the trends have been reversed. The results indicate that, from grade 4 on, the immersion students are outperforming the

TABLE 4.1 Summary of findings for Cohorts I, II and III in grades K-8, French immersion (I) and comparison (C) groups.[+]

Variable	Cohort	Grade								
		K	1	2	3	4	5	6	7	8
IQ	I	ns	ns	ns	ns	I > C***	I > C*	I > C***	I > C***	I > C**
	II	I > C**	ns	ns	ns	ns	ns	I > C*	-	
	III	I > C*	ns	ns	ns	ns	ns	I > C**		
English	I	(C > I: letter recog.*)	C > I: wd. know*** wd. disc.*** read.***	ns	C > I: spell.*	ns	I > C: vocab.** punct.*** usage* lg. tot.**	I > C: spell.** capit.*** punct.*** usage** lg. tot.***	I > C: spell.* punct.* lg. tot.*	I > C: spell.** lg. tot.*
	II	(C > I: letters & sounds**)	C > I: wd. know** wd. disc.*** read.***	C > I: wd. know.* read.* tot. read.* spell.***	C > I: wd. know** tot. read.* spell.***	I > C: vocab.* usage* C > I: capit.*	ns	I > C: punct.* usage*** lg. tot.** C > I: story compl.*	-	
	III	ns	C > I: wd. know** wd. disc.*** read.***	C > I: spell.*	C > I: capit.*** punct.** lg. tot.**	ns	I > C: punct.** usage* lg. tot.*	I > C: punct.* usage** lg. tot.**		
Maths	I	ns	ns	ns	C > I: prob. solv.*	ns	ns	ns	ns	ns
	II	ns	ns	ns	C > I: concepts* prob. solv.*	ns	ns	ns	-	ns
	III	ns	I > C: comput.***	ns	ns	ns	I > C: prob. solv.*	ns		

Work-study skills	I	I > C: map read.* graphs & tables*	wk.-st.tot.*	I > C: gr./tables* ref. mat.*** wk.st.tot.**	I > C: ref. mat.*	ns	ns
	II		ns	ns	I > C: ref. mat.**	ns	–
	III	ns	ns		I > C*	ref. mat.**	–
CTBS composite score	I		ns	ns	I > C**	ns	ns
	II		ns	ns	ns	ns	–
	III		I > C*		ns	ns	5
Science	I			ns	ns	ns	ns
	II			ns	ns	ns	–
	III			ns	ns		
Test de rend. en Français (stanine)	I	4[a]	4	4	5	5	5
	II	3.5[a]	4	4	4	4	–
	III	3	3[c]	4	5		

([a] 2-1/2 months lag with norms, [b] 4-1/2 months lag, [c] 7 months lag)

***p ≤ .001 **p ≤ .01 *p ≤ .05

+ IQ findings based on unadjusted scores; all others, except *Test de rendement en français*, based on data adjusted for IQ (1979 results) or age and IQ (1971–1978 results) Andrew, Lapkin and Swain 1979a; Barik and Swain 1975, 1977b, 1978a; Swain and Barik 1976a, 1977; and present chapter.

comparison students on several of the English and work-study skills which have been tested. There has been one significant difference noted in mathematics, and none in science. Many earlier concerns about the immersion students' achievement in English and other academic areas have thus been addressed by the data of the last few years.

Findings concerning the French achievement of the immersion students are more difficult to summarize. First, there has been no comparison group for most of the French tests, since the tests administered to the immersion students are too difficult for the English programme students who study French as a second language in relatively short daily periods. Secondly, except for the *Test de rendement en français*, the French tests used here have all been developed by the Bilingual Education Project. Consequently, the tests are revised from year to year, making comparisons across cohorts difficult. However, where the same test has been given to two different grades, the students in the higher grade have consistently performed better. With respect to the *Test de rendement en français*, the immersion students have been performing consistently at the stanine 4 level or better since grade 3. This is seen as satisfactory, since a group of average francophone students in Montreal would be expected to score at the stanine 5 level. Thus the immersion students' scores are only slightly below the average scores for francophone students on this test. French results on the other tests have also been considered satisfactory. Where comparison data are available, the immersion pupils' scores have been slightly below those of native French-speaking pupils.

Comparisons between different groups of EFI students on the basis of programme variations have only recently been discussed, and findings to date have been tentative. Swain and Barik (1977) suggested that, within the EFI context, varying the amount of time allocated to instruction via English may influence students' achievement. In a further discussion of this question, Andrew, Lapkin and Swain (1979a) suggested that teaching mathematics in English beginning at grade 5 may result in increased mathematics achievement.

A second factor concerns the setting in which the immersion programme is found: 'immersion centres' (schools where all the students are in the immersion programme) may offer advantages relative to 'dual-track schools' (schools where some classes are in immersion and others are in the English programme). Andrew, Lapkin and Swain (1979a) reported, on the basis of the grade 5 results of their 1978 Ottawa–Carleton evaluation, that studying in an immersion centre appears to improve the students' achievement, both in French language skills *and* English language skills. They suggested that the advantage of the immersion centres *vis-à-vis* the students' French achievement might lie in the greater use of French in the school environment that the centres may provide. Further, this increased proficiency in French might be the underlying factor in promoting better English proficiency as well. A further study conducted in 1979 (Lapkin, Andrew, Harley, Swain and Kamin 1981) confirmed that the immersion centres provide the students with more exposure to French in various settings in the school than do dual-track schools, and that the immersion centre students perform significantly better than dual-track students on measures of French listening and reading comprehension, and in English reading comprehension, and spelling.

Description of samples and programmes

In the past, the students tested were those in the first three cohorts enrolled in the EFI programmes in OBE and CBE. In 1979, however, only Cohorts I and III were tested. At the time of testing in the spring of 1979, these students were in grade 8 (Cohort I) and 6 (Cohort III). As in the previous three years (Andrew, Lapkin and Swain 1979a; Barik and Swain 1978a; Swain and Barik 1977), only a few representative classes at each grade level were tested in 1979. A similar number of classes consisting of English programme students was also tested for comparison purposes.

As in past evaluations, the data of some students were excluded from the analysis. For example, all test scores of students with physical or emotional problems, repeaters, and recent immigrants with a limited ability in English were excluded. The French scores of students with a home background of French were also excluded. In addition, students who had transferred within the last three years from immersion to the English programme or vice versa, or who had transferred from a francophone school were excluded from all analyses. The set of data analyses in the present report is thus intended to be representative of the test results of English-speaking students in the immersion and English programmes in OBE and CBE.

Table 4.2 provides a summary of the classes tested, and the characteristics of the immersion and English programmes in the OBE and CBE at the relevant grade levels. The language of instruction for

TABLE 4.2   Description of samples and programmes, grades 6 and 8

Grade	Samples				Programmes[a]	
	No. classes		No. Pupils		Immersion programme description	Subjects taught in English
	Imm.	Comp.	Imm.	Comp.		
6	7 (4 + 3)[b]	4 (2 + 2)	197	112	OBE— 50%–60% French 40%–50% Eng.	ELA, science, music, art, phys. ed.
					CBE— 50%–60% French 40%–50% Eng.	ELA, maths or science[c] music, art, phys. ed.[d]
8	4 (2 + 2)	4 (2 + 2)	100	134	OBE— 50% English 50% French	ELA, science, music, art, phys. ed, home ec., ind. arts
					CBE— 50% French 50% English	ELA, maths or science,[e] art, phys. ed.

[a] Students in the regular English programme for the classes tested here receive 40 minutes per day of instruction in French as a second language.
[b] Number of classes in CBE and OBE respectively. One of the CBE classes was tested only in mathematics and IQ.
[c] One CBE school teaches maths in French and science in English (2 classes in maths at this school); the other two CBE schools teach maths in English and science in French (see Tables 4.3 and 4.4).
[d] One CBE school teaches art and phys. ed. in French.
[e] One CBE school teaches maths in English and science in French; the other teaches maths in French and science in English (see Tables 4.3 and 4.4).

TABLE 4.3 Immersion programme variations: language of instruction in mathematics, 1976–79

	Cohort I			Cohort III		
	Grade 6 (1976–77)	Grade 7 (1977–78)	Grade 8 (1978–79)	Grade 4 (1976–77)	Grade 5 (1977–78)	Grade 6 (1978–79)
Carleton	class A English class B French	English	class A English class B French	French	English	classes C&D English classes E & F French[1]
Ottawa	French	French	French	French	French	French

[1] Class 'F' was tested in mathematics and IQ only.

TABLE 4.4 Immersion programme variations: language of instruction in science, 1976–79

	Cohort I			Cohort III		
	Grade 6 (1976–77)	Grade 7 (1977–78)	Grade 8 (1978–79)	Grade 4 (1976–77)	Grade 5 (1977–78)	Grade 6 (1978–79)
Carleton	French	French	class A French class B English	French	French	classes C & D French class E English
Ottawa	English	English	English	French	French	English

mathematics and science is specified in Tables 4.3 and 4.4 since these programme differences are relevant to the present evaluation.

Description of the Test Battery

Testing in the areas of cognitive ability, English language skills, French language skills, mathematics, science and work-study skills was conducted in April and May of 1979. The following tests were administered in English to both the immersion and comparison groups:

1. Canadian cognitive abilities test, nonverbal battery (CCAT)
This test provides an IQ measure. The nonverbal battery is intended to measure what has been called 'fluid intelligence', that is, ability that is not bound by formal school instruction.

2. Canadian tests of basic skills (CTBS)
The five main tests in this battery are:
a) vocabulary;
b) reading;
c) language skills (spelling, capitalization, punctuation and usage);
d) work-study skills (map reading, reading graphs and tables, and knowledge and use of reference materials);
e) mathematics skills (concepts and problem solving).
The scores on all subtests of the CTBS are expressed in terms of grade equivalents, and the scores of the five main tests are averaged to yield a composite score for the total test battery.

3. Metropolitan achievement tests: science (MAT)
The test consists of items relating to several science areas (life science, earth science, physical science, conservation and health). Since no Canadian-normed science test was available for use in the elementary school grades, the Metropolitan test, which was normed in the United States, was employed. None of the items in the versions used related to an American context, however. The intermediate level was administered in grade 6; the advanced level was given in grade 8.

4. English story completion test
This is a cloze procedure test which provides a measure of overall English language proficiency. The test consists of passages of prose in which the first and last paragraphs are left intact and every seventh word is deleted from the body of the passages, to be completed by

the students. Level D was used in grade 6, while Level C was given in grade 8. The exact word method of scoring was used (see Lapkin and Swain 1977).

5. *English composition*
Students were asked to write a short composition. The results of this test have not yet been analysed. For previous findings relating to writing skills, see Swain (1975a) and Lapkin (1982).

The following tests were administered in French only to the immersion students:

6. *Test de rendement en français*
This test measures general achievement in French. Norms are available for native French-speaking pupils in Montreal. Level 6 (1973–74 edition) was given to grade 6. The 'secondaire II' level (1974–75 edition) was given to the grade 8 pupils. This test was given in late November to correspond to its time of administration to the norming population in Montreal.

7. *Test de mots à trouver*
This cloze procedure test provides an overall measure of French language proficiency. See test 4 above. Niveau D was given in grades 6 and 8.

8. *Composition française*
Students were asked to write a short composition in French. The results of this test have not yet been analysed. For previous findings relating to writing skills, see Swain (1975a).

9. *Test de compréhension auditive*[1]
This test, developed by the Bilingual Education Project, measures the understanding of spoken French, reflecting a variety of real-life situations. The test consists of a number of passages recorded from radio broadcasts and other real-life situations including news items, sports items, weather forecasts, advertisements, radio drama, etc. The students listened to a passage, which was then followed by one or more questions based on its contents. Niveau B, a revised version of the test administered the previous year, consisting of eight recorded items and 22 questions, was given in grades 6 and 8.

10. *Test de compréhension de l'écrit*
This test, developed by the Bilingual Education Project, measures the

comprehension of written French, once again reflecting a variety of real-life situations. The test consists of a number of written passages taken from various sources – newspaper articles, magazine articles, weather forecasts, newspaper ads, television schedules, horoscopes, etc., each of which is followed by a number of multiple-choice questions. The revised niveau B, consisting of 10 passages and 22 questions, was given in grades 6 and 8 (see note 1, p. 79.)

1979 results

Immersion versus English programme groups

The test results for the immersion and English programme students were compared at each grade level by using a one-way analysis of covariance which adjusted for differences in IQ between the two groups.

The results from grades 6 and 8 are given in Tables 4.5 and 4.6 respectively. For these tables, OBE and CBE classes were combined. The tables show, for both the immersion and comparison groups, the number of students who were included in the analysis of covariance for each test, the actual (unadjusted) mean score for that group of students and the standard deviation for the scores of that group. The F ratio and significance level reported for the age and IQ results are based on analysis of variance. For all other tests, the mean scores adjusted for differences in IQ between the two groups are given in the tables. The F ratio and significance level for these tests are based on analysis of covariance, with IQ as the covariate.

Age
In both cohorts tested (Cohorts I and III), the comparison group is older than the immersion group by approximately a month and a half. This corresponds to the age differences noted the previous year for these cohorts, although this year the Cohort I difference is not statistically significant.

IQ
The immersion students' IQ scores are significantly higher than the comparison students' IQ scores both for Cohort I and for Cohort III. Longitudinally, the results are consistent with the result for Cohort I in their grade 7 year (1978), with approximately a 12 point difference in IQ noted both in 1978 and in 1979 between the immersion and comparison groups. For Cohort III, the difference of approximately 5

TABLE 4.5   Ottawa-Carleton: Immersion versus regular programme, grade 6 (Cohort III)

| | Unadjusted means | | | | | | Adjusted means (cov. = IQ) | | |
| | Immersion group | | | | Comparison group | | Immersion group | Comparison group | F ratio |
	N	Mean	St. dev.	N	Mean	St. dev.	Mean	Mean	
Age (mos, May '79)	184	142.26	5.04	93	144.01	4.93			5.93*
Cdn. Cog. Ab. T. (Stand. Age Sc. = IQ)	184	112.80	13.34	93	107.68	13.55			9.03**
Cdn. T. Bas. Sk. Grade equivs.									
English skills:									
a) Vocab.	160	7.42	1.16	93	7.13	1.15	7.36	7.23	0.85
b) Read. comp.	160	7.12	1.13	93	6.92	1.00	7.05	7.04	0.01
c) Spelling	158	7.41	1.43	90	7.01	1.42	7.36	7.10	2.02
d) Capitalization	158	6.90	1.21	90	6.76	1.43	6.84	6.86	0.02
e) Punctuation	158	7.31	1.23	90	6.79	1.32	7.24	6.91	5.13*
f) Usage	158	7.19	1.27	90	6.61	1.36	7.15	6.67	8.38**
g) Lang. Tot. (c-f)	158	7.21	1.07	90	6.79	1.13	7.15	6.89	4.15*
Maths skills:									
h) Concepts	172	7.40	1.19	89	7.31	1.24	7.32	7.46	0.99
i) Prob. Solv.	172	6.86	1.22	89	6.74	1.14	6.79	6.87	0.42
j) Maths. Tot. (h-i)	172	7.13	1.14	89	7.03	1.09	7.06	7.17	0.88
Work-study skills:									
k) Map read.	155	7.03	1.10	88	6.64	1.29	6.97	6.77	2.00
l) Graphs & Tables	155	7.00	1.31	88	6.65	1.23	6.92	6.79	0.80
m) Use ref. mat.	155	7.14	1.13	88	6.67	1.13	7.07	6.78	4.58*
n) Wk.-study Tot. (k-m)	155	7.06	1.02	88	6.65	1.03	6.99	6.78	3.15
o) CTBS Comp. Sc. (a.b.g;i.n.)	141	7.19	0.97	81	6.98	0.93	7.13	7.09	0.14
MAT Science (st. score)	153	89.77	9.61	90	90.42	9.16	89.34	91.16	2.60
Eng. Story Compl., Level D (max = 52)	157	22.87	5.62	90	21.84	5.77	22.58	22.36	0.10

*** p ≤ .001   ** p ≤ .01   * p ≤ .05

TABLE 4.6   Ottawa–Carleton: Immersion versus regular programme, grade 8 (Cohort I)

| | Unadjusted means | | | | | | Adjusted means (cov. = IQ) | | |
| | Immersion group | | | | Comparison group | | Immersion group | Comparison group | F ratio |
	N	Mean	St. dev.	N	Mean	St. dev.	Mean	Mean	
Age (mos., May '79)	85	165.20	4.66	114	166.63	5.97			3.36
Cdn. Cog. Ab. T. (Stand. Age Sc. = IQ)	85	120.18	14.31	114	108.82	12.42			35.74***
Cdn. T. Bas. Sk. Grade equivs.									
English skills:									
a) Vocab.	80	9.55	1.16	111	9.41	1.16	9.35	9.55	1.31
b) Read. comp.	80	9.37	1.19	111	8.92	1.03	9.19	9.05	0.71
c) Spelling	78	9.91	1.38	112	8.95	1.49	9.83	9.00	13.01***
d) Capitalization	78	9.31	1.42	112	8.65	1.44	9.11	8.79	2.08
e) Punctuation	78	9.36	1.57	112	8.67	1.53	9.09	8.86	0.99
f) Usage	78	9.49	1.72	112	8.95	1.60	9.28	9.10	0.52
g) Lang. Tot. (c-f)	78	9.52	1.28	112	8.80	1.19	9.33	8.94	4.49*
Maths skills:									
h) Concepts	78	9.48	1.40	92	8.86	1.36	9.20	9.09	0.29
i) Prob. Solv.	78	8.47	1.52	92	8.38	1.37	8.31	8.51	0.73
j) Maths. Tot. (h-i)	78	9.00	1.29	92	8.62	1.14	8.76	8.80	0.06
Work-study skills:									
k) Map read.	81	9.42	1.25	109	9.09	1.11	9.23	9.24	0.00
l) Graphs & Tables	81	9.33	1.68	109	8.85	1.55	9.08	9.04	0.03
m) Use ref. mat.	81	9.15	1.53	109	8.70	1.49	8.89	8.89	0.00
n) Wk.-study Tot. (k-m)	81	9.30	1.34	109	8.88	1.15	9.07	9.05	0.01
o) CTBS Comp. Sc. (a.b.g,i,n.)	69	9.37	1.07	87	8.92	0.88	9.16	9.08	0.25
MAT Science (st. score)	71	99.76	8.67	95	99.42	9.69	97.99	100.74	3.76
Eng. Story Compl, Level C (max = 41)	70	23.54	3.44	105	21.92	4.47	22.81	22.41	0.39

points in IQ, in favour of the immersion group, is statistically significant. This difference was not found for Cohort III last year. Replicationally, the Cohort III result is consistent with the results of both previous cohorts in grade 6: for all three cohorts, the immersion students' mean IQ was significantly higher than that of the comparison group.

English language skills
On tests of the CTBS relating to English skills, where differences are found they are in favour of the immersion group. This is consistent with previous findings at the grade 4 level or higher.

Cohort III
These immersion students (grade 6) obtained higher scores than their comparison group in punctuation, usage and language total. This is consistent with their own performance the previous year in grade 5. These results also replicate the results obtained on these three CTBS tests by Cohorts I and II in grade 6. Cohort I had in addition performed better than its comparison group on two other CTBS English tests in grade 6.

Cohort I
These immersion students (grade 8) obtained higher scores than their comparison group in spelling and language total. This is consistent with their results on the CTBS English tests in the 1978 evaluation, except that a significant difference in favour of the immersion group on the punctuation test in grade 7 did not occur again in 1979.

In summary, virtually all results to date at grades 4 to 8 show that any differences in performance on CTBS tests relative to English skills are in favour of the immersion students. Over the three cohorts, a trend is noted on the punctuation and language usage tests where the immersion students are ahead of the comparison students for most of the groups tested in grades 5 to 7.

On the English story completion test, a cloze procedure measure of general English competence, no differences were found between immersion and comparison groups at the grade 6 and 8 levels. Longitudinally, this is consistent with all previous results for this test for Cohorts I and III. Replicationally, the present result for Cohort III (no significant difference) is consistent with the result obtained by Cohort I in grade 6. The one result which is not consistent with the observed pattern was the Cohort II result in grade 6 (1978), when the comparison students had outperformed the immersion students on this test.

Work-study skills
In previous years, no differences between immersion and comparison groups had been found for Cohort I in grades 5 to 7. Similarly this year, Cohort I (in grade 8) showed no differences. For Cohort III this year, the immersion students were ahead of their comparison group on the reference materials test. In 1978, Cohort III immersion students (then in grade 5) had shown the same advantage, and had also scored better than the comparison group on the graphs and tables test and on the work-study skills total. Replicationally, the 1979 result for Cohort III (grade 6) is consistent with the previous year's finding for Cohort II. In summary, there is a trend in the grades 4 to 6 range for immersion students to be ahead of their comparison groups on work-study skills (see also Andrew, Lapkin and Swain 1980).

Mathematics and science
For grades 6 and 8 there were no significant differences between the immersion and comparison groups in mathematics and science test results. Longitudinally, this is consistent with all previous findings for the last four years for Cohort I. Replicationally, Cohort III's results in these areas correspond to all previous results at grade 6. Longitudinally for Cohort III, this group had shown a difference in mathematics problem-solving in favour of the immersion students in the 1978 evaluation, but this appears to be an isolated finding.

General academic performance: the CTBS composite score
Previously, there has tended to be no difference between the immersion and English programme groups on the CTBS composite score, with the exception of a difference in favour of Cohort I immersion students in grade 6, and another in favour of Cohort III immersion students in grade 5. In 1979, no differences were found between the immersion and comparison groups for Cohort I or Cohort III. Thus, the 1979 results follow the general trend.

All CTBS test scores are expressed in terms of grade equivalents. For all the CTBS tests, the unadjusted grade equivalent scores of both the immersion and English programme groups are generally close to or slightly above their own grade placement at the time of testing (6.8 and 8.8 for grades 6 and 8 respectively). On the CTBS composite score, for example, the English programme students obtained scores of 7.0 and 8.9 for Cohorts III and I respectively and the immersion students were four to six months ahead of their grade placement with unadjusted scores of 7.2 and 9.4 for Cohorts III and I respectively.

Comparison of the achievement of the immersion students and the English programme students in four academic areas (English, mathematics, science, and work-study skills) at the grade 6 and 8 levels has yielded the following findings: at both grade levels, the performance of the two groups is equivalent in the areas of mathematics and science, following the general trend for previous findings in these areas. Also consistent with previous findings is the trend, from grade 4 onward, for the immersion students to outperform the English programme students on several measures of English language skills and work-study skills. The advantage of the immersion students in work-study skills may be restricted to grades 4 to 6, but some advantages in English have continued through grade 8.

With respect to work-study skills, results from another immersion programme have also revealed differences in favour of the immersion group at grades 4 to 7 (Barik and Swain 1978c; Andrew, Lapkin and Swain 1979b, 1980). This finding appears to indicate that the immersion programme leads to earlier development of effective work-study skills than does the English programme.

Similarly, the English results correspond generally to those found in other immersion programmes. Lambert and Tucker (1972) suggested that the advantages in English skills shown by immersion children may be due to 'a process of comparing and contrasting two linguistic codes' (p. 207), and to 'the early development of a linguistic "detective" capacity, that is, an attentive, patient, inductive concern with words, meanings, and linguistic regularities' (p. 208).

Cummins (1979a) has also discussed this analytic orientation toward language, and the interdependence of skills in the immersion child's first (L1) and second (L2) languages. He has stated that 'as [immersion] children develop high levels of L2 skills, their fluent access to two languages can give rise to enhancement both of L1 skills and other aspects of cognitive functioning' (p. 31).

French language skills
The French test results are summarized in Table 4.7 for grades 6 and 8. On the *Test de rendement en français*, a test of general French achievement, Cohorts I and III obtained mean scores in the stanine 5 range relative to native French speakers. Longitudinally, Cohort I's mean score on this test has been consistently in the stanine 5 range for three years (since grade 6). Cohort III students have been scoring

TABLE 4.7 CBE and OBE: French performance, grades 6 and 8 immersion

	N	Mean	Standard deviation
Test de rendement en français (French achievement test)			
Grade 6: Gr 6 level (max = 45)	151	24.03	5.98 Stanine 5
Grade 8: Secondaire II (max = 35)	80	19.43	5.20 Stanine 5
Test de compréhension auditive (Listening comprehension test)			
Grade 6: niv. B (max = 22)	152	11.11	3.25
Grade 8: niv. B (max = 22)	80	14.95	3.74
Test de compréhension de l'écrit (Reading comprehension test)			
Grade 6: niv. B (max =22)	156	11.20	3.27
Grade 8: niv. B (max = 22)	80	14.75	4.16
Test de mots à trouver (French cloze test)			
Grade 6: niv. D (max = 41)	153	15.82	4.15
Grade 8: niv. D (max = 41)	79	19.90	4.30

in the stanine 4 range; the 1979 result represents an improvement in their performance on this test since the previous year. The Cohort III result replicates the result for Cohort I in grade 6. Combining the test results of the three cohorts, it can be seen that four of the five results recorded at the grade 6 level or higher have been in the stanine 5 range of the *Test de rendement en français*. Thus, in general, by grade 6 the immersion students do as well on this test as a group of average French-speaking students from the Province of Quebec.

On niveau B of the *Test de compréhension auditive*, the grade 6 students scored 11.1 out of 22, compared to the grade 8 students' scores of 15.0 on this test. A group of grade 8 francophone bilinguals obtained a score of 14.5 on this test (Edwards *et al.* 1979). On niveau B of the *Test de compréhension de l'écrit*, the grade 6 and 8 students received scores of 11.2 and 14.8 out of 22, respectively.

On niveau D of the *Test de mots à trouver*, Cohort III students (grade 6) obtained a mean score of 15.8 out of 41,[2] compared to a score of 16.4 obtained on the same test in 1977 by Cohort I students when they were in grade 6 (see Swain and Barik 1977). This year, Cohort I students (in grade 8) obtained a mean score of 19.9 on this level of the test. A class of 24 unilingual French-speaking students in grade 6 obtained a mean score of 18.9 (see Swain and Barik 1977), somewhat higher than the present grade 6 immersion students' score. A group of grade 8 francophone bilinguals (n = 78) obtained a mean score of 19.6 on this test (Edwards *et al.* 1979), the same as the grade 8 immersion students' score. Comparisons on this test and on the *Test de compréhension auditive* between the OBE/CBE immersion classes and the francophone classes must be treated with caution because of possible IQ, socio-economic, and other uncontrolled differences in the testing situation between the two groups.

These four French tests together provide measures on a variety of French language skills, including grammatical and vocabulary knowledge, spelling, stylistics, communicative ability with respect to various real-life situations involving listening and reading, as well as overall French proficiency. In each case, the cross-sectional data reveal growth from grade 6 to grade 8. Where comparison data are available, grade 8 students are achieving native-like performance.

Variations within the immersion programme

The immersion programme variations in the OBE and CBE are summarized in Table 4.2.[2] In grade 6, both boards report approximately 60% of the curriculum being taught in French, and 40% in English. For grade 8, both boards report a 50% French/ 50% English format. From Tables 4.3 and 4.4 it is clear that the language of instruction for mathematics and science has varied for some classes in Cohorts I and III. This is of interest in considering whether the language of instruction has an effect on student achievement: are there differences in achievement in favour of students who study mathematics and science in their native language?

In order to avoid introducing a Board variable, it was decided to examine the variations in the language of instruction of mathematics and science, using only the test data from the CBE classes. The relevant programme differences in the CBE as shown on Tables 4.3 and 4.4 are the following:

1. Class A (Cohort I) of the CBE has studied mathematics in English for three years (grades 6, 7 and 8) while class B studied mathematics in French for two of those years (grades 6 and 8).

2. Class A (Cohort I) of the CBE has studied science in French for three years (grades 6, 7 and 8), while class B has studied science in French for two of those years (grades 6 and 7).

3. During the past three years of their schooling, classes C and D (Cohort III) of the CBE have studied mathematics in English for two years (grades 5 and 6) while classes E and F have studied mathematics in French for two of the three years (grades 4 and 6).

4. Classes C and D (Cohort III) of the CBE have studied science in

French for three years (grades 4, 5 and 6), while class F has studied science in English for one of those years (grade 6).

Analyses of covariance, with IQ as the covariate, were carried out in order to compare the achievement of CBE immersion students who study mathematics (or science) in English with that of CBE immersion students who study the subject in French.

Mathematics and science

In grades 6 and 8, do students who study mathematics in English achieve better scores on CTBS mathematics tests than students who study the subject in French? The results are summarized in Table 4.8. As shown in Table 4.8, in grade 6 there is no difference in mathematics achievement between those CBE immersion students who study mathematics in French and those who study it in English. In grade 8, however, the CBE immersion students who study mathematics in English have an advantage over those who study it in French on the mathematics concepts test and the mathematics total score. This finding should be interpreted with caution, because it is based on only one class of 'English mathematics' and one class of 'French mathematics' students.

To investigate this question further, an analysis of covariance was done within each of the two schools to compare the mathematics achievement of immersion and English programme students in the school. It was found that the 'French mathematics' immersion students did not differ from the English programme students in their school on either of the CTBS mathematics tests, indicating that they seem not to be at a disadvantage within their own school by having their mathematics instruction in French. The 'English mathematics' immersion students on the other hand, were better than the regular programme class in their school on the mathematics concepts test ($p \leqslant .05$), and tended to be better in the mathematics total scores ($p = .06$). Thus, it appears that it is the especially high achievement in mathematics of this immersion class which has produced the significant difference in favour of 'English mathematics' students over 'French mathematics' students.

The second question arising from the variations within the CBE immersion programme is the following: in grades 6 and 8, do students who study science in English achieve better scores on the MAT science test than students who study it in French? At both of these grade levels, no difference was found on the MAT science test between CBE immersion students who are studying science in French and those who are studying science in English. Again, this finding

TABLE 4.8 Mathematics achievement of CBE immersion students according to language of instruction

	Unadjusted scores				
	English instruction		French instruction		F ration[1]
	Mean	*St. dev*	*Mean*	*St. dev*	
Grade 6					
Number of students	49		36		
a) Maths concepts	7.47	1.05	7.57	1.33	.18
b) Problem solving	6.95	1.01	6.85	1.38	.68
c) Maths total	7.21	.97	7.26	1.27	.50
Grade 8					
Number of students	25		18		
a) Maths concepts	10.30	1.39	9.44	1.18	5.21*
b) Problem solving	9.41	1.65	8.85	1.29	1.76
c) Maths total	9.86	1.32	9.14	1.14	4.07*

[1] The F ratio is based on analysis of covariance, with IQ as the covariate.
* $p \leq .05$

must be treated cautiously, for two reasons. First, the results are based on small numbers of classes – for example, only one 'English science' and one 'French science' class in grade 8. Therefore, the findings could vary in another evaluation, depending on class-specific factors. Secondly, the science test used here was normed in the United States. Therefore, the content is not specific to the CBE science curriculum. It would be preferable to administer a science test developed by the CBE teachers to a larger number of immersion classes, in order to determine whether the immersion students who are taught science in French are at any disadvantage with respect to science achievement. Further, in view of the mathematics findings reported here, such testing would be desirable at the grade 8 level and above in other subjects, such as history and geography, which are taught in French to the immersion students.

Summary of 1979 findings

The achievement of the immersion students in French continues to be satisfactory with the immersion students' performance approaching or equivalent to that of native speakers of French in some tests of French.

In English language skills and work-study skills, the immersion students continue to perform as well as or better than the English programme groups. This has been a noteworthy trend since the grade 4 level.

In science, those immersion students who study the subject in French are performing as well as the immersion students who study the subject in English at both grades 6 and 8. Similarly, there are no differences in mathematics achievement at the grade 6 level. In grade 8, in spite of a slight difference in favour of immersion students studying mathematics in English, the interpretation put forward here is that this isolated finding is insufficient to discourage the use of French as the language of instruction for mathematics. The possibility that some subjects are better taught in English in order that the immersion students reach the same achievement levels as their English-educated counterparts is one that deserves more detailed study, especially in the higher grades.

Conclusions

The results of the long-term evaluation of the EFI programme in the CBE and OBE (and others as well, e.g. Andrew, Lapkin and Swain

1980; Genesee 1979) suggest two important conclusions. First, they suggest that it is possible through appropriately designed FSL programmes to develop a considerable degree of bilingualism among majority language students. The programmes may be radical in nature, but they appear to lead to a degree of bilingualism not found with other FSL programmes, while having no long term detrimental effects on cognitive growth, first language skills, or academic achievement. Indeed there are indications that the cumulative effects of the bilingual programme may at least have positive effects on the development of first language skills.

Secondly, the results point to the value of long term evaluations. Had we stopped our examination of the programme in the earlier grades, we might never have observed the positive outcomes of early French immersion later on.

Notes

1. In previous reports, including that of the 1978 evaluation, the listening comprehension test was called the *Test de compréhension aurale*. In addition, the names of the levels of all three French tests developed by the Bilingual Education Project for use in grades 5 to 8 have been changed, as follows:

   a) Niveau A of the *Test de compréhension auditive* and of the *Test de compréhension de l'écrit* were previously called Level 6. They are unchanged from the 1978 versions of these tests. (This level of both tests was first introduced in 1977 and was revised in 1978.)

   b) Niveau B of the *Test de compréhension auditive* and of the *Test de compréhension de l'écrit* are revised versions (revised in 1979) of Level 7 of the same tests, which were first developed in 1978.

   c) Niveaux C (max = 49) and D (max = 41) of the *Test de mots à trouver* were previously called Levels 7 and 6 respectively. The tests themselves have not been changed.

   These changes have been made in order to reflect the degree of difficulty of the tests (for example, niveau B is more difficult than niveau A), without suggesting that each level is suitable for use in only one particular grade. In fact, these tests have been used appropriately at several different grade levels, in a variety of French immersion programmes.

2. The exact-word scoring method was used; hence the apparently low scores reported for all groups on this test.

5 Linguistic interdependence: a central principle of bilingual education

It is frequently argued in opposition to bilingual education for minority students that if students are deficient in the school language (henceforth English) then they need intensive instruction in that language. Attempting to remedy English language deficiencies through instruction in students' first language (L1) appears counter-intuitive to many policy-makers and educators. The bilingual approach appears to imply that less English instruction will result in more English achievement. The scepticism of many policy-makers and educators with respect to bilingual education is expressed in the *New York Times* editorial of 10th October 1981:

> The Department of Education is analysing new evidence that expensive bilingual education programmes don't work ... Teaching non-English speaking children in their native language during much of their school day constructs a roadblock on their journey into English. A language is best learned through immersion in it, particularly by children ... Neither society nor its children will be well served if bilingualism continues to be used to keep thousands of children from quickly learning the one language needed to succeed in America.

The assumption underlying this position is that the development of English academic skills is directly related to exposure to English and hence minority students require *maximum exposure* to English if they are to succeed academically.

Although intuitively appealing, there is a considerable amount of research evidence that refutes a simplistic 'maximum exposure' hypothesis. Clearly, sufficient exposure to the school language is essential for the development of academic skills; however, equally or more important, is the extent to which students are capable of understanding the academic input to which they are exposed. In the case of minority students this is directly related to the conceptual attributes which have developed as a result of interaction in their L1.

The evidence supporting this latter position is reviewed in this chapter. The issues revolve around two alternative conceptions of bilingual proficiency which can be termed the separate underlying proficiency (SUP) and common underlying proficiency (CUP) models.

The SUP and CUP models of bilingual proficiency

The argument that if minority children are deficient in English, then they need instruction in English, not in their L1, implies:

a) that proficiency in L1 is separate from proficiency in English;
b) that there is a direct relationship between exposure to a language (in home or school) and achievement in that language.

The SUP model is illustrated in Figure 5.1.

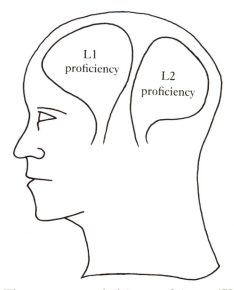

FIGURE 5.1   The separate underlying proficiency (SUP) model of bilingual proficiency

The second implication of the SUP model follows from the first, that if L1 and L2 proficiency are separate, then content and skills learned through L1 cannot transfer to L2 and vice versa. In terms of the balloon metaphor illustrated in Figure 5.1, blowing into the L1 balloon will succeed in inflating L1 but not L2. When bilingual education is approached with these 'common-sense' assumptions about bilingual proficiency, it is not at all surprising that it appears illogical to argue that one can better inflate the L2 balloon by blowing into the L1 balloon.

However, despite its intuitive appeal, there is little evidence to support the SUP model.[1] In order to account for the evidence reviewed, we must posit a CUP model in which the literacy-related aspects of a bilingual's proficiency in L1 and L2 are seen as common or interdependent across languages. Two ways of illustrating the CUP model (the interdependence principle) are shown in Figures 5.2 and 5.3.

Figure 5.2 expresses the point that experience with either language can promote development of the proficiency underlying both languages, given adequate motivation and exposure to both either in school or in the wider environment. In Figure 5.3 bilingual proficiency is represented by means of a 'dual iceberg' in which common cross-lingual proficiencies underlie the obviously different surface manifestations of each language. In general the surface features of L1 and L2 are those that have become relatively automatized or less cognitively demanding whereas the underlying proficiency is that involved in cognitively demanding communicative tasks.

There are three major sources of evidence for the CUP model:
1. results of bilingual education programmes;
2. studies relating age on arrival and immigrant students' L2 acquisition;
3. studies relating bilingual language use in the home to academic achievement.

Evaluations of bilingual programmes

Although there is a widespread perception in the United States that bilingual education has yet to prove its effectiveness (Baker and de Kanter 1981), findings of the available, well-controlled research are strongly supportive of the basic principle underlying bilingual education, i.e. the CUP model of bilingual proficiency. A recent review of international bilingual education evaluations (Cummins 1983) reported that virtually all the evaluation results are interpretable within the context of the CUP model. The immersion programme results, reviewed in Chapter 3, along with several programme evaluations reviewed here, illustrate the pattern of findings.

English–Ukrainian programme in Edmonton, Alberta

In September 1974, the Edmonton Public School Board (EPSB) introduced the English–Ukrainian bilingual programme at the kindergarten and grade 1 levels. In kindergarten 100% of instruc-

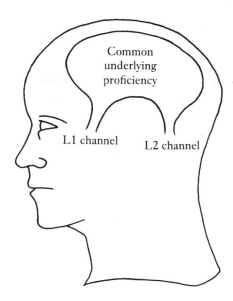

FIGURE 5.2   The common underlying proficiency model (CUP) of bilingual proficiency

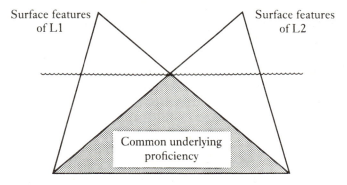

FIGURE 5.3   The 'dual-iceberg' representation of bilingual proficiency

tional time was in Ukrainian, after which instructional time was divided equally between English and Ukrainian. Mathematics, English language arts, and science were taught in English, while social studies, physical education, Ukrainian language arts, art, and music were taught in Ukrainian.

More than three-quarters of the students came from homes in which one or both parents could speak Ukrainian and only about 10% of the students had no Ukrainian ancestry. However, only about 15% of the students were fluent in Ukrainian on entry to school. Unlike many students in French immersion programmes, the bilingual programme students were representative of the EPSB system in terms of both ability level and parental socio-economic status. For example, their grade 1 score (averaged over five years from 1974 to 1978) on the Metropolitan Readiness Test was only one point above the EPSB mean, and less than 50% of parents had post-secondary education (Edmonton Public Schools 1980a).

In the first year of the evaluation, comparison students were chosen from among students in regular unilingual English programme classes across the EPSB system whose parents had the same socio-economic level and knowledge of Ukrainian as the programme parents. In subsequent years comparison students were randomly chosen from the same schools as students in the bilingual programme. The selection was stratified on the basis of sex, school, and ability level.

No consistent pattern of differences emerged in comparisons of English and mathematics skills between the bilingual and unilingual programme students in the early grades. However, at the grade 5 level the first cohort of bilingual programme students performed significantly better than the comparison students in mathematics and on both decoding and comprehension subtests of the standardized English reading test that was administered. The evaluation was discontinued at this point so that it is impossible to say whether subsequent cohorts also outperformed the unilingual comparison group.

The evaluation carried out by the EPSB also examined the issue of whether the programme was equally appropriate for students of different ability levels. This was done by dividing students into high, medium, and low ability levels and testing programme-by-ability interaction effects in a two-way analysis of variance design. No evidence of interaction effects was found, indicating that low-ability students had no more difficulty in the bilingual programme than they would have had in the regular programme.

As reported in Chapter 1, a study carried out by Cummins and Mulcahy (1978a) revealed that grade 1 and 3 students who were relatively fluent in Ukrainian because their parents used it consistently in the home were significantly better able to detect ambiguities in *English* sentence structure than either equivalent unilingual English-speaking children not in the programme or children in the programme who came from predominantly English-speaking homes.

The EPSB evaluation also reported that students' Ukrainian skills developed in accord with programme expectations and they also developed an appreciation for and knowledge about the Ukrainian culture. In addition, a large majority of the parents and programme personnel were pleased with the programme, felt the students were happy, and wished the programme to be continued to higher grade levels.

The Bradford Punjabi mother tongue project

The Bradford mother tongue and English teaching (MOTET) project consisted of a one-year bilingual education programme for five-year-old native speakers of Punjabi who, at the start of the project, had little or no knowledge of English. Approximately seventy students were randomly assigned to either experimental (bilingual) or control (monolingual English) groups, and their performance on nonverbal tasks and both English and Punjabi verbal tasks was assessed after one academic year (Rees 1981).

No group differences were observed on the nonverbal ability measures. On the verbal tasks, the bilingual group tended to perform better in Punjabi than the control group, while performance in English was, on balance, equivalent (the control group showed a slight superiority on the productive task while the bilingual group performed better on the receptive tasks). Rees (1981) concludes cautiously that:

> Provision of a bilingual education programme in the first year at school does not in practice necessarily constitute a danger to a child's progress. In the areas examined peer progress is as good as that in monolingual conditions on balance. Given that there are institutional and personal benefits and a positive effect on the mother tongue, the provision of a bilingual education programme might be beneficial for some young Asian children. (p. 74)

It is worth noting that this evaluation is exceptionally well-designed in that students were randomly assigned to experimental and control treatments and a variety of L1 and L2 dependent measures are employed. It clearly shows no detrimental consequences for English language development as a result of using L1 as an initial medium of instruction.

The San Diego Spanish-English language 'immersion' programme

This demonstration project, implemented in 1975 in the San Diego City Schools, involved approximately 60% Spanish L1 and 40% English L1 students. Instruction was predominantly in Spanish from pre-school to grade 3, after which half the time was spent through the medium of each language. Twenty minutes of English instruction was included at the pre-school level, 30 minutes at grades K to 1, and 60 minutes at grades 2 to 3. Originally implemented in just one school, the project subsequently spread to several others. The original project was located in a lower-middle-class area and, although participation was (and is) voluntary, the Spanish background students appear typical of most limited-English proficient students in regular bilingual programmes.

The project evaluation shows that although students lag somewhat behind grade norms in both Spanish and English reading skills until near the end of elementary school, by grade 6 they were performing above grade norms in both languages. Mathematics achievement also tended to be above grade norms. The evaluation results for both groups of students are summarized as follows:

> Native English-speaking project students – because they do not receive instruction in English reading as early as do students in the district's regular elementary level program – begin to develop English reading skills somewhat later than regular-program students. However, project students make rapid and sustained progress in English reading once it is introduced and, as has been noted, ultimately meet or exceed English-language norms for their grade levels. Also, though native Spanish-speaking project students are not exposed to English reading and writing as early as they would be in the regular English-only instructional program, they eventually acquire English-language skills which are above the norm for students in regular, English-only instructional programs and, in addition, develop their native-language skills.
>
> (San Diego City Schools 1982, p. 183)

Although clearly these demonstration project results must be treated with caution, confidence in their potential generalizability is increased by the fact that they are entirely predictable from the interdependence principle (the CUP model) and consistent with data from similar programmes involving minority francophones in the Canadian context (Carey and Cummins 1983; Hébert *et al.* 1976). The results strongly support the feasibility of bilingual programmes designed to promote additive bilingualism among minority children who are academically at risk.

In summary, the results of research on bilingual programmes show that minority children's L1 can be promoted in school at no cost to the development of proficiency in the majority language. In other words, the educational argument against bilingual education is invalid; in order to explain the findings, it is necessary to posit a common proficiency dimension that underlies the development of academic skills in both languages. The data show that well-implemented bilingual programmes have had considerable success in developing English academic skills despite the fact that students receive less exposure to English than in monolingual English programmes.

How do we reconcile the success of L1-medium programmes for minority children with the fact that majority language children fare very well academically in French immersion programmes? There are many differences between these situations, e.g. prestige of L1, security of children's identity and self-concept, and level of support for L1 development in home and environment. Thus it is not surprising that different forms of educational programmes should be appropriate for children with very different background characteristics. The apparent contradiction between findings in minority and majority contexts completely disappears when we stop thinking in terms of 'linguistic mismatch' or 'home–school language switch'. In immersion programmes for majority language children, as well as in bilingual programmes for minority children, instruction through the *minority* language has been effective in promoting proficiency in *both* languages. These findings, which have been replicated in a number of studies, support the following 'interdependence' principle: *To the extent that instruction in Lx is effective in promoting proficiency in Lx, transfer of this proficiency to Ly will occur provided there is adequate exposure to Ly (either in school or environment) and adequate motivation to learn Ly.* In other words, far from being contradictory, the same theoretical principle, the CUP model, underlies immersion programmes for majority language students as well as bilingual programmes for minority language students.

Age on arrival and L2 acquisition

It would be predicted on the basis of the interdependence principle that older learners who are more cognitively mature and whose L1 proficiency is better developed would acquire cognitively demanding aspects of L2 proficiency more rapidly than younger learners. Recent reviews of research on the age issue confirm this prediction (Cummins 1981c; Genesee 1978c; Krashen *et al.* 1979). One area where research suggests older learners may not have an advantage is pronunciation, which, significantly, appears to be one of the least cognitively demanding aspects of both L1 and L2 proficiency.

Two studies are reviewed which illustrate the extent to which older L2 learners have an advantage in acquiring cognitively demanding aspects of L2. The first study involved a re-analysis (Cummins 1981c) of data derived from 1,210 immigrant students in grades 5, 7 and 9 in the Toronto Board of Education (Ramsey and Wright 1970, 1974), while the second consisted of an analysis of the determinants of L2 acquisition among Japanese immigrant students in Toronto (Cummins *et al.* 1984).

The Toronto Board reanalysis

Figure 5.4 presents the data for a group-adapted version of the Ammons Picture Vocabulary Test (PVT) which was one of seven English proficiency measures administered to the 1,210 students. The independent influence of both age on arrival (AOA) and length of residence (LOR) on test performance is clear from these data. In every case older learners acquired more vocabulary in the same

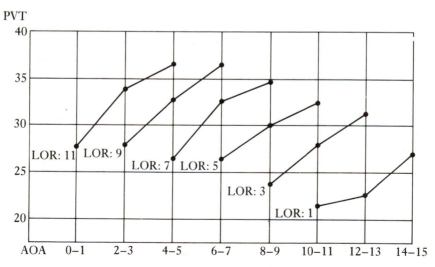

FIGURE 5.4   Age on arrival, length of residence, and PVT raw scores

amount of time than did younger learners. In the study it was possible to make ninety comparisons between older and younger learners on cognitively demanding aspects of L2. In eighty-nine of these, older learners performed better.

It may appear surprising that older learners make more rapid progress in acquiring L2 in view of the popular myth that there is an optimal pre-pubertal age for L2 acquisition. However, a major reason for the advantage is obvious when the data are viewed from within the context of the CUP model. For example, in learning the term 'democracy' the task for a fourteen-year-old immigrant child consists of acquiring a new label for a concept already developed in L1; for a six-year-old immigrant child the term will not be acquired until the concept has been developed. The advantage of older learners lies in the interdependence of conceptual knowledge across languages.

Acquisition of English by Japanese students in Toronto

This study (Cummins *et al.* 1984) was designed to investigate the extent to which L1 and L2 academic skills are interdependent. The subjects were children of Japanese 'temporary residents' in Toronto, i.e. business people or others on temporary assignment abroad. All were of middle to upper-class background. For some analyses, ninety-one children were involved but most of the detailed analyses involved a sub-group of fifty-nine students.

At the time of testing, students were in either grades 2 to 3 or grades 5 to 6 of Canadian schools and all were attending a Japanese language school on Saturdays. The Japanese school attempted to cover much of the regular curriculum of Japanese schools in order to facilitate students' re-entry into the Japanese academic system on their return.

The assessment procedures in English and Japanese involved individual interviews which were rated according to a variety of criteria, e.g. grammatical, discourse, fluency and elaborateness of responses, etc. Students were also given a variety of measures designed to assess cognitive/academic aspects of English and Japanese proficiency. In Japanese this consisted of a standardized diagnostic reading test widely used in Japan; the English measures consisted of the Gates-McGinitie grade 2 tests of vocabulary and reading comprehension, a prepositional usage test adopted from the Ramsey and Wright (1974) study, and two individually administered measures of antonyms and sentence repetition (derived from the *Language Assessment Umpire* (Cohen 1980)). In addition, interviews with parents yielded a substantial number of predictor variables related to students' exposure to and use of both English and Japanese and also information regarding students' personal attributes (e.g. ratings of introversion/extroversion).

Factor analyses of the English variables resulted in three factors which were defined respectively by syntax, elaborateness of response, and cognitive/academic proficiency measures. The second factor was labelled 'interactional style' since the variables reflected students' ease in the interview situation and their disposition to provide elaborate responses to questions. Ratings of cohesion (an indicator of discourse competence) were split between the second and third factors.

The Japanese factor analyses also yielded three factors: a general factor upon which most of the interview variables (reflecting primarily interactional style) loaded, a second factor defined by pronunciation, fluency and academic proficiency, and a third factor defined by students' tendency to use English in the interview situation. The composition of these factors can be understood in the context of the fact that age was strongly related (positively) to the first factor while length of residence (LOR) in Canada was related (negatively) to the second factor. In other words, the aspects of proficiency that loaded on the second factor were those that declined with increasing residence in a non-Japanese context.

The interdependence hypothesis was tested by means of a variety of analyses: partial correlations across languages controlling for LOR, regression analyses, and comparisons of the fourteen sets of siblings in the sample. The partial correlations showed significant correlations between English and Japanese cognitive/academic measures and also between measures of interactional style in both languages. Older siblings performed better than younger siblings on most of the English cognitive/academic measures but there were few differences on the indices of syntax or interactional style.

The pattern of results is revealed in the regression analyses of the English factor scores shown in Table 5.1. Predictor variables were entered in the order shown in order to assess the effects of exposure to the language (LOR) alone and the incremental effects of both cognitive (age and L1 cognitive/academic proficiency) and personal (personality, Japanese interactional style and gender) variables. It can be seen that LOR alone accounts for more variance in syntax (26%) than in interactional style (21%) or cognitive/academic proficiency (17%). Entry of the cognitive/academic variables accounts for an additional 18% in English cognitive/academic proficiency, but only

TABLE 5.1 Exposure and attribute predictors of English proficiency

	Syntax (factor 1)			Interactional style (factor 2)			Academic proficiency (factor 3)		
	R square	Rsq change	Beta	R square	Rsq change	Beta	R square	Rsq change	Beta
1. LOR	0.26	0.26	0.54	0.21	0.21	0.49	0.17	0.17	0.73
2. Japanese academic proficiency	0.26	0.00	0.13	0.25	0.04	0.11	0.26	0.09	0.25
3. AOA: older group	0.28	0.02	-0.06	0.27	0.01	0.06	0.35	0.09	0.40
4. Age in months	0.29	0.01	-0.05	0.27	0.00	-0.14	0.35	0.00	0.08
5. Personality*	0.30	0.01	-0.03	0.32	0.05	0.09	0.37	0.01	-0.09
6. L1 interactional style	0.33	0.03	-0.21	0.44	0.12	0.42	0.37	0.01	-0.11
7. Sex**	0.36	0.02	-0.16	0.48	0.04	0.21	0.38	0.01	0.07

* 5 point scale, 1 = very shy, 5 = very outgoing
** 2 = Female, 1 = Male

5% in interactional style and 3% in syntax. By contrast, the personal attributes account for an additional 21% in interactional style but only 3% in cognitive/academic proficiency and 6% in syntax.

Further analyses involving the predictor variables derived from the parental interviews showed that exposure to and use of English accounted for considerably more variance in English syntax than was the case for either of the other two sets of English proficiency variables. By the same token, background and attributes of the individual accounted for more variance on interactional style and cognitive/academic proficiency than was the case for syntax.

These results suggest a distinction between 'input-based' and 'attribute-based' aspects of L2 proficiency. More specifically, the development of grammatical L2 skills appears to be more related to the extent of exposure to and use of the L2 in the environment than to cognitive or personal attributes of the individual whereas the opposite is true for L2 interactional style and cognitive/academic proficiency. Our hypothesis of why we find relatively strong cross-lingual relationships for these variables is because they reflect relatively stable attributes of the individual (i.e. personality and cognition) (see Figure 5.5).

L1 development in the home

Several studies show that the use of a minority language in the home is not, in itself, a handicap to children's academic progress (Carey and Cummins 1983; Cummins and Mulcahy 1978b; Dolson 1984;

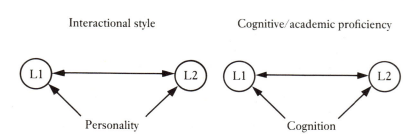

FIGURE 5.5   Model of attribute-based interdependent language proficiency

National Assessment of Educational Progress 1983a; Spence, Mishra and Ghozeil 1971; Yee and Laforge 1974). There is evidence, in fact, that in some situations exclusive use of the majority language in the home may be associated with poor academic progress in that language (e.g. Bhatnagar 1980; Chesarek 1981). Bhatnagar, for example, examined the academic progress of 171 Italian immigrant children in English language elementary schools in Montreal and 102 in French language schools in relation to language spoken at home and with friends and siblings. He summarized his findings as follows:

> The results reported here do not support the popular assumption that the more immigrant children speak the local language the better their adjustment to the host culture. It is interesting to note that immigrant children who used Italian and a Canadian language interchangeably were better even at English or French, of both the spoken and written variety, than children who used English or French all the time . . . Language retention . . . should lead to higher academic adjustment, better facility in the host language, and better social relations of immigrant children.
>
> (Bhatnagar 1980, pp. 150–55)

Bhatnagar (1980) also reported that immigrant students who used L1 exclusively with parents and siblings also performed significantly worse than those who used both L1 and L2. However, it seems likely that this finding can be attributed to the fact that only those students who had immigrated relatively recently would use L1 exclusively. Length of residence is not considered in Bhatnagar's study, but there is considerable research documentation (see, for example, Skutnabb-Kangas 1984) about how rapidly a switch to the majority language occurs among siblings and the peer group.

A recent National Assessment of Educational Progress (NAEP) (1983a) study provides the most comprehensive data on the implications of speaking a minority language in the home. It was found that although students from other-language-dominant homes tended to lag behind students from English-dominant homes in reading achievement, the pattern of findings could not be attributed to any simple relationship between linguistic mismatch and achievement. The trends in the data are summarized in the NAEP Newsletter (1983b, p. 3):

> . . . some students from homes where English is not spoken often are much better readers than others. And some, in fact, read better than many students from English-dominant homes . . . Consequences of coming from an other-language-dominant home are not the same for students of different racial and ethnic backgrounds . . .
>
> White youngsters from other-language-dominant homes have a strike against them when it comes to reading skills. At age 17, these pupils are

about 5 percentage points below whites from English-speaking homes in reading performance.

For Hispanos, however, language spoken in the home doesn't appear to make much difference in reading abilities. For 17-year-olds, students from both other-language-dominant and English-speaking homes lagged about 9 percentage points behind the nation in reading skills.

The complexity of the interactions between home language use and other variables can be seen in the results presented by Yee and Laforge (1974). Their study of fifty-three American-born Chinese nine- and ten-year-olds in San Francisco revealed that the more exposure to and emphasis on Chinese outside the home (e.g. closeness of home to Chinatown, attendance at Chinese school), the better students performed on the English WISC. Amount of English use in the home was unrelated to WISC scores.

Dolson (1984) investigated the academic performance of 108 Hispanic students in grades 5 and 6 in relation to the extent that Spanish had been maintained as the major home language. He reported significantly poorer academic performance on five out of ten scholastic measures among students who had switched to English as the main home language (subtractive bilinguals) in comparison to students who had maintained Spanish as the main home language (additive bilinguals).

These findings also show the inadequacy of attempts to explain minority students' achievement solely by means of 'acculturation' (e.g. Troike 1984). If acculturation to the values and norms of the majority culture were the primary causal factor, then we would expect to find that students who made more use of the majority language would perform better. Clearly, this is not the case.

In conclusion, the evaluation and research data reviewed above refute the 'maximum exposure' hypothesis with regard to the causes of minority student underachievement. This does not mean that exposure to a language is unimportant; rather, it implies that minority students' L1 cognitive/academic skills are just as important as L2 exposure for the development of cognitive/academic skills in L2. For other aspects of L2 proficiency (e.g. grammatical competence), the Japanese data suggest that exposure and use may be more important than cognitive/academic attributes of the learner. However, the policy debate has centred on minority students' academic development and it would appear that the intuitions of many policy-makers are removed from the reality indicated by research. The data do in fact provide a solid basis for policy predictions and programme planning when they are viewed within the framework of the CUP model of bilingual proficiency.

Notes

1. Macnamara (1970) points out that a strict interpretation of an SUP model would leave the bilingual in a curious predicament in that 'he would have great difficulty in "communicating" with himself. Whenever he switched language he would have difficulty in explaining in L2 what he had heard or said in L1' (pp. 25–26). It is not surprising that the SUP model is not seriously proposed by any researcher. Nevertheless, it is important to examine the research evidence in relation to this model, since many educators and policy-makers espouse positions in regard to bilingual education which derive directly from this implicit model.

Section 3
Programme planning for bilingualism

In this concluding section of Part One, we synthesize and elaborate the themes of the previous two sections by outlining three principles of bilingual programme planning. These principles of programme planning are some of the common denominators of successful programmes independent of the characteristics of the children being served. The first principle is the principle of 'first things first'; the second is the principle of 'bilingualism through monolingualism'; and the third is the principle of 'bilingualism as a bonus'.

The principle of first things first implies that development and maintenance of a child's first language is critically important to his or her psychological, linguistic and cognitive well-being. It is therefore important that schools foster first language development. This principle could be construed to imply a neglect of second language development were it not for the recognition of a common underlying proficiency – of an interdependence between first and second languages in cognitive academic aspects of language proficiency. The concept of linguistic interdependence was introduced and discussed in Section 2. Having a common underlying proficiency means that certain aspects of what is learned in the first language will be 'passed along', so to speak, to the second language.

The second principle, that of bilingualism through monolingualism, proposes that the languages of instruction be used separately rather than concurrently. Separate use implies that each language will be exploited to its fullest: material which is taught in one language will be fully presented in that language and not be sacrificed to the vocabulary and structural exposition of the other language. It creates the opportunity for linguistic thresholds (see Section 1) to be attained in both languages. Separate language use is also one way to overcome the strong influence of the external sociolinguistic forces that promote the use of the majority language. It ensures a healthy balance of language use: pedagogically, psychologically and sociolinguistically.

Bilingualism as a bonus is the third principle. By this is meant that teachers must understand that there may be advantages – political, economic, cultural, psychological, linguistic and cognitive – associated with bilingualism. Section 1 dealt with some of the metalinguistic and cognitive benefits that have been found to be associated with bilingualism. The point is that these benefits are associated with certain types of bilingualism, specifically those where high levels of proficiency in both languages have been attained. Educational programmes need to compensate for linguistic deficiencies of the external environment by providing them in school; a strong second language programme for majority language children; a strong first language programme for minority language children.

6 Bilingualism without tears*

I suspect there is no such thing as 'bilingualism without tears', any more than there is 'growing up without tears', or 'life without tears'. But somehow, the myth has been perpetuated in our society that becoming bilingual as a child is a 'snap' – or perhaps I should say that this is a myth perpetuated by the anglophone majority of our society, who, themselves, have never been faced with the necessity of learning a second language, and who have watched from a distance, young immigrant or minority children playing in English with their friends. Whatever the source, the belief that learning a second language is easy for young children is at the heart of many of our current educational policies. Why else do *early* total French immersion programmes exist in Canada? Why else is there currently such an emphasis in the United States that bilingual education be completed by grade 1 or grade 2? For the most part, it is because it is thought that 'early = easy', as far as second language learning is concerned.

Each of us could, I am sure, provide anecdotal evidence which would counter the claim that early bilingualism is achieved easily. Let me give just one example of a four-year-old girl, Elizabeth, who was fluently bilingual in French and English. One time Elizabeth and a French-speaking friend of hers were playing together. Elizabeth was in the process of telling her friend a story in French when a third person, an English speaker, walked into the room. Initially the two children ignored her, and Elizabeth went on with her story. Eventually, however, the third person interrupted with, 'tell me too'. Elizabeth's response was to say angrily to her friend, in French, of course: 'All the time, I have to explain things to her. C'mon, just the two of us, let's get out of here. I don't want to talk to *her*.' Elizabeth

* This chapter originally appeared as an article of the same title by M. Swain in
M. Clarke and J. Handscombe (eds.) *On TESOL '82: Pacific Perspectives on Language Learning and Teaching*. Washington, D.C.: TESOL, 1983: 35–46. Copyright 1983 by Teachers of English to Speakers of Other Languages. This article is reprinted with permission of the publisher and the author.

then stormed out of the room. I found her shortly afterwards in her bedroom – crying.

Maybe Elizabeth was just upset over having her story interrupted. I suspect, though, there was more to it than that. I suspect that the competing demands her two linguistic worlds were simultaneously making on her were at the root of her frustration. My point in telling this story is not, however, to determine why Elizabeth was unhappy, but simply to indicate her unhappiness and frustration. This story, and many, many others, attest to the social and emotional crises that can accompany bilingualism. What can schools do about them? How can they help?

The answer for some, is simple: do not develop bilingualism, develop monolingualism. Teach immigrant minority children English. Assimilate them, and the problems will go away. The trouble with this answer is that it is wrong. The problems do not necessarily go away; they may even increase, for the individual, and for the society.

So the answer lies in developing bilingualism. And if we are looking to schools to aid in this process, the answer must lie in bilingual education. But what sort of bilingual education? And what sort of bilingual teaching?

There are a bewildering array of children to serve, from children with limited proficiency to full proficiency in either their first language, their second language, or both. There are children who already have some literacy skills, and some that do not. There are children whose home language is a socially or economically prestigious language, and there are those whose home language is not. Can common denominators of bilingual education be identified that will serve this complex array of child characteristics?

I think so. And that is what I would like to focus on in this chapter. I will call these common denominators, 'principles' of successful bilingual education. By successful bilingual education, I mean a programme which leads to the development and maintenance of bilingual skills, high levels of academic achievement and personal social-psychological enrichment. There are three principles of successful bilingual education that I would like to suggest. There are surely others. But for now, I will consider only three principles. The first is the principle of 'first things first'; the second is the principle of 'bilingualism through monolingualism'; and the third is the principle of 'bilingualism as a bonus'.

Principle of first things first

The first principle, that of first things first, establishes the central role of the child's first language in all aspects of his or her educational development. It says: ensure that the child's home language is adequately developed before worrying about progress in the second language. It implies that the first language is so instru-mental to the emotional and academic well-being of the child, that its development must be seen as a high, if not the highest, priority in the early years of schooling.

Why is the development of the first language so crucial to second language development, academic success, and emotional well-being? Perhaps the role of the home language is easiest to understand with respect to the psychological and emotional development of the child, and is so obvious as to need little explanation. To be told, whether directly or indirectly, explicitly or implicitly, that your language and the language of your parents, of your home and of your friends is non-functional in school is to negate your sense of self. One can imagine any number of responses on the part of the children who hear this message. They could accept the school's dictum and reject their families; they could feel anger and frustration towards their teachers and school, which could lead to hostility and aggression and eventu-ally dropping-out of school, or to a denial of the value of school. And so on. Needless to say, none of these are healthy responses, but each of them has been observed (e.g. Gardner and Lambert 1972). Moreover, in addition to the negative feelings that might be generated towards members of the majority language community, socially and culturally, there is, at least with many minority groups, the real possi-bility of developing feelings of ambivalence towards their *own* language and social-self. This 'bicultural ambivalence' (Cummins 1982) is particularly destructive both to one's self and to society.

Acceptance of the home language in the home and school is clearly, then, one of the first steps in creating an environment where learning can occur, an environment which fosters feelings of self-worth and self-confidence. But acceptance of the home language is only the beginning. Active encouragement to make use of the home language in school is equally important. This can be done in a variety of ways. One way, of course, is to use the language as a medium of instruction, which not only enhances students' comprehension, thereby improving academic performance, but also provides concrete evidence that the home language is a useful and valued tool. Teachers can also ask children for the cooperation of their parents in preparing assignments concerned with cultural traditions, family histories, family stories, folk tales, jokes, etc. Local people such as artists, musicians, athletes and businessmen who are fluent in the children's first language can be brought in to talk with them (Legaretta-Marcaida 1981). Whatever can be done to involve the home and community in the school programme will help to convince the students that the school is sincere in its regard for their language and culture.

Under these conditions, most research indicates that children from linguistic minorities feel better about themselves, their language and their culture than children in English-only programmes (e.g. Rivera 1972; Skoczylas 1972). The trend noted in some studies (e.g. Morris 1974) of a decreasing self-concept among minority children with increasing years in regular English classes can be reversed, with the result that the basic conditions for learning are, at least, present.

It has been argued that primary French immersion programmes in Canada provide a counter-example for the need to make use of the home language in school. Nothing could be further from the truth. In the first place, the home language of the immersion students *is* used in the school. The home language, which is English for the French immersion children, is the language of the school. That is, most French immersion programmes are housed in English schools and so the language of the corridors and the playground is English. Moreover, although the language of instruction is French right from the first day of kindergarten, the children frequently use English when speaking to their teacher and their classmates for the first year or two of school. This is made possible by the fact that French immersion teachers are bilingual. Although the teachers do not *speak* English in class, they understand whatever the children say to them. In this way, the teachers can respond relevantly, appropriately and supportively to their students, and build from the child's existing linguistic repertoire and interests.

Secondly, instruction in, and about, English is introduced in primary French immersion programmes from the second or third grade. From then on, it remains part of the curriculum with increasing allotments of time given to it.

And thirdly, this is done even though the French immersion children come from the dominant, majority group culture. For them, there is no threat in learning a second language to feelings of self-worth or personal identity. There is virtually no possibility, given the overwhelming use of English in the wider environment, that they could lose their home language. So do not let anyone try to tell you that

French immersion education as practised in Canada does not allow for the use of the home language in school.

Having suggested, then, that one reason for introducing the first language of minority students first is to create, at minimum, the conditions under which learning can take place, we now need to examine the role the first language plays in achieving improved academic performance and second language development.

The usual rationale for using the home language to teach academic content is that the children will be able to understand what is being taught, and therefore, they will not fall behind in school while they are learning English. This argument makes sense as far as it goes. The problem is that it does not go far enough. Not only will the children be learning academic content, but they will be improving their first language skills in the process. Developing full proficiency in their first language will promote the same in their second language.

This is an important point: that developing full proficiency in the first language promotes the same in the second language. What it assumes is that there is an underlying proficiency that is common to both languages (see this volume, Section 2). Consider, for example, literacy-related skills. The difficult task is learning to read. Once reading, as a skill and as a knowledge source, has been learned, then it is a relatively simple matter to transfer the skill and knowledge to a second language context. In other words, one does not relearn to read every time a new language is learned. One makes use of already learned skills and knowledge in learning to read the second time around. Similarly, once one has learned how to use language as a tool for conceptualizing, drawing abstract relations or expressing complex relationships in one language, then these processes, or language functions, are applicable to any language context. Thus, spending time learning in one language does not impede the development of these language functions in a second language, it enhances them. Or, to put it another way, spending time learning in one language benefits both languages with respect to developing those language-related skills associated with cognitive functioning and literacy-related activities.

Given that this is the case, and there is considerable research evidence to suggest that it is (e.g. Cummins *et al.* 1984), then the implications for the role of the first language and bilingual education are profound. Simply stated, they are that learning in the first language benefits both first and second language development, and that, therefore, more time spent developing the first language, which implies less time spent teaching the second language, should lead to superior first and second language development.

The evidence for this claim comes from a variety of sources. (See Cummins (1981b) for a review, and this volume, Chapters 3 and 5.) There are a growing number of bilingual education programmes for minority language children in the United States, and elsewhere, where the students in the programme exhibit improved first and second language skills, *and* superior academic performance relative to bilingual students in monolingual programmes. These bilingual education programmes are characterized by the use of the first language for instructional purposes for a major portion of the curriculum in the early primary years of schooling, with increasing portions of the curriculum taught in English in later elementary schooling.

Once again, the results from the early total French immersion programmes in Canada have been used to argue that initial education in the first language is not necessary for successful second language learning or academic progress. However, the data from French immersion studies, when examined longitudinally, suggest otherwise.

The evidence from the early immersion programmes indicates that after several years of schooling in French, immersion children interact with relative ease and naturalness in face-to-face play sessions with native French-speaking peers (Szamosi, Swain and Lapkin 1979). However, at the same time, that is, at about the grade 2 level, the immersion children's performance on a standardized test of French achievement placed them at approximately the 16th percentile relative to native French speakers in Quebec (Swain and Barik 1976b). It was not until about the *sixth* grade that the immersion students' performance on a standardized test of French placed them at about the 50th percentile in relation to francophones (see, for example, this volume, Chapter 4). Now, recall that I mentioned earlier that instruction in, and about, English, the immersion children's first language, is introduced into the programme in grade 2 or grade 3. Up until that time their performance on standardized tests of English was inferior to that of comparable groups of English-speaking students educated only in English (e.g. Barik and Swain 1975). But once English literacy was introduced into the programme, the immersion students quickly caught up, and eventually surpassed their English-educated peers in some aspects of measured English language skills (e.g. Barik and Swain 1978a).

There are two important points to note in these data. The first point is that the scores on tests of French achievement of the immersion children remained below average until marked improvement was noted in their English achievement scores. In other words, it was not until their first language achievement scores had improved considerably that their second language achievement scores increased to indicate average performance relative to francophones. The message here is that first language literacy-related instruction is associated with improved second language performance in literacy-related tasks. Thus, even the French immersion data support the claim of the crucial role played by the first language in second language development.

The second point to note from these data is that although the French immersion children were able to interact in face-to-face play situations with French children after several years in the programme, it took some *six to seven* years in the programme to produce average performance on second language achievement tests. The message here is that language learning takes time. The message is also that we should re-examine our expectation that bilingual education should be, or even can be, a short and transitory experience, if it is to be a successful one. We should be thinking of the long term, and watching for the cumulative benefits to emerge.

So, to summarize the principle of first things first: it means that a priority of education should be to ensure that the child has a sound basis in his or her first language. By doing this, we will provide for the child a social-emotional environment in which the basic conditions for learning can occur; and in which the linguistic and cognitive development in the first language will support the same in the second language.

The principle of bilingualism through monolingualism

The second principle of successful bilingual education is the principle of bilingualism through monolingualism. This principle refers to the way in which the languages of instruction are used by the teaching staff. On the one hand, the two languages can be used *concurrently*, that is, with frequent shifting back and forth between the two languages within a class lesson. This approach to bilingual teaching has been called the 'mixing approach' (McLaughlin 1978). On the other hand, the two languages can be used *separately*, separate by person, by time, by lesson, or by subject content. This approach to bilingual teaching I will call the 'separation' approach. The principle of bilingualism through monolingualism proposes that the development of bilingual skills on the part of the students will be enhanced by the separated use of languages on the part of the teachers.

What is the evidence to support this claim? One piece of evidence comes from a study completed by Legaretta (1979) of six bilingual classrooms. In five classrooms the concurrent, or mixing, approach was used, and in one classroom the separation approach was used such that only one language was used in the morning and the other language was used in the afternoon. The kindergarten children in these classes were pre-tested and tested again six months later in both Spanish and English. The children in the bilingual programme using the separation approach made significantly greater gains in oral comprehension of English and in communicative skills in general in both English and Spanish than the children in the classes using the mixing approach.

We might ask why the separation approach would produce superior results relative to the mixing approach. There are at least four fairly powerful reasons that I can think of.

One reason is that children apparently learn to ignore the language they do not understand. If the same, or a related, message is typically given in both languages, then there is no motivation to try to figure out what is being said in English. Lily Wong Fillmore (1980a), describing video-tapes of children in a classroom where a concurrent translation approach was used, reports the students 'alternatively being attentive and inattentive as the teachers switch between languages in their lessons. During the time the language they do not understand is being spoken, the students simply stop listening.' (p. 29).

A second reason for the greater effectiveness of the separation approach may be that students and teachers have to work harder: students are trying to make sense of what the teacher's message is; and teachers are trying to present a message that makes sense. For the teacher, this means, as Lily Wong Fillmore (1980a) suggests:

> that the lesson must involve enough of the kinds of experiences (e.g. demonstrations, participation in ongoing activities) which permit the child to figure out what the point of the lesson is even if they do not understand what is being said, or could not understand it out of context. This kind of approach requires a lot of planning, preparation and imagination on the part of the teacher.
>
> (p. 99)

Our experience in Canada with French immersion, an example of a bilingual education programme that has used the separation approach, has shown that not only does the teaching draw on all the creative resources of the teacher, but that it works – the children learn the second language and progress satisfactorily in subject matter learning as well.

A third reason for the relative effectiveness of the separation approach may be that, although it draws on the creative resources of the teachers, it is less demanding of their linguistic resources. That is to say, switching back and forth between languages is an exhausting task. Simultaneous interpretation, to which the task of a teacher using a concurrent approach to bilingual teaching can be likened, is recognized by their profession as extremely demanding, and in Canada, at least, the union representing simultaneous interpreters insists that no one can work for longer than twenty minutes without a break. Surely an exhausted teacher cannot be the best teacher. By definition, the separation approach does not make these sorts of exhausting demands on the teacher.

A fourth reason for the superiority of the separation approach may be related to the first principle, that of first things first. Although many bilingual teachers may be convinced that in a concurrently taught programme, they are using each language about equally as often, they may be wrong. Bilingual individuals are frequently unaware of which language they are using at a given time, or that they have switched from one language to another. This means that they may well be inaccurate in their own perception of how much, and for what purposes, they use each language. For example, Legaretta-Marcaida (1981), commenting on her research in bilingual classrooms, noted that:

> teachers and aides have been confident that they use Spanish and English about equally. When classroom interaction was assessed quantitatively, however, to arrive at actual percentages of Spanish and English used, it was found that in classrooms using Concurrent Translation, English was used by both the teacher and the aide, on an average, nearly three-quarters (72 per cent) of the time; and Spanish was being used just over one-quarter (28 per cent) of the time.
>
> (p. 104)

It is interesting to note that this was done by teachers and aides whose first language was Spanish. In contrast, in the separation approach class, nearly equal amounts of Spanish and English were used.

What these sorts of data suggest is that the separation approach, that is, an approach that ensures that the languages will be kept separate instructionally, counteracts the natural 'pull' exerted by the dominant position of the majority language. It helps to overcome the *natural* tendency of minority language speakers to shift to the majority language. It, in effect, ensures that the first language will keep its position, both psychologically for the children and sociologically within the confines of the school as an institution, as an equally important and accepted language along with English.

Consider, for example, what Legaretta-Marcaida (1981) reports was observed in an unmonitored mixing approach as opposed to a separation approach: '. . . bilingual teachers in the Concurrent Translation classrooms used an average of 77 per cent English for "solidarity" functions (e.g. warming, accepting, or amplifying pupil talk), while the separation teaching staff used much more Spanish (72 per cent) for this function' (p. 105).

The hidden message of this kind of distribution of language use over sociolinguistically important functions of language as observed in the concurrent classrooms can be serious. It can negate all the overt signs of the first principle, of first things first, and, by so doing, reinforce or re-establish the negative consequences of bicultural ambivalence.

So, to summarize, the principle of bilingualism through monolingualism argues that it is pedagogically more sound to use languages separately in an instructional unit than to use them concurrently. The most obvious reasons for the greater pedagogical effectiveness of the separation approach are four-fold. First, if languages are used concurrently, students tend to tune out the language they do not know, or are least competent in. This leads to boredom, and lack of motivation to learn the second language on the part of the students. Secondly, using the two languages in separate contexts, that is, not being able to rely on the other language when the going gets tough, means that both teachers and students may have to work harder. For the students this may mean greater concentration on what the teacher is saying, knowing that there is no other way to understand what is going on. For the teacher this means, by necessity, a reliance on a multitude of nonverbal, gestural, visual cues, a reliance on personal ingenuity and creativity, and a nonreliance on the other language. Ultimately this means the children will benefit more, because any material which is taught in the first language will be fully presented in that language, and not be sacrificed to the vocabulary and structural exposition of the second language. Thirdly, the exhausting linguistic demands of translating from language to language, or even of covering the same topics in both languages, will not be imposed on the teacher. Fourthly, through the use of the minority language over a lengthy time period, the linguistic pull of the dominant culture can be counteracted. In effect, it is one way to overcome the strong influence of the external sociolinguistic forces that promote the use of the majority language. It ensures a healthy balance of language use: pedagogically, psychologically and sociolinguistically. These, then, are the reasons behind the principle of bilingualism through monolingualism.

The principle of bilingualism as a bonus

The third principle I want to mention with respect to the successful functioning of a bilingual education programme is 'bilingualism as a bonus'. The intent of this principle is simple: let your students know how and why bilingualism will work for them. And the corollary to this principle is 'believe it, and it will become a self-fulfilling prophecy'. In other words, 'boast the benefits of bilingualism' to your students, their parents, educators in the system, to anyone you talk to.

There are lots of benefits that you can boast about bilingualism. They range from political to economic to cultural to linguistic to cognitive to personal benefits.

For example, several years ago children at the grade 5 and 6 levels in the French immersion programme and in the regular English programme in Toronto and Ottawa were asked to write an opinion essay on the topic of 'Why I like (or don't like) being a Canadian'. Their responses were not analysed linguistically. Instead, the content of what they said was examined. The results indicated that the immersion children gave three times as many reasons, on the average, as the monolingual children did for why they liked being Canadian. In addition, they gave as reasons for why they liked being Canadian, statements that could be classified as relating to the linguistic and cultural diversity of Canada. That is, both the immersion and monolingual groups wrote in their essays about the physical beauty of Canada – the fact that in Canada you can find mountains, plains and lakes. However, the immersion children, and only the immersion children, also wrote about the linguistic and cultural diversity of Canada (Swain 1980). To quote one grade 5 immersion student:

> I like being Canadian because we have people from all over the world
> who may live just next door. Here in Canada you hear different
> languages and [different] styles ... And most of all we care.

Another example representing a heightened linguistic and cultural understanding – 'an insight into different cultures and ways of organizing knowledge' (Cummins 1982) comes from the writings of a teenager who was a New Canadian Student (Henry Ma) from Hong Kong. He wrote:

> English style is very different from my style. English people do not like sentences to go round and round, and the idea must be clear, but in our tradition we tend to go around and around and then at least the focus becomes narrower and narrower.

These are personal individual examples. The professional literature includes considerable research evidence which suggests that bilingualism is correlated with cognitive flexibility (see this volume, Chapter 1, for a review), superior first language skills (Swain and Lapkin 1981), and higher measured IQ (Barik and Swain 1976a). However, this is true only for 'additive' forms of bilingualism and not for subtractive forms.

Thus what we need to be assured of, in order to produce these benefits of bilingualism is that an additive form of bilingualism exists. And that brings us back to the principle of 'first things first'. It is only through the careful support, development and maintenance of the *first* language in a minority linguistic group situation that there is any guarantee of the development of 'additive' bilingualism, that is, where the second language is *added* to the first without any threat of loss to the first language. This is in contrast to the situation of 'subtractive' bilingualism, where the learning of a second language, because of its majority status, its prestige value, or whatever results in the lack of maintenance, or loss, of the first language. Ultimately this condition can lead to monolingualism in a second language, rather than bilingualism.

Conclusion

In conclusion, then, three principles have been suggested which underlie the operation of successful bilingual education programmes. The principle of first things first, argues for the development and maintenance of the first language in school on the grounds that this will provide the essential psychological and sociological support for linguistic and academic learning in both languages. The second principle, that of bilingualism through monolingualism, argues for the separated use of the two languages for instructional purposes. And the third principle, that of bilingualism as a bonus, argues that it is our responsibility to know about the possible benefits of bilingualism and the conditions which will lead to them. It is our responsibility as educators to aid in the creation of the conditions that will foster positive forms of bilingualism.

Part Two
Bilingual proficiency

Section 4
The construct of bilingual proficiency

There is still little consensus among researchers as to the nature of language proficiency. For example, a model proposed by Hernandez-Chavez, Burt and Dulay (1978) comprised sixty-four separate proficiencies, each of which, hypothetically, is independently measurable. At the other extreme is Oller's (1978, 1979) claim that 'there exists a global language proficiency factor which accounts for the bulk of the reliable variance in a wide variety of language proficiency measures' (1978, p. 413). This factor is strongly related to cognitive ability and academic achievement measures and is about equally well measured by certain types of listening, speaking, reading and writing tasks.

In this section, two quite different perspectives on the nature of language proficiency are discussed. Each of the two perspectives was developed to serve different functions. The framework of communicative competence outlined in Chapter 7 was developed to serve as a descriptive basis for the preparation of tests measuring communicative proficiency (Canale and Swain 1980a; Canale 1983). The framework of language proficiency outlined in Chapter 8 was developed to account for differences in performance on academic and non-academic language tasks.

The framework of communicative competence outlined in Chapter 7 grew mainly from a review of the theoretical literature. The proposal is that communicative competence consists minimally of discourse, sociolinguistic, grammatical and strategic competence. Grammatical competence is defined to include knowledge of vocabulary, rules of word formation, pronunciation/spelling and sentence formation. Sociolinguistic competence reflects the degree to which specific utterances are appropriate given, for example, the topic, the status of the participants, and the purpose of the interaction. Discourse competence includes the mastery of cohesion (e.g. the ability to connect text with appropriate conjunctions or adverbs) and coherence, the ability to arrange ideas in logical sequence and organize meanings effectively. Strategic competence involves the use of 'coping' strategies to avoid breakdown in communication or to enhance the effectiveness of spoken discourse or written text.

The research discussed in Chapter 7 illustrates the importance of using a variety of analytical tools to probe the meaning of one's data. For example, using factor analytic (correlational) techniques, the results did not support the existence of the hypothesized components. However, by comparing the performance of native speakers with that of non-native speakers, it was seen that they performed similarly on most discourse measures and on some sociolinguistic measures, whereas they performed very differently on grammatical measures. This finding suggests that there is something different about grammatical performance as compared to discourse and sociolinguistic performance, supporting the notion that grammatical performance, at least, is differentiable from other aspects of communicative performance.

The research discussed in Chapter 7 also serves to remind us that conclusions are only as good as our measures – the operationalizations of our theoretical constructs. The conclusions we have drawn with respect to discourse, sociolinguistic and grammatical competence are solidly anchored in the way we have chosen to measure them. Although we are not dissatisfied with the indices that have been used, we continue to be concerned about what has *not* been measured.

There are two ways in which aspects of communicative performance have not been measured in our research. First, we have not applied our indices of performance to a wide variety of spoken and written language collected under a variety of situations. Rather, for the most part, each measure has been applied to one type of task performed under fairly contrived settings.

Secondly, there are some aspects of performance that our methods of data collection simply did not elicit. This appears to be a particular problem in the domain of sociolinguistic proficiency. For example, a friend of ours recently had several foreign guests to visit her home. One of the guests, on examining a painting that was hung on the wall, exclaimed 'By no means is that beautiful!', meaning 'That's ugly!'. Capturing this sort of social *faux pas* in a productive test of sociolinguistic performance will take some ingenuity on the part of the researchers. It is also possible that the language learners will be equally ingenious in avoiding such spontaneous comments in any activity resembling a test situation. Future research needs to address itself to both of these areas of missing data.

The framework outlined in Chapter 8 represents a completely different way to conceptualize language proficiency. The view of language proficiency developed in Chapter 8 is linked to the interdependence hypothesis proposed in Part One of this book. The assumption is that at least those aspects of language which are at the context-reduced end of a dimension representing the range of contextual cues available to aid in the interpretation of meaning are interdependent across languages. This provides a link between language proficiency and academic achievement.

These two views of language proficiency are not irreconcilable. Reconciliation of the two conceptualizations is an empirical issue, and in Section 6 we attempt to synthesize the two perspectives through a consideration of the research evidence. In the interim, it is important to note that both Chapters 7 and 8 present the view that language proficiency is developed through language use embedded in meaningful contexts. In Chapter 7, it is argued that language learners need to have opportunities for both receptive and productive uses of the target languages. In other words, language proficiency is not developed through input alone. Opportunities for language output in situations that cause learners to push the limits of their linguistic resources is important. Contexts in which the learner wants to understand or convey a message will therefore be significantly more effective than rehearsal of meaningless drills. Similarly, in Chapter 8, it is noted that being able to manipulate and interpret cognitively demanding, context-reduced text grows from using language in contextually-embedded situations.

7 Communicative competence: some roles of comprehensible input and comprehensible output in its development[*]

The role of input is, without a doubt, of critical importance in under-standing the what and why of second language acquisition. To this end, we are seeing an increasing number of studies which focus on fine-grained analyses of the nature of foreigner talk, teacher talk and learner talk, as well as on the variables intervening between input and intake. The data base for the majority of these studies is input to learners of English as a second or foreign language, and input to adults.

The focus of this chapter, and the data base employed, are consider-ably different. Rather than focusing on a micro-analysis of learner input in specific interactional events, attention will be paid to the input-output relationships at the level of language proficiency *traits*, specifically the traits of grammatical, discourse and sociolinguistic competence. The data come from children whose first language is English, and who are learning French as a second language in the school setting of a French immersion programme. Compared with ESL learners, these children make infrequent use of the target language outside of the school setting. Thus, the second language input to these students is largely that of native-speaker teacher talk and non-native peer talk, as well as, of course, experience with literacy activi-ties. Within a theoretical framework that incorporates traits and contexts of language use, the structure of the immersion students' output, that is, the structure of their language proficiency can be seen to relate rather directly to the nature of the input received. However,

[*] This chapter originally appeared as an article of the same title by M. Swain in S. Gass and C. Madden (eds.) *Input in Second Language Acquisition*. Rowley, Mass.: Newbury House, 1985: 235–253. Permission to reprint this article has been granted by Newbury House.

aspects of the immersion students' second language proficiency cannot be totally accounted for on the basis of the input received.

This chapter, then, will consider the second language proficiency exhibited by these French immersion students, relating their output at a macro level to their language learning environment. Of the conclusions I will draw, one that I think is fundamental to our understanding of the role of input in second language acquisition, is that although comprehensible input (Krashen 1981, 1982) may be essential to the acquisition of a second language, it is not enough to ensure that the outcome will be native-like performance. In fact, I will argue that while comprehensible input and the concomitant emphasis on interaction in which meaning is negotiated (e.g. Long 1983; Varonis and Gass 1985) is essential, its impact on grammatical development has been overstated. The role of these interactional exchanges in second language acquisition may have as much to do with 'comprehensible output', as it has to do with comprehensible input.

The data I will be drawing on in this chapter come from one study undertaken within the context of a large-scale research project concerned with the development of bilingual proficiency.[1] The overall aim of the research is to explore the influences of social, educational and individual variables on the processes and outcomes of second language learning. The specific goal of the study I will be discussing here was to determine the extent to which certain components of language proficiency represented in our theoretical framework as linguistic traits were empirically distinguishable, and were differentially manifested in oral and written tasks. Other studies currently underway as part of the same large-scale research programme will compare the structure of language proficiency of French immersion students with that of other learners who have learned their second language under considerably different conditions. Thus, although of theoretical interest, the research programme has been designed to have direct bearing on language policy issues in schools through the identification of strengths and weaknesses in certain aspects of the students' language proficiency.

The basic theoretical framework within which the study was carried out is diagrammed in Figure 7.1. The framework incorporates as traits several components of communicative competence proposed by Canale and Swain (1980a) and Canale (1983) – grammatical, discourse and sociolinguistic; and incorporates as methods, oral and literacy based tasks.

For each cell in the matrix of traits by methods shown in Figure 7.1,

FIGURE 7.1

		Traits	
	Grammar	Discourse	Sociolinguistic
Oral production	structured interview	film retelling and argumentation	– requests – suggestions – complaints
Multiple choice	45 items	29 items	28 items
Written production	←————— 2 narratives —————— ←————— 2 letters ——————→	2 notes	directives

Methods (vertical label at left)

a test and relevant scoring procedures were developed. The details of the tests, scoring procedures and reliability indices are described elsewhere (Allen *et al.* 1982, 1983). Here, I will confine myself to a brief trait-by-trait description of the tests and main features of the scoring procedures utilized. The scoring breakdown has theoretical interest in that it pinpoints which aspects of language competence are being assessed in each test.

The trait of grammatical competence was operationalized as rules of morphology and syntax, with a major focus on verbs and prepositions. The oral production task consists of a structured interview which embeds thirty-six standardized questions in a conversation. The topics are concrete and familiar, designed to focus the student's attention on communication rather than on the second language code. The standardized questions are designed to elicit a range of verb forms and prepositions in French, as well as responses that are sufficiently elaborated to score for syntactic accuracy. Grammatical scoring, then, was based on the student's ability to use certain grammatical forms accurately in the context of particular questions.

The grammatical multiple choice test consists of forty-five items assessing knowledge of similar aspects of syntax and morphology as were elicited in the interview situation.

In the grammatical written production tasks the student is presented with four situations and asked to write a short text about each. The four topics were designed to bias towards the use of the past and present tenses through two narrations, and future and conditional tenses through two letters of request. Grammatical errors were tallied for each of four categories: syntactic errors, preposition errors, homophonous verb errors and non-homophonous verb errors.

The error counts were translated into accuracy scores by considering them, in the case of syntactic errors, relative to the number of finite verbs produced; in the case of prepositions, relative to the number of obligatory contexts for prepositions; and in the case of verb errors, relative to the number of verb forms produced.

Before moving on to a description of the tasks and scoring procedures used in measuring the discourse and sociolinguistic traits, it is useful to examine the results obtained by the grade 6 immersion students who took the grammar tests relative to native speakers of French also in grade 6. The results reported in this paper are based on a sub-sample of sixty-nine French immersion students who were administered the entire battery of oral production, multiple choice and written production tests. These immersion students have been in a programme in which they were taught entirely in French in kinder-garten and grade 1, about 80% in French in grades 2 to 4, about 60% in French in grade 5, and about 50% in French in grade 6 – the year they were tested. The comparison group of native French speakers consists of ten grade 6 students who likewise were admin-istered the entire test battery. The native speakers of French were in a unilingual French school in Montreal.

The results for the grammatical oral production, multiple choice and written production tasks are shown in Tables 7.1, 7.2 and 7.3 respectively. The essential point to note in these tables is that with the exception of correct use of homophonous verb forms, the native speakers score significantly higher (p<.01) than the immersion students, indicating clearly that, although the immersion students are doing quite well, they have not acquired native-like abilities in the grammatical domain.

The second trait measured, that of discourse competence, was defined as the ability to produce and recognize coherent and cohesive text. The discourse oral production task is designed to elicit narrative and argumentation. The students are shown a short nonverbal film, *The Mole and the Bulldozer*, chosen for its appropriateness to the age group of the students being tested, and for its provocative content which illustrates the conflict between modern technology and the preservation of nature. The day following the film's showing, students are taken individually from class and asked to tell the story of the film. A series of pictures of key events is placed in front of the child to minimize the burden on memory. Following the narration, the student is asked to role-play the mole and try to convince the bulldozers not to change the route of a road, using all the arguments he or she can think of.

TABLE 7.1   Grammatical oral production: percentage correct

	Immersion students		Native speakers		Comparison	
	Mean	*SD*	*Mean*	*SD*	*t*	*sig of t*
Syntax	81.3	13.1	96.5	6.8	3.60	.01
Prepositions	80.5	12.1	100.0	0.0	–	–
Verbs	57.0	18.1	96.4	5.1	6.79	.01
Total	73.2	8.6	96.9	4.0	8.56	.01

TABLE 7.2   Grammatical multiple choice: percentage correct

Immersion students		Native speakers		Comparison	
Mean	*SD*	*Mean*	*SD*	*t*	*sig of t*
60.7	4.41	81.3	4.40	6.20	.01

TABLE 7.3   Grammatical written production: percentage correct

	Immersion students		Native speakers		Comparison	
	Mean	*SD*	*Mean*	*SD*	*t*	*sig of t*
Syntax	75.5	12.1	93.6	6.9	4.60	.01
Prepositions	78.8	10.5	96.0	6.3	5.01	.01
Non-hom. verbs	85.5	7.2	95.9	4.6	4.49	.01
Hom. verbs	78.5	9.0	79.1	10.3	.20	ns
Total	70.9	8.7	85.0	8.5	4.82	.01

Scoring of the story-retelling task was based on four categories:
1. setting the scene;
2. identification;
3. logical sequence of events;
4. time orientation.

Under the category of 'setting the scene', the student's establishment of the idyllic habitat and lifestyle of the mole was assessed. This was important for the coherence of the story as it was this idyllic atmosphere that was at risk throughout. Under the category of 'identification', the student was rated for the explicitness and clarity with which key characters, objects and locations were introduced into the narrative. Because the student had been given to understand that the interviewer had not seen the movie, it was incumbent on the student to name the characters, objects and locations. Under the category 'logical sequence of events', a rating was given for the logical coherence with which the events of the story were narrated. Thus it was important to explain how the mole knew the bulldozers were coming and would endanger his garden, and what the various steps were that the mole took to insure the safety of his property. And finally, under the category of 'time orientation', a rating was given for the coherent use of verb tenses, temporal conjunctions, adverbials and other elements that clarified the temporal relationship between the events of the story. Each of these categories was rated on a scale of 1 (low) to 5 (high). The role-playing situation was also rated on a scale of 1 (low) to 5 (high) for the extent to which logical arguments were presented to support the mole's case that the road should not be straightened. And finally a global score of 1 (low) to 5 (high) was obtained representing the raters' subjective integration of scene setting, identification, logic, time sequence and argument.

The multiple choice test of discourse competence consists of twenty-nine items primarily measuring coherence. Each item is a short passage of two to five sentences. One sentence is omitted from the passage, and the task is to select the appropriate completion from a set of three alternatives. The criterion for selection is primarily the logical coherence of the passage. Intersentential cohesive devices are explicitly incorporated in some items as a basis for choice. An example is given below:

Le premier voyage en ballon dirigible a eu lieu en France en 1783.
_____. Cependant
ça a été un grand événement pour les français.
a)   Il n'a duré que 8 minutes.
b)   Il avait été bien planifié.
c)   Il était rempli d'air chaud.

The written discourse production tasks were the same ones used in the grammatical production tasks, two compositions involving narrative discourse and two letters involving suasion. Scoring for discourse involved six categories:
1. basic task fulfilment;
2. identification;
3. time orientation;
4. anaphora;
5. logical connection;
6. punctuation.

The assessment of 'basic task fulfilment' involved rating how well the written work fulfilled the basic semantic requirements of the discourse task. To qualify as narratives, for example, the compositions needed to include a series of events. To qualify as suasion, the letters had to contain a request with at least one supporting argument. The category of 'identification' was similar to that for the oral production task in which an assessment was made of whether new characters, objects and locations were sufficiently identified, or whether too much prior knowledge on the part of the reader was assumed. The category of 'time orientation' was also similar to that used in the oral production task, assessing how adequately events or situations were located in time, and, where relevant, whether the temporal relationship between events or situations was clear. Under the category of 'anaphora', the use of anaphoric reference to already identified characters, objects, or locations through the use of subject pronouns, possessive adjectives and articles was assessed. The category of 'logical connection' assessed the logical relationship between segments of the text: whether there were non-sequiturs, semantically obscure or fragmentary incidents, or logically missing steps in the argument or sequence of events. The final category, that of 'punctuation' was rated as an indication of the information structure of a text. Ratings were based on the extent to which punctuation clarified the information structure of the text by indicating boundaries of information units. Each of these categories was rated on a five-point scale of 0 (low) to 2 (high).

Following the detailed scoring, the raters who had scored the six discourse categories independently assigned a global discourse score by first sorting the written tasks into three categories of below average, average and above average, and then rating them as relatively high or low within each of these three categories. This resulted in a six-point scale. The criteria for assigning a global score were not closely specified: the scorers were simply asked to keep in mind the general criterion of coherent discourse.

The discourse results are shown in Tables 7.4, 7.5 and 7.6 for oral production, multiple choice and written production tasks respectively. On the separate aspects of discourse which were rated, examination of the comparisons between the immersion and native-speaker students reveals only two significant differences: in the case of oral production, native speakers are rated significantly higher than immersion students on time orientation ($p<.01$); and in the case of written production, native speakers are rated significantly lower than immersion students on punctuation ($p<.01$). The non-significant trend revealed by these

TABLE 7.4 Discourse oral production: ratings on a scale from 1 (low) to 5 (high)

	Immersion students		Native speakers		Comparison	
	Mean	*SD*	*Mean*	*SD*	*t*	*sig of t*
Scene	3.0	1.16	3.5	.85	1.43	ns
Identification	3.2	1.07	3.9	1.37	1.89	ns
Logic	2.9	1.29	2.9	1.37	.04	ns
Time	3.5	1.18	4.5	.71	2.54	.01
Argument	2.9	1.55	3.4	1.26	1.06	ns
Total	3.1	.79	3.6	.79	2.10	.05
Global	2.9	.88	3.6	1.04	2.16	.05

TABLE 7.5 Discourse multiple choice: percentage correct

Immersion students		Native speakers		Comparison	
Mean	*SD*	*Mean*	*SD*	*t*	*sig of t*
66.6	3.78	71.0	2.84	1.03	ns

TABLE 7.6 Discourse written production: ratings on a scale from 0 (low) to 2 (high)

	Immersion students		Native speakers		Comparison	
	Mean	*SD*	*Mean*	*SD*	*t*	*sig of t*
Basic	1.7	.28	1.8	.30	1.61	ns
Identification	1.3	.31	1.2	.25	−.58	ns
Time	1.5	.30	1.4	.38	−.47	ns
Anaphora	1.7	.24	1.6	.33	−.98	ns
Logic	1.5	.30	1.6	.35	1.34	ns
Punctuation	1.6	.41	1.2	.54	−2.67	.01
Total	1.5	.19	1.5	.24	−.72	ns
Global	3.3	1.04	4.1	1.42	2.22	.05

comparisons, but indicated in the comparison of total discourse scores is that native speakers generally perform better than the immersion students on the oral story retelling task, but do not differ in their performance on the written production tasks. The only indication to the contrary is that the global score for the written production tasks shown in Table 7.6 reveals a significant difference (p<.05) between the mean scores obtained by the two groups in favour of the native speakers.

There would seem to be two possible interpretations for the different results obtained by a comparison of the *total* written discourse scores from those obtained by a comparison of the *global* written discourse scores (Table 7.6). It may indicate that the raters were able to detect qualitative differences in the written discourse of native speakers and immersion students that were not captured in the detailed component scores, or it may be that the raters did not stay strictly within the bounds of discourse in making their global ratings. For example, if the raters inadvertently attended to grammatical aspects, which, as has been seen, are clearly better in the native-speaking sample, they may have rated the native speakers better for the wrong reason.

At this point then, it can be seen that differences between the native and non-native groups depend on the trait being measured. For grammar, the difference is large regardless of method; for discourse, the difference is small regardless of method. These results suggest that the grammatical trait is distinguishable from the discourse trait.

The third trait measured, that of sociolinguistic competence, was defined as the ability to produce and recognize socially appropriate language within a given sociocultural context. The oral production sociolinguistic test consists of presenting a series of twelve situations using slides and audio accompaniment describing the situation. Each situation is a particular combination of one of three functions – request, suggestion or complaint; of one of two levels of formality – high or low; and of one of two settings – in school or out of school. The test begins with the tester explaining to the student being tested how different registers of speech may be used in different situations and illustrates this with an example. The student then watches a set of three slides and listens to the synchronized description. With the showing of the last slide, the student responds in the most appropriate way as if addressing the person shown in the slide. For example, one set of slides shows two children in the school library who are the same age as the student being tested. The student hears a description, in French, that says 'You're in the library to study. But there are two persons at the next table who are speaking loudly, and are bothering you. You decide to ask them to make less noise. What would you say if the two persons were friends of yours?' To change the level of formality, another set of slides shows two adults in the library, and the final question is 'What would you say if the two persons were adults that you don't know?'.

The objective of the scoring was to determine the extent to which students could vary their language use appropriately in response to the social demands of the different situations. In other words, the scores were to indicate the student's ability to use linguistic markers of formal register in formal situations and to refrain from using them in informal situations. Thus, for each situation, a student's response was scored for the presence ($=1$) or absence ($=0$) of six markers of formal register. The six formal features were:

1. the use of an initial politeness marker such as *pardon* or *madame* in the utterance opening;
2. the use of *vous* as a form of address;
3. the use of question forms with *est-ce que* or inversion;
4. the use of the conditional verb form;
5. the inclusion of formal vocabulary and/or the use of additional explanatory information;
6. the use of concluding politeness markers such as *s'il vous plaît*.

A student's score on a particular marker in a particular situation was taken as the difference between use of the marker in the formal variant of the situation and use in the informal variant. A good sociolinguistic score was thus a relatively high difference score, and a poor sociolinguistic score was a relatively low or negative difference score.

The multiple choice test of sociolinguistic competence consists of twenty-eight items designed to test the ability of a student to recognize the appropriateness of an utterance with respect to its sociocultural context. The items describe a specific sociocultural situation and the student is asked to select the best of three possible ways to express a given idea in that situation. The items are designed to include both written and spoken language use in varying degrees of formality, and include the identification of certain written styles such as those used in proverbs, in publications such as journals, encyclopedias and magazines, and in public notices. Before starting the test, the distinction between oral and written language is drawn to the students' attention, and the students are told that the register of the responses, not their grammaticality, is the important consideration. Each item is scored according to the degree of appropriateness based on native-speaker responses, with values ranging from nought to three points. Two examples are given below:

1. A l'école, dans la cour de récréation, dite par une élève à son ami
   a) Pourrais-je te voir un instant?
   b) Est-ce que je pourrais te parler quelques minutes?
   c) Je peux te parler une minute?

2. Devant l'hôtel de ville, écrit sur un panneau public
   a) Prière de ne pas passer sur le gazon.
   b) Ne pas passer sur le gazon.
   c) Vous ne devez pas passer sur le gazon.

The sociolinguistic written production tasks focus on two extremes of directive. The students wrote two letters requesting a favour of a higher status, unfamiliar adult. In addition, the students wrote two notes in which they assumed the role of a familiar adult (mother, teacher) imposing authority by means of a brief informal note to get action from the student who is at fault in some way (has left room untidy, homework undone).

As with the sociolinguistic oral production tasks, the scoring of the sociolinguistic written production tasks was designed to capture the student's ability to use formal sociolinguistic markers of politeness that were appropriate in the context of the letters, and to abstain from using such markers in the context of the notes. Thus each letter and note were scored for the presence or absence of several formal markers:

1. the use of conditional verb forms;
2. the use of modal verbs, and/or *est-ce que*, inverted and indirect question forms, and/or the use of idiomatic polite expressions (e.g. *ayez l'obligeance de*);
3. the use of *vous* as a form of address;
4. the use of formal closings (e.g. *merci à l'avance, merci de votre collaboration*).

As with the sociolinguistic oral task, a difference score was calculated between the use of each marker in the formal contexts and its use in the informal contexts.

The sociolinguistic scores are shown in Tables 7.7, 7.8 and 7.9 for the oral production, multiple choice and written production tasks respectively. The results suggest that overall, native speakers perform significantly better on the sociolinguistic tasks than the immersion students. Excluding for the moment the use of *vous* as a polite form of address, the only discernible pattern in the results is that in those categories of sociolinguistic performance where formulaic politeness terms are possible, immersion students tend to perform as well as

TABLE 7.7   Sociolinguistic oral production: difference scores, formal-informal use

	Immersion students		Native speakers		Comparison	
	Mean	*SD*	*Mean*	*SD*	*t*	*sig of t*
Introduction	.522	.263	.400	.263	−1.37	ns
Vous	.300	.220	.800	.132	6.97	.01
Question	.117	.180	.417	.180	4.96	.01
Conditional	.042	.150	.267	.210	4.22	.01
Other	.102	.167	.517	.183	7.25	.01
Finale	.095	.203	.200	.258	1.49	ns
Total	1.170	.530	2.600	.570	7.94	0.1

TABLE 7.8   Sociolinguistic multiple choice: percentage correct

Immersion students		Native speakers		Comparison	
Mean	*SD*	*Mean*	*SD*	*t*	*sig of t*
35.29	6.13	40.50	10.10	2.29	.05

TABLE 7.9   Sociolinguistic written production: difference scores, formal-informal use

	Immersion students		Native speakers		Comparison	
	Mean	*SD*	*Mean*	*SD*	*t*	*sig of t*
Conditional	.195	.335	.700	.350	4.43	.01
MQP	.645	.365	.750	.355	.85	ns
Vous	.230	.350	1.000	.000	–	–
Closing	.405	.455	.650	.410	1.60	ns
Total	1.480	.840	3.100	.667	5.83	.01

native speakers, whereas in those categories where grammatical knowledge inevitably plays a role in the production of the appropriate form, immersion students' performance is inferior to that of native speakers. This is especially obvious in the use of the conditional where immersion students perform relatively poorly on both written and oral tasks. This result is not particularly surprising in light of the grammatical results reviewed earlier. As Tables 7.1 and 7.3 indicate, immersion students are relatively weak in verb morphology.

Here, then, appears to be a good example of the dependence of some aspects of sociolinguistic performance on grammatical knowledge.

The underuse of *vous* as a polite marker in formal contexts by immersion students as indicated in both Tables 7.7 and 7.9 can be linked directly to the input the students have received. Teachers address the students as *tu*, and students address each other as *tu*. The use of *vous* in the classroom setting is likely to be reserved for addressing groups of students, thus signalling its use as a plural form, or as a means of signalling annoyance on the part of the teacher. There are thus few opportunities in the classroom for the students to observe the use of *vous* as a politeness marker used in differential status situations.

The picture which emerges from these results, then, is one of a group of language learners who, although they have in some respects reached a high level of target language proficiency, are still appreciably different in their use of some aspects of the language from native speakers. This appears to be particularly evident in those aspects of communicative performance which demand the use of grammatical knowledge. These results are consistent with those we have found with grade 9 immersion students using a completely different set of tests (Lapkin, Swain and Cummins 1983).

Krashen (1981) has argued that learners 'acquire structure by understanding messages and not focusing on the form of input, by "going for meaning" ' (p. 54). According to Krashen, this comprehensible input 'delivered in a low (affective) filter situation is the only "causative variable" in second language acquisition' (p. 57). Comprehensible input I take to mean language directed to the learner that contains some new element in it but that is nevertheless understood by the learner because of linguistic, paralinguistic or situational cues, or world knowledge back-up. It is different in nature, I think, from what Schachter (1984) has referred to as negative input. Negative input is feedback to the learner which indicates that his or her output has been unsuccessful in some way. Negative input includes, for example, explicit corrections, confirmation checks and clarification checks. There is no reason to assume that negative input necessarily includes some new linguistic element in it for the learner. It may, for example, consist of a simple 'What?' in response to a learner utterance. As such it is basically information given to learners telling them to revise their output in some way because their current message has not been understood.

The hypothesis that comprehensible input is the *only* causal variable in second language acquisition seems to me to be called into question by the immersion data just presented in that immersion students do receive considerable comprehensible input. Indeed, the immersion students in the study reported on here have been receiving comprehensible input in the target language for almost seven years.

One might question, then, whether the immersion students have, in fact, been receiving comprehensible target language input. The evidence that they have, however, seems compelling. The evidence comes from their performance on tests of subject-matter achievement. For years now, in a number of French immersion programmes across Canada, immersion students have been tested for achievement in such subjects as mathematics, science, history and geography, for which the language of instruction has been French, and their performance has been compared to that of students enrolled in the regular English programme who are taught the same subject-matter content in their first language. In virtually all the comparisons the French immersion students have obtained achievement scores equivalent to those obtained by students in the regular English programme (Swain and Lapkin 1982). Furthermore, on tests of listening comprehension in French, the immersion students perform as well as native speakers of French by grade 6 (see this volume, Chapter 4). This strongly suggests that the immersion students understood what they were being taught, that they focused on meaning. Yet, as we have seen, after seven years of this comprehensible input, the target system has not been fully acquired.

This is not to say that the immersion students' input is not limited in some ways. We have already seen that there are few opportunities in the classroom for the students to observe the use of *vous* as a politeness marker in differential status situations. I suspect also that the content of every-day teaching provides little opportunity for the use of some grammatically realized functions of language. The use of the conditional may be a case in point. But until data are collected pertaining to the language actually used by immersion teachers, nothing further can be said on this point. It is our intention to collect such immersion teacher talk data in the near future.

Another way in which the immersion students' input may be limited is by virtue of peer input. The students hear their peers speaking as they do. But as is pointed out below, in the later grades of school, students are likely to hear more teacher talk than peer talk. And our own informal observations indicate that most peer–peer interaction that is not teacher directed is likely to occur in English rather than in French at this grade level.

Given these possible limitations in input, the fact still remains that these immersion students have received comprehensible input in the target language for seven years. Perhaps what this implies is that the notion of comprehensible input needs refinement. Long (1983), Varonis and Gass (1985), and others have suggested that it is not input *per se* that is important to second language acquisition, but input that occurs in interaction where meaning is negotiated. Under these conditions, linguistic input is simplified and the contributions made by the learner are paraphrased and expanded, thereby making the input more comprehensible. Given then, that comprehensible input is the causal variable in second language acquisition (Krashen 1981), the assumption is that second language acquisition results from these specific interactional, meaning-negotiated conversational turns.

If this is the case, then, we may have part of the explanation for the immersion students' less than native-like linguistic performance. In the context of an immersion class, especially in the later grade levels, and like in any first language classroom where teachers perceive their primary role as one of imparting subject-matter knowledge, the teachers talk and the students listen. As Long (1983) has indicated in the context of language classes, there are relatively few exchanges in classroom discourse motivated by a two-way exchange of information where both participants – teacher and student – enter the exchanges as conversational equals. This is equally true of content classes, and immersion classrooms are no exception.

Immersion students, then, have – relative to 'street learners' of the target language – little opportunity to engage in two-way, negotiated meaning exchanges in the classroom. Under these circumstances, the interaction input hypothesis would predict that second language acquisition would be limited. This prediction is consistent with the immersion students' performance if it is confined to grammatical acquisition. Confining this prediction to grammatical acquisition is compatible with what appears to be an assumption underlying the input interaction hypothesis – that second language acquisition is equivalent to grammatical acquisition. As has been indicated by the theoretical framework of linguistic proficiency used in this study, however, we consider second language acquisition to be more than grammatical acquisition, and to include at least the acquisition of discourse and sociolinguistic competence as well, in both oral and written modes. From this perspective, the relative paucity of two-way, meaning negotiated exchanges does not appear to have impeded the acquisition of discourse competence. Indeed, it seems likely that the diet of comprehensible, non-interactive, extended discourse received by the immersion students may account – at least in part – for their strong performance in this domain relative to native speakers. In short, what the immersion data suggest is that comprehensible input will contribute differentially to second language acquisition depending on the nature of that input, and the aspect of second language acquisition one is concerned with.

As I have suggested, the interaction input hypothesis is consistent with the prediction that immersion students will be somewhat limited in their grammatical development relative to native speakers because of their relatively limited opportunity to engage in such interaction. Although this provides a theoretically motivated and intuitively appealing explanation, I have several doubts about its adequacy. The doubts relate to two inter-related assumptions:

1. the assumption that it is the exchanges, themselves, in which meaning is negotiated that are facilitative to grammatical acquisition as a result of comprehensible input;
2. the assumption that the key facilitator is input, rather than output.

The first assumption, that the exchanges themselves are facilitative to grammatical acquisition, rests on the possibility that a learner can pay attention to meaning and form simultaneously. However, this seems unlikely. It seems much more likely that it is only when the substance of the message is understood that the learner can pay attention to the means of expression – the form of the message being conveyed. As Cross (1978), examining the role of input in first language acquisition, stated:

> By matching the child's semantic intentions and ongoing cognitions, (the mother's) speech may free the child to concentrate on the formal aspects of her expressions and thus acquire syntax efficiently.
>
> (p. 214)

In other words, it would seem that negotiating meaning – coming to a communicative consensus – is a necessary first step to grammatical acquisition. It paves the way for future exchanges, where, because the message is understood, the learner is free to pay attention to form. Thus comprehensible input is crucial to grammatical acquisition, *not* because the focus is on meaning, *nor* because a two-way exchange is occurring, but because by being understood – by its match with the learner's ongoing intentions and cognitions – it permits the learner to focus on form. But this would appear to be the sort of comprehensible input that immersion students do, in large part, receive.

What, then, is missing? I would like to suggest that what is missing is output. Krashen (1981) suggests that the only role of output is that of generating comprehensible input. But I think there are roles for output in second language acquisition that are independent of comprehensible input. A grade 9 immersion student told me about what happens when he uses French. He said, 'I understand everything anyone says to me, and I can hear in my head how I should sound when I talk, but it never comes out that way.' (Immersion student, personal communication, Nov. 1980). In other words, one function of output is that it provides the opportunity for meaningful use of one's linguistic resources. Smith (1978b, 1982) has argued that one learns to read by reading, and to write by writing. Similarly, it can be argued that one learns to speak by speaking. And one-to-one conversational exchanges provide an excellent opportunity for this to occur. Even better, though, are those interactions where there has been a communicative breakdown – where the learner has received some negative input – and the learner is pushed to use alternate means to get across his or her message. In order for native-speaker competence to be achieved, however, the meaning of 'negotiating meaning' needs to be extended beyond the usual sense of simply 'getting one's message across'. Simply getting one's message across can and does occur with grammatically deviant forms and sociolinguistically inappropriate language. Negotiating meaning needs to incorporate the notion of being pushed towards the delivery of a message that is not only conveyed, but that is conveyed precisely, coherently and appropriately. Being 'pushed' in output, it seems to me, is a concept parallel to that of the $i+1$ of comprehensible input. Indeed, one might call this the 'comprehensible output' hypothesis.

There are at least two additional roles in second language acquisition that might be attributed to output other than that of 'contextualized' and 'pushed' language use.[2] One, as Schachter (1984) has suggested, is the opportunity it provides to test out hypotheses – to try out means of expression and see if they work. A second function is that using the language, as opposed to simply comprehending the language, may force the learner to move from semantic processing to syntactic processing. As Krashen (1982) has suggested:

> in many cases, we do not utilize syntax in understanding – we often get the message with a combination of vocabulary, or lexical information plus extra-linguistic information.

> (p. 66)

Thus, it is possible to comprehend input – to get the message – without a syntactic analysis of that input.[3] This could explain the phenomenon of individuals who can understand a language and yet can only produce limited utterances in it. They have just never got round to a syntactic analysis of the language because there has been no demand on them to produce the language. The claim, then, is that producing the target language may be the trigger that forces the learner to pay attention to the means of expression needed in order to successfully convey his or her own intended meaning.

The argument, then, is that immersion students do not demonstrate native-speaker productive competence, *not* because their comprehensible input is limited, but because their comprehensible output is limited. It is limited in two ways. First, the students are simply not given – especially in later grades – adequate opportunities to use the target language in the classroom context. Secondly, they are not being 'pushed' in their output. That is to say, the immersion students have developed, in the early grades, strategies for getting their meaning across which are adequate for the situation they find themselves in: they are understood by their teachers and peers. There appears to be little social or cognitive pressure to produce language that reflects more appropriately or precisely their intended meaning: there is no push to be more comprehensible than they already are. That is, there is no push for them to analyse further the grammar of the target language because their current output appears to succeed in conveying their intended message. In other words, although the immersion students do receive comprehensible input, they no longer receive much negative input.

This discussion has so far referred primarily to the acquisition of spoken language. However, much of the experience these immersion students have had with French has been literacy based. The primary task of early education is the development of reading and writing skills, and early immersion education is no different, except that it occurs in the students' second language.

The results already presented relate not only to spoken language, but to language which makes use of literacy skills as well. However, performance across tasks within traits are not directly comparable in any way. Thus the results presented so far cannot address the issue of the relationship between spoken and written language. For this, we need to rely on factor analytic analyses.

The factor analyses carried out to date have involved only the total or global scores for each trait by method cell. The correlations among the scores of the nine cells for the sixty-nine students in the immersion sample only are presented in Table 7.10. Inspection of this table shows that the simplest interpretation of the correlations in terms of the three traits and three methods is not possible. If the only causes

TABLE 7.10   Correlations among overall cell scores

	GO	GM	GW	DO	DM	DW	SO	SM
GM	.180							
GW	.286	.600						
DO	.160	.100	.074					
DM	.240	.432	.432	.245				
DW	.178	.467	.496	.261	.460			
SO	.139	.073	.175	.103	.085	.023		
SM	.268	.314	.417	.295	.260	.326	.171	
SW	−.067	.198	.170	.219	.344	.530	−.038	.109

of correlations were shared trait and method, tests that shared neither would not correlate, or at least they would not correlate as highly as tests that shared a common trait, a common method, or both. Yet some pairs of tests that share neither trait nor method do correlate more highly, such as grammatical multiple choice and discourse written production (.47).

Several hypotheses concerning the structure underlying the correlations among the nine scores were tested using confirmatory factor analyses (LISREL). One very acceptable solution was found ($x^2 = 14.13$, df = 21, p = .864) and is shown in Table 7.11. It is a two factor solution with a general factor and a method factor. The method factor reflects the school experience of the students with the target language – one that highlights written rather than oral language – and is most strongly represented by the written discourse task. It is to be noted that the written discourse task, as indicated in Table 7.6, is the one in which native speakers and immersion students performed most similarly. It also represents the sort of task which all students have had considerable experience with in school. That immersion

TABLE 7.11   Confirmatory factor analysis – LISREL

	Factor 1 general	Factor 2 written	Uniqueness
GO	.53	—	.72
GM	.49	.55	.47
GW	.68	.39	.38
DO	.30	—	.91
DM	.41	.42	.65
DW	.20	.66	.52
SO	.23	—	.95
SM	.47	.24	.72
SW	−.03	.49	.76

$x^2 = 14.13$, df = 21, p = .864

students do as well as native speakers may reflect, then, their comprehensible output in this domain of language use. These results also indicate that there is no strong relationship between performance on the literacy-based tasks and performance on the oral tasks, except that captured by the global proficiency factor.

These results do not show the validity of the three postulated traits. However, it has already been shown that in the wider context of immersion students *plus* native speakers, at least two of the three traits – grammar and discourse – are distinct.[4] The fact that these two traits do not emerge in the factor analysis is probaby due largely to the homogeneity of the immersion sample. In the wider sample, the native speakers have had considerably different experiences from the immersion students, but among the immersion students the main experience for all the students is in the same sort of immersion classroom. There are not major opportunities for some students to acquire certain aspects of language proficiency, and others to acquire different aspects. What is in common for these students is their literacy-based experience as revealed by the structure of their target language proficiency. The fact that no strong relationship is shown between their written and oral performance can be interpreted within the context of the previous discussion: whatever knowledge they have of the language that is literacy-based is only weakly demonstrated in their oral performance because in general, they have had limited opportunity to use and practise their speaking skills in communicative exchanges that require a precise and appropriate reflection of meaning, whereas they have had considerable practice in doing so in written tasks.

To summarize and conclude, the results of a series of tests administered to grade 6 French immersion students indicate that, in spite of seven years of comprehensible input in the target language, their grammatical performance is not equivalent to that of native speakers. Immersion students, however, perform similarly to native speakers on those aspects of discourse and sociolinguistic competence which do not rely heavily on grammar for their realization. In addition, results from the immersion data reveal a structure of proficiency reflective of their school-based language learning situation: one which emphasizes written rather than spoken language.

The findings are compatible with an explanation of grammatical acquisition resulting in part through conversational exchanges in which meaning is negotiated. It was suggested, however, that these sorts of exchanges, although a prerequisite to acquisition are not themselves the source of acquisition derived from comprehensible input. Rather they are the source of acquisition derived from comprehensible output: output that extends the linguistic repertoire of the learner as he or she attempts to create precisely and appropriately the meaning desired. Comprehensible output, it was argued, is a necessary mechanism of acquisition independent of the role of comprehensible input. Its role is, at minimum, to provide opportunities for contextualized, meaningful use, to test out hypotheses about the target language, and to move the learner from a purely semantic analysis of the language to a syntactic analysis of it. Comprehensible output is, unfortunately, generally missing in typical classroom settings, language classrooms and immersion classrooms being no exceptions.

Notes

1. The Development of Bilingual Proficiency Project is funded by a grant (no. 431-79-0003) from the Social Sciences and Humanities Research Council of Canada to Merrill Swain, Patrick Allen, Jim Cummins and Raymond Mougeon.

2. Roger Andersen (personal communication, 7 March 1984) has suggested another possible function of output. 'My argument is that if the learner has some sort of expectation to have to *use* the L2 in clearly definable ways, that future use of the language can cause the learner to perceive aspects of the input very differently from what his/her perception would be if there is no clear, definable, future expected *use* of the language.'

3. Gary Cziko suggests (personal communication, 17 January 1984) that 'you can make a stronger case for the importance of output in second language acquisition by considering the notion of a fuzzy, open, non-deterministic syntactic parsing strategy that can be used for *comprehending* discourse but would be inadequate in *producing* it. (See Clark and Clark (1977) and van Dijk and Kintsch (1983), especially pages 28–31.) It may not be just that only semantic processing is required for comprehension but that in addition any syntactic processing involved in comprehension might be very different from the closed logical system of rules required to *produce* a grammatical utterance.'

4. That evidence for a distinction between grammatical and discourse competence was found by the fact that the French immersion students lagged further behind the native speakers in grammatical

competence than in discourse competence, yet the factor analysis failed to reveal a similar distinction, may be an example of one of the problems of using a correlational approach to investigate models of communicative competence (Cziko 1984). Cziko suggests (personal communication, 17 January 1984) that 'what you found may be similar to Examples 6 or 7 on Table 2 where norm-referenced (or correlational) interpretation might suggest a common factor underlying two dimensions of communicative competence while a criterion-referenced interpretation might suggest separate factors'.

8 Language proficiency and academic achievement*

Many of the most contentious debates in the areas of psycholinguistics and educational psychology during the past twenty years have revolved around the issue of how 'language proficiency' is related to academic achievement. Disagreement about appropriate ways of conceptualizing the nature of language proficiency underlies controversies as diverse as the extent to which 'oral language' is related to the acquisition of reading (e.g. Wells 1981), the extent to which learning disabilities are in reality language disabilities (e.g. Vellutino 1979), and the extent to which the poor school achievement of low socio-economic status (SES) and minority group students is caused by differences in the language use patterns of these students in comparison with middle-class students (e.g. Labov 1970).

The question of what constitutes 'language proficiency' and the nature of its cross-lingual dimensions is also at the core of many hotly debated issues in the areas of bilingual education and second language pedagogy and testing. Researchers have suggested ways of making second language teaching and testing more 'communicative' (e.g. Canale and Swain 1980a; Oller 1979) on the grounds that a communicative approach better reflects the nature of language proficiency than one which emphasizes the acquisition of discrete language skills. Issues such as the effects of bilingual education on achievement, the appropriate age to begin teaching L2, and the consequences of different patterns of bilingual language use in the home on minority students' achievement are all intimately related to the broader issue of how L1 proficiency is related to the development of L2 proficiency. This issue, in turn, clearly cannot be resolved without an adequate conceptualization of the nature of 'language proficiency'.

* This chapter originally appeared as an article of the same title by J. Cummins in J. W. Oller, Jr. (ed.) *Issues in Language Testing Research*. Newbury House, Rowley, Mass.: 1983, 108–126. Reprinted by permission of the publisher.

In this chapter I shall first describe some of the practical educational consequences of the lack of such a theoretical framework. Then theoretical approaches to the question of what constitutes 'language proficiency' will be reviewed, following which the theoretical framework itself will be presented. Finally, some applications of the framework will be discussed.

The lack of a theoretical framework: practical consequences

An example from a Canadian study in which the teacher referral forms and psychological assessments of 428 children from English-as-a-second-language (ESL) backgrounds are analysed (Cummins 1980c) will illustrate the need for such a framework and also serve to root the theoretical discussion into a concrete context which is replicated every day in our schools. The psychological assessment is a particularly appropriate language encounter to illustrate the invidious consequences of the theoretical confusion which characterizes debate about many of the issues outlined above, because in diagnosing the cause of ESL children's academic difficulties, psychologists often reveal implicit assumptions about issues such as the relationships of oral language performance to reading and other academic skills, the role of language deficits in learning disabilities, the relationship between L2 face-to-face communicative skills and other L2 language and academic skills, the relationships of L1 to L2 development, and the influence of bilingual background experiences on ESL children's academic functioning.

PR (283)

PR was referred for psychological assessment because he was experiencing difficulty in the regular grade 1 work despite the fact that he was repeating grade 1. The principal noted that 'although PR was in Portugal for part (6 months) of the year there is a suspicion of real learning disability. WISC (Wechsler Intelligence Scale for Children) testing would be a great help in determining this'. PR's scores on the WISC-R were verbal IQ, 64; performance IQ, 101; full scale IQ, 80. After noting that 'English is his second language but the teacher feels that the problem is more than one of language,' the psychologist continued:

> Psychometric rating, as determined by the WISC-R places PR in the dull normal range of intellectual development. Assessment reveals

performance abilities to be normal while verbal abilities fall in the mentally deficient range. It is recommended that PR be referred for resource room placement for next year and if no progress is evident by Christmas, a Learning Centre placement should be considered.

This assessment illustrates well the abuses to which psychological tests can be put. It does not seem at all unreasonable that a child from a non-English background who has spent six months of the previous year in Portugal should perform very poorly on an English verbal IQ test. Yet, rather than admitting that no conclusion regarding the child's academic potential can be drawn, the psychologist validates the teacher's 'suspicion' of learning disability by means of a 'scientific' assessment and the use of inappropriate terminology ('dull normal', 'mentally deficient'). An interesting aspect of this assessment is the fact that neither the teacher nor the psychologist makes any reference to difficulties in English as a second language and both considered that the child's English proficiency was adequate to perform the test.

It is clear from this, and many other assessments in the study, that psychologists often assume that because ESL children's L2 face-to-face communicative skills appear adequate, they are therefore no longer handicapped on a verbal IQ test by their ESL background. In other words, it is assumed that the 'language proficiency' required for L2 face-to-face communication is no different from that required for performance on an L2 cognitive/academic task. This assumption leads directly to the conclusion that poor performance on an L2 verbal IQ test is a function of deficient *cognitive* abilities (i.e. learning disability, retardation).

The same type of inference based on implicit assumptions about the nature of 'language proficiency' and its relationship to achievement and cognitive skills is common in the context of bilingual education in the United States. Language minority students are frequently transferred from bilingual to English-only classrooms when they have developed superficially fluent English communicative skills. Despite being classified as 'English proficient' many such students may fall progressively further behind grade norms in the development of English academic skills (e.g. see Mazzone 1980). Because these students are relatively fluent in English, it appears that their poor academic performance can no longer be explained by their English language deficiency, and thus cognitive or cultural 'deficiencies' are likely to be invoked as explanatory factors.

Other assessments reveal the assumptions of some psychologists about the influence of bilingual experiences. For example, in the assessment report of an ESL grade 1 child who obtained a verbal IQ of 94 and a performance IQ of 114, the psychologist noted:

> A discrepancy of 20 points between the verbal and performance IQs would indicate inconsistent development, resulting in his present learning difficulties. . . . It is quite likely that the two spoken languages have confused the development in this area.

It is clear that educators' implicit assumptions in regard to the nature of 'language proficiency' are by no means innocuous; on the contrary, they emerge clearly in many educational encounters and militate against the academic progress of both ESL and monolingual English students. It is perhaps not surprising to find questionable assumptions about 'language proficiency' emerging in school contexts since the issues are equally unclear at a theoretical level.

Theoretical approaches to the construct of 'language proficiency'

The practical examples considered above raise the issue of how face-to-face communicative skills (in L1 and/or L2 contexts), 'oral language abilities' (often operationalized by vocabulary tests) and language skills (e.g. reading) are related. All clearly involve 'language proficiency', but the precise ways in which language proficiency is involved in these types of performance is anything but clear. Even the question of individual differences in language proficiency is problematic since certain theorists (e.g. Chomsky 1972; Lenneberg 1967) have characterized language 'competence' as a species-specific ability which is universally acquired by all humans with the exception of severely retarded and autistic children. Measures of those aspects of 'oral language abilities' which relate strongly to reading skills would thus be regarded as assessing, at best, cognitive skills (and therefore not language skills) and, at worst, 'test-taking ability'.

It seems clear that some basic distinctions must be made in order to accommodate these very different understandings of the nature of 'language proficiency'. The need for such distinctions can be illustrated by contrasting the views of Oller (1979; Oller and Perkins 1980) and Labov (1970), who have emphasized very different aspects of language proficiency. After we examine the anomalies to which extreme versions of these theories lead, we will briefly outline four other theoretical positions in which an attempt is made to describe differences between the linguistic demands of the school and those of face-to-face situations outside the school.

Language proficiency as intelligence (Oller)

In sharp contrast to theorists such as Hernandez-Chavez, Burt and Dulay (1978), who have attempted to analyse 'language proficiency' into its constituent parts (the Hernandez-Chavez *et al.* model contains sixty-four separate proficiencies), Oller (1979; Oller and Perkins 1980) has reviewed considerable research which suggests that one global factor underlies most aspects of linguistic, academic and intellectual performance. Oller and Perkins (1980) express this view as follows:

> A single factor of global language proficiency seems to account for the lion's share of variance in a wide variety of educational tests including nonverbal *and* verbal IQ measures, achievement batteries, and even personality inventories and affective measures . . . the results to date are . . . preponderantly in favor of the assumption that language skill pervades every area of the school curriculum even more strongly than was ever thought by curriculum writers or testers.

(p. 1)

This global dimension is not regarded by Oller (1981) as the only significant factor in language proficiency, but the amount of additional variance accounted for by other factors is relatively modest.

The strong relationships between language proficiency and academic and cognitive variables exist across all four of the general language skills (listening, speaking, reading and writing). From a psycholinguistic point of view these relationships are attributed to the fact that 'in the meaningful use of language, some sort of pragmatic expectancy grammar must function in all cases' (1979, p. 25). A pragmatic expectancy grammar is defined by Oller as 'a psychologically real system that sequentially orders linguistic elements in time and in relation to extralinguistic elements in meaningful ways' (1979, p. 34).

Several aspects of Oller's theory of language proficiency are consonant with recent theoretical approaches to perceptual processes, reading theory, language pedagogy, and language testing. Neisser's (1967, 1976) conceptualization of perception (including language perception), for example, emphasizes the importance of anticipated information from the environment. The psycholinguistic analysis of reading developed by Goodman (1967) and Smith (1978a) assigns a central role to prediction, defined as the prior elimination of unlikely alternatives, as the basis for comprehending both written and oral language. This predictive apparatus appears to function in a similar way to Oller's pragmatic expectancy grammar. In fact, Tannen (1979) has reviewed a large variety of theoretical approaches in cognitive psychology, anthropology and linguistics, all of which assign a central role to the power of expectation:

> What unifies all these branches of research is the realization that people approach the world not as naive, blank-slate receptacles who take in stimuli as they exist in some independent and objective way, but rather as experienced and sophisticated veterans of perception who have stored their prior experiences as 'an organized mass', and who see events and objects in the world in relation to each other and in relation to their prior experience.
>
> (1979, p. 144)

The pedagogical implications of Oller's theory are very much in line with the current emphasis on 'language across the curriculum' (e.g. Bullock 1975; Fillion 1979) in which language is seen as playing a central role in all aspects of the learning process in schools. Oller (1979) makes these pedagogical implications explicit for both first and second language curricula by stressing that 'every teacher in every area of the curriculum should be teaching all of the traditionally recognized language skills' (p. 458). The central role assigned to the pragmatic expectancy grammar in using and learning language implies that a 'discrete skills' approach to language teaching (either L1 or L2) is likely to be futile, since the pragmatic expectancy grammar will be involved only in meaningful or 'communicative' uses of language. Again, the emphasis on the necessity for effective language teaching to be 'communicative' has strong empirical support (e.g. Swain 1978a) and is currently widely accepted.

Finally, Oller's position that language proficiency cannot meaning-fully be broken down into a variety of separate components implies that integrative tests of language proficiency (e.g. cloze, dictation) are more appropriate than discrete-point tests, a view which currently has considerable support among applied linguists.

However, many theorists are unwilling to accept that there are close relationships between 'language proficiency', intelligence, and academic achievement, despite the strong empirical support which Oller has assembled for this position, and the apparent attractiveness of its implications for both assessment and pedagogy. One reason for this opposition is that an approach which emphasizes individual differences among native speakers in language proficiency is not especially compatible with the Chomsky/Lenneberg position that all native speakers acquire linguistic 'competence'. Also, sociolinguists have vehemently rejected any close relationship between 'language proficiency', intelligence, and academic functioning in the context of the debate on the causes of poor educational performance by low SES and minority group children. Shuy (1977, p. 5), for example, argues that 'rather compelling evidence rejects every claim made by those who attempt to show linguistic correlates of cognitive deficit'. This position is considered in the next section.

Language proficiency and educational failure (Labov)

Much of the impetus for compensatory education programmes in the 1960s derived from the belief that language proficiency was a crucial component of educational success. The educational difficulties of many lower-class and minority group children were attributed to lack of appropriate verbal stimulation in the home, and the remedy, therefore, was to expose the child to an intensive programme of verbal stimulation prior to the start of formal schooling.

Apart from the fact that this approach 'diverts attention from real defects of our educational system to imaginary defects of the child' (Labov 1973, p. 22), its main problem lay in its naive assumptions about the nature of language proficiency and the relationship between language proficiency and educational success. Basically, language proficiency was identified with control over the surface structures of standard English which, in turn, was viewed as a prerequisite to both logical thinking and educational progress. This is illustrated by Labov with reference to Bereiter's comment that 'the language of culturally deprived children ... is not merely an underdeveloped version of standard English, but is a basically nonlogical mode of expressive behaviour' (Bereiter, Engelmann, Osborn and Reidford 1966). Thus according to Labov (1973), social class and ethnic differences in grammatical form were often equated with differences in the capacity for logical analysis, and then attempts were made to teach children to think logically by requiring them to mimic certain formal speech patterns used by middle-class teachers.

Labov shows clearly that this position confuses logic with surface detail and that the logic of nonstandard forms of English cannot be distinguished from the logic of standard English. However, he goes on to state a position regarding the relationship between language proficiency and conceptual thinking which is implicitly reflected in the approach of many linguists to the assessment of language proficiency in minority children. Labov (1973, p. 63) claims that:

> Linguists are also in an excellent position to assess Jensen's claim that the middle-class white population is superior to the working-class and Negro populations in the distribution of Level II, or conceptual

intelligence. The notion that large numbers of children have no capacity for conceptual thinking would inevitably mean that they speak a primitive language, for, even the simplest linguistic rules we discussed above involve conceptual operations more complex than those used in the experiment Jensen cites.

This implies that the conceptual operations reflected in children's ability to produce and comprehend language in interpersonal communicative situations are not essentially different (apart from being more complex) from those involved in the classification and analogies tasks that typically appear in verbal IQ tests. Labov and many other linguists (e.g. Burt and Dulay 1978; Dieterich *et al.* 1979; Shuy 1977) would claim that the latter tasks are invalid as measures of language proficiency because they assess proficiency outside of a naturally occurring communicative context. Labov attributes the fact that low SES black children often tend not to manifest their conceptual abilities in academic tasks to the influence of low teacher expectations brought about by teachers' equation of nonstandard dialect with deficient academic ability.

Thus, whereas much of the compensatory education effort derived from the assumption that the deficient language proficiency of low SES and minority children reflected, and gave rise to, deficiencies in conceptual abilities, Labov's position, as expressed in the quotation above, is that these children's language is not in any way deficient, and consequently, their conceptual abilities are not in any way deficient. This is because complex conceptual operations are involved in language comprehension and production. In both instances, therefore, a close relationship is assumed between conceptual abilities and language proficiency, although the respective interpretations of this relationship are clearly very different.

Insofar as 'language proficiency' is regarded as closely allied to 'conceptual intelligence', both these positions are similar (at least superficially) to that of Oller. However, it will be argued that none of these positions provides an adequate theoretical basis for conceptualizing the relationship between language proficiency and academic achievement. The language deficit view naively equates conceptual intelligence with knowledge of the surface structure of standard English; Labov, on the other hand, places the onus for explaining educational failure on sociolinguistic and sociocultural factors in the school situation, rejecting any direct relationship between language proficiency and failure. While this position can account for differences in educational achievement *between* SES groups, it does not appear adequate to account for the strong relationships observed between language proficiency measures and achievement *within* SES groups. Oller's (1979) position appears to be subject to the objections of sociolinguists to language deficit theories in that, for Oller, deficient academic achievement is, ipso facto, deficient language proficiency. Most researchers, however, would agree with Labov when he states that despite the low level of academic achievement of black students, their 'language proficiency' is in no way deficient.

This apparent incompatibility arises from the fact that Labov and Oller are discussing two very different dimensions under the rubric of 'language proficiency'. The necessity of distinguishing a dimension of language proficiency which is strongly related to cognitive and academic skills (Oller's global language proficiency) from manifestations of language proficiency which are embedded within face-to-face communicative contexts is the common thread uniting the theories of language proficiency discussed in the next section. The distinctions emphasized by these theorists in educational contexts find parallels in the current anthropological distinction between oral and literate traditions (see Tannen 1980).

Communicative and analytic competence (Bruner)

In discussing language as an instrument of thought, Bruner (1975) distinguishes a 'species minimum' of linguistic competence from both communicative and analytic competence. Species minimum competence implies mastery of the basic syntactic structures and semantic categories emphasized in theories of language acquisition such as those deriving from the views of Chomsky (1965) and Fillmore (1968). Bruner suggests that mere *possession* of species minimum competence has relatively little effect on thought processes. It is only when language use moves toward 'context-free elaboration' that it transforms the nature of thought processes. He points out that

> in assessing the elaborated use of language as a tool of thought, it does not suffice to test for the *presence* [emphasis original] in a speech sample of logical, syntactical, or even semantic distinctions, as Labov (1970) has done in order to determine whether non-standard Negro dialect is or is not impoverished. The issue, rather, is how language is being used, what in fact the subject is doing with his language.
>
> (p. 71)

In this regard Bruner distinguishes between 'communicative competence' and 'analytic competence'. The former is defined as the ability to make utterances that are appropriate to the context in which they are made and to comprehend utterances in the light of the context in which they are encountered. Analytic competence, on the other hand, involves the prolonged operation of thought processes exclusively on linguistic representations. It is made possible by the possession of communicative competence and is promoted largely through formal schooling. According to Bruner, schools decontextualize knowledge and demand the use of analytic competence as a feature of the communicative competence of their members.

Although Bruner's basic distinction between communicative and analytic aspects of language proficiency is echoed in the theories considered below, there are several shortcomings in his specific formulation of this distinction. First, it identifies analytic competence as a manifestation of a higher cognitive level than communicative competence. As pointed out by Cole and Griffin (1980), this is a dangerous assumption and we should be extremely cautious

> in attributing cultural differences in the ability to think 'theoretically', 'rationally', or in a 'context-free manner'. There is reason to believe that such statements have a basis in fact, but the nature of the facts is not so clear as our metaphors may have seduced us into believing.
>
> (p. 361)

The latter point raises a second objection to Bruner's formulation, one that is equally applicable to the other theories considered below, namely, that dichotomies between two *types* of thinking or language proficiency are likely to greatly oversimplify the reality. However, despite these shortcomings, Bruner's notion of analytic competence does highlight some facets of language proficiency which are both promoted at school and also required for academic success.

Utterance and text (Olson)

Olson's (1977) distinction between 'utterance' and 'text' attributes the development of 'analytic' modes of thinking specifically to the acquisition of literacy skills in school. The distinction relates to whether meaning is largely extrinsic to language (utterance) or intrinsic to language (text). In interpersonal oral situations the listener has access to a wide range of contextual and paralinguistic information with which to interpret the speaker's intentions, and in this sense the meaning is only partially dependent upon the specific linguistic forms used by the speaker. However, in contrast to utterance, written text

> is an autonomous representation of meaning. Ideally, the printed reader depends on no cues other than linguistic cues; it represents no

intentions other than those represented in the text; it is addressed to no one in particular; its author is essentially anonymous; and its meaning is precisely that represented by the sentence meaning.

(p. 276)

Olson explicitly differentiates the development of the ability to process text from the development of the mother tongue (utterance) in the pre-school years:

> But language development is not simply a matter of progressively elaborating the oral mother tongue as a means of sharing intentions. The developmental hypothesis offered here is that the ability to assign a meaning to the sentence per se, independent of its nonlinguistic interpretive context, is achieved only well into the school years.
>
> (1977, p. 275)

He points out that the processing of text calls for comprehension and production strategies which are somewhat different from those employed in everyday speech and which may require sustained 'education' for their acquisition. He also suggests that acquisition of text processing skills may have profound implications for cognitive functioning in general:

> The child's growing competence with this somewhat specialized and distinctive register of language may contribute to the similarly specialized and distinctive mode of thought we usually associate with formal education.
>
> (1980, p. 107)

Olson's distinction between utterance and text is useful in highlighting important differences between the linguistic demands (and possible consequences) of formal education and those of face-to-face situations outside school. The same distinction is emphasized from a different perspective by Donaldson (1978).

Embedded and disembedded thought and language (Donaldson)

Donaldson (1978) distinguishes between embedded and disembedded cognitive processes from a developmental perspective and is especially concerned with the implications for children's adjustment to formal schooling. She points out that young children's early thought processes and use of language develop within a 'flow of meaningful context' in which the logic of words is subjugated to perception of the speaker's intentions and salient features of the situation. Thus, children's (and adults') normal productive speech is embedded within a context of fairly immediate goals, intentions, and familiar patterns of events. However, thinking and language which move beyond the bounds of meaningful interpersonal context make entirely different demands on the individual, in that it is necessary to focus on the linguistic forms themselves for meaning rather than on intentions.

Donaldson offers a reinterpretation of Piaget's theory of cognitive development from this perspective and reviews a large body of research which supports the distinction between embedded and disembedded thought and language. Her description of pre-school children's comprehension and production of language in embedded contexts is especially relevant to current practices in assessment of language proficiency in bilingual programmes. She points out that

> the ease with which pre-school children often seem to understand what is said to them is misleading if we take it as an indication of skill with language per se. Certainly they commonly understand us, but surely it is not our words alone that they are understanding – for they may be shown to be relying heavily on cues of other kinds.
>
> (1978, p. 72)

She goes on to argue that children's facility in producing language that is meaningful and appropriate in interpersonal contexts can also give a misleading impression of overall language proficiency:

> When you produce language, you are in control, you need only talk about what you choose to talk about . . . [The child] is never required, when he is himself producing language, to go counter to his own preferred reading of the situation – to the way in which he himself spontaneously sees it. But this is no longer necessarily true when he becomes the listener. And it is frequently not true when he is the listener in the formal situation of a psychological experiment or indeed when he becomes a learner at school.
>
> (1978, p. 73)

The relevance of this observation to the tendency of psychologists and teachers to overestimate the extent to which ESL students have overcome difficulties with English is obvious.

Conversation and composition (Bereiter and Scardamalia)

Bereiter and Scardamalia (1982) have analysed the problems of learning to write as problems of converting a language production system geared to conversation over to a language production system capable of functioning by itself. Their studies suggest that some of the major difficulties involved in this process are the following:

1. learning to continue producing language without the prompting that comes from conversational partners;

2. learning to search one's own memory instead of having memories triggered by what other people say;
3. planning large units of discourse instead of planning only what will be said next;
4. learning to function as both sender and receiver, the latter function being necessary for revision.

Bereiter and Scardamalia argue that the absence of normal conversational supports makes writing a radically different kind of task from conversation:

> We are proposing instead that the oral language production system cannot be carried over intact into written composition, that it must, in some way, be reconstructed to function autonomously instead of interactively.
>
> (1982, p. 3)

This emphasis on the increasing autonomy or disembeddedness of literacy activities in comparison with face-to-face communication is a common characteristic of the views of Bruner, Olson, Donaldson, and Bereiter and Scardamalia.

However, it is also important to ask what is the *developmental* nature of the cognitive involvement in these literacy tasks. In the context of writing skills acquisition, Bereiter and Scardamalia (1983) suggest that, developmentally, cognitive involvement can be characterized in terms of progressive automatization of lower-level skills (e.g. handwriting, spelling of common words, punctuation, common syntactic forms) which releases increasingly more mental capacity for higher-level planning of large chunks of discourse. This characterization is similar to Posner's (1973) distinction between effortless and effortful processing.

The process of increasing automatization is also evident in reading skills acquisition where, as fluency is acquired, word recognition skills are first automatized and then totally short-circuited insofar as the proficient reader does not read individual words but engages in a process of sampling from the text to confirm predictions (see, for example, Smith 1978a). The release of mental capacity for higher-level operations is consistent with research reviewed by Singer (1977) which shows a change between grades 1 and 5 in the amount of common variance between IQ and reading achievement from 16% to 64% (correlations of .40 to .79). This he interprets in terms of the nature of the component skills stressed in reading instruction at different grade levels.

As reading achievement shifts from predominant emphasis on word recognition to stress on word meaning and comprehension, the mental functions being assessed by intelligence and reading tests have more in common.

(p. 48)

In summary, several theorists whose primary interest is in the developmental relationships between thought and language have argued that it is necessary to distinguish between the processing of language in informal everyday situations and the language processing required in most academic situations. In concrete terms, it is argued that reading a difficult text or writing an essay makes fundamentally different information processing demands on the individual compared with engaging in a casual conversation with a friend. In addition to the different information processing requirements in these two types of situation, it has been suggested (Bereiter and Scardamalia 1983) that the amount of active cognitive involvement in the language activity may vary as a function of the degree of mastery of its constituent skills.

What are the implications of these theories for clarifying the relationships between language proficiency and academic achievement?

A theoretical framework

On the basis of the preceding discussion several minimal requirements of a theoretical framework for conceptualizing the relationships between language proficiency and academic achievement in both monolingual and bilingual contexts can be distinguished: first, such a framework should incorporate a developmental perspective such that those aspects of language proficiency which are mastered early by native speakers and L2 learners can be distinguished from those that continue to vary across individuals as development progresses; second, the framework should be capable of allowing differences between the linguistic demands of the school and those of interpersonal contexts outside the school to be described; third, the framework should be capable of allowing the developmental relationships between L1 and L2 proficiency to be described.

Current theoretical frameworks of 'communicative competence' (e.g. Canale 1983; Canale and Swain 1980a) do not (and were not intended to) meet these requirements. Canale (1983) for example, distinguishes grammatical, sociolinguistic, discourse, and strategic competencies but states that their relationships with each other and with world knowledge and academic achievement is an empirical question yet to be addressed. Although this framework is extremely useful for some purposes, its applicability is limited by its static nondevelopmental nature and by the fact that the relationship between academic performance and the components of communicative competence in L1 and L2 are not considered. For example, both pronunciation and lexical knowledge would be classified under grammatical competence. Yet L1 pronunciation is mastered very early by native speakers, whereas lexical knowledge continues to develop throughout schooling and is strongly related to academic performance.

The framework outlined below is an attempt to conceptualize 'language proficiency' in such a way that the developmental interrelationships between academic performance and language proficiency in both L1 and L2 can be considered. Essentially, the framework tries to integrate an earlier distinction between basic interpersonal communicative skills (BICS) and cognitive/academic language proficiency (CALP) (Cummins 1980a) into a more general theoretical model. The BICS-CALP distinction is similar to the distinctions proposed by Bruner, Olson, and Donaldson and was intended to make the same point that was made earlier in this chapter, namely, that academic deficits are often created by teachers and psychologists who fail to realize that it takes language minority students considerably longer to attain grade/age-appropriate levels in English academic skills than it does in English face-to-face communicative skills. However, dichotomizing 'language proficiency' into two categories oversimplifies the phenomenon and makes it difficult to discuss the developmental relationships between language proficiency and academic achievement.

The framework presented in Figure 8.1 proposes that 'language proficiency' can be conceptualized along two continua. First is a continuum relating to the range of contextual support available for expressing or receiving meaning. The extremes of this continuum are described in terms of 'context-embedded' versus 'context-reduced' communication.[1] They are distinguished by the fact that in context-embedded communication the participants can actively negotiate meaning (e.g. by providing feedback that the message has not been understood) and the language is supported by a wide range of meaningful paralinguistic and situational cues; context-reduced communication, on the other hand, relies primarily (or at the extreme of the continuum, exclusively) on linguistic cues to meaning and may in some cases involve suspending knowledge of the 'real' world in order to

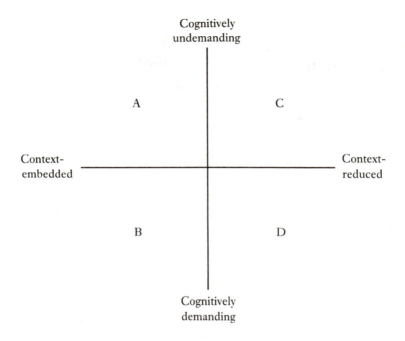

FIGURE 8.1   Range of contextual support and degree of cognitive involvement in communicative activities

interpret (or manipulate) the logic of the communication appropriately.[2]

In general, context-embedded communication derives from interpersonal involvement in a shared reality which obviates the need for explicit linguistic elaboration of the message. Context-reduced communication, on the other hand, derives from the fact that this shared reality cannot be assumed, and thus linguistic messages must be elaborated precisely and explicitly so that the risk of misinterpretation is minimized. It is important to emphasize that this is a continuum and not a dichotomy. Thus, examples of communicative behaviours going from left to right along the continuum might be: engaging in a discussion, writing a letter to a close friend, writing (or reading) an academic article. Clearly, context-embedded communication is more typical of the everyday world outside the classroom, whereas many of the linguistic demands of the classroom reflect communication which is closer to the context-reduced end of the continuum.

The vertical continuum is intended to address the developmental aspects of communicative proficiency in terms of the degree of active cognitive involvement in the task or activity. Cognitive involvement can be conceptualized in terms of the amount of information that must be processed simultaneously or in close succession by the individual in order to carry out the activity.

How does this continuum incorporate a developmental perspective? If we return to the four components of communicative competence (grammatical, sociolinguistic, discourse, and strategic) discussed by Canale (1983), it is clear that within each one, some subskills are mastered more rapidly than others. In other words, some subskills (e.g. pronunciation and syntax within L1 grammatical competence) reach plateau levels at which there are no longer significant differences in mastery between individuals (at least in context-embedded situations). Other subskills continue to develop throughout the school years and beyond, depending upon the individual's communicative needs in particular cultural and institutional milieus.

Thus, the upper parts of the vertical continuum consist of communicative tasks and activities in which the linguistic tools have become largely automatized (mastered) and thus require little active cognitive involvement for appropriate performance. At the lower end of the continuum are tasks and activities in which the communicative tools have not become automatized and thus require active cognitive involvement. Persuading another individual that your point of view rather than his or hers is correct, or writing an essay on a complex theme are examples of such activities. In these situations, it is necessary to stretch one's linguistic resources (e.g., in Canale and Swain's terms, grammatical, sociolinguistic, discourse, and strategic competences) to the limit in order to achieve one's communicative goals. Obviously, cognitive involvement, in the sense of amount of information processing, can be just as intense in context-embedded as in context-reduced activities.

As mastery is developed, specific linguistic tasks and skills travel from the bottom toward the top of the vertical continuum. In other words, there tends to be a high level of cognitive involvement in task or activity performance until mastery has been achieved or, alternately, until a plateau level at less than mastery levels has been reached (e.g. L2 pronunciation in many adult immigrants, 'fossilization' of certain grammatical features among French immersion students). Thus, learning the phonology and syntax of L1, for example, requires considerable cognitive involvement for the two and three-year-old child, and therefore these tasks would be placed in quadrant B (context-embedded, cognitively demanding). However, as mastery of these skills develops, tasks involving them would move from quadrant B to quadrant A since performance becomes increasingly automatized and cognitively undemanding. In a second language context the same type of developmental progression occurs.[3]

Another requirement for a theoretical framework applicable to both monolingual and bilingual contexts is that it permit the developmental interrelationships between L1 and L2 proficiency to be conceptualized. There is considerable evidence that some aspects of L1 and L2 proficiency are interdependent, i.e. manifestations of a common underlying proficiency (see Cummins 1981b). The evidence reviewed in support of the interdependence hypothesis primarily involved academic or 'context-reduced' language proficiency because the hypothesis was formulated explicitly in relation to the development of bilingual academic skills. However, any language task which is cognitively demanding for a group of individuals is likely to show a moderate degree of interdependence across languages. In general, significant relationships would be predicted between communicative activities in different languages which make similar contextual and cognitive demands on the individual.

In addition to the interdependence which has been shown to exist between L1 and L2 context-reduced, cognitively demanding proficiency, there is evidence that some context-embedded, cognitively undemanding aspects of proficiency are also interdependent across languages. For example, Cummins, Swain, Nakajima, Handscombe, Green and Tran (1984) reported that among Japanese immigrant students in Toronto, strong relationships were found between Japanese and English proficiency factors representing aspects of 'interactional style', e.g. amount of detail communicated, richness of vocabulary, and use of cohesive devices. The relationship between these linguistic manifestations of interactional style and academic achievement is likely to be complex (Wells 1981; Wong Fillmore 1980b) and also less direct than the cognitively demanding dimension of language proficiency highlighted in the present framework. The implications for bilingual education of the interdependence between L1 and L2 in context-reduced cognitively demanding aspects of proficiency have been explored by Cummins (1979b, 1981b) while current research on interactional styles in bilingual programmes (Wong Fillmore 1980b) should greatly increase our understanding of their significance.

In conclusion, the theoretical framework differs from the conceptualizations of 'language proficiency' proposed by Oller (1979) and Labov (1973) in that it allows the linguistic demands of academic situations to be distinguished from those of face-to-face situations outside of school contexts. In so doing, the framework incorporates elements of the distinctions discussed by Bruner, Olson, Donaldson, and Bereiter and Scardamalia. However, the present framework conceptualizes the degree of cognitive involvement and the range of contextual support for communicative activities as independent continua, whereas these two continua tend to merge to some extent in the distinctions proposed by other theorists. The dangers of regarding context-reduced communicative activities as more 'cognitively loaded' than context-embedded activities have been pointed out by Cole and Griffin (1980). Cultures (or subcultures) that tend to engage in relatively few context-reduced communicative activities are not necessarily any less cognitively adept, in general terms, than cultures which place a strong emphasis on such activities.

Applications of the theoretical framework

In this section potential applications of the framework to several of the issues raised earlier in the chapter will be briefly sketched. These issues concern:

1. language proficiency and intellectual assessment of ESL students;
2. validation of theories of 'communicative competence';
3. language pedagogy;
4. the relationships between language proficiency, socio-economic status (SES), and achievement.

Assessment of ESL students

The location of any particular language task or activity on the vertical and horizontal continua is a function not only of inherent task characteristics but also of the level of proficiency of the language user. Thus, tasks that are cognitively undemanding for a native speaker (e.g. using appropriate syntax) may be highly cognitively demanding for an L2 learner. The more context-reduced a particular task (i.e. the fewer nonlinguistic cues to meaning) the longer it will take L2 learners to achieve age-appropriate performance. For example, it has been shown (Cummins 1981c) that although face-to-face L2 communicative skills are largely mastered by immigrant students within about two years of arrival in the host country, it takes between five and seven years, on the average, for students to approach grade norms in L2 academic skills.

It should be clear that psychological assessment procedures as well as the regular English curriculum are likely to be considerably more context-reduced and cognitively demanding for most ESL students than they are for native English speakers. Failure to take account of the difference between 'quadrant A' and 'quadrant D' (Figure 8.1) language skills often leads to invalid interpretations of ESL students' classroom or test performances and to the labelling of students as mentally retarded or learning disabled (Cummins 1980c).

Validation of constructs of 'communicative competence'

The present framework is directed specifically at the relationships between academic achievement and language proficiency and thus its applicability to manifestations of 'communicative competence' in academically unrelated contexts is limited. For example, there may be many language activities which would be grouped into quadrant A in the present framework, insofar as they tend to be context-embedded and cognitively undemanding, which nevertheless show consistent individual differences in performance. For example, ability to 'get the message across', or in Canale and Swain's terms 'strategic competence', may be a reliable dimension of this type. Such linguistic traits may be strongly related to dimensions of personality or inter-actional style and show only weak relationships to cognitive variables (see Cummins *et al.* 1984; Wong Fillmore 1980b). In other words, there may be several language factors 'deeper than speech' (Oller 1981) but only one which is directly related to academic achievement. It is this dimension which is of major concern to the present chapter, and the proposed framework is not necessarily applicable to other manifestations of 'communicative competence'.

However, despite this limitation, there are implications of the present framework for current attempts to validate theories of communicative competence (e.g. Bachman and Palmer 1982). In the first place, the framework could be used as a basis for carrying out a task analysis of language measures with a view to predicting the degree to which different measures relate to cognitive and academic variables for specific groups of individuals. In this regard, different relationships among tasks would be likely to be predicted in an L1 as compared with an L2 context because tasks located close to the top of the vertical continuum for native speakers may be close to the bottom for L2 learners. Also, skills which are acquired in a context-embedded situation by native speakers may be acquired in a context-reduced situation (e.g. a formal classroom) by L2 learners.

A second implication related to this is that there is likely to be considerable 'method' variance as well as 'trait' variance in language assessment procedures, depending upon their relative location along the horizontal and vertical continua. This is in fact what Bachman and Palmer (1982) found, and it is not surprising given, for example, the obvious differences between a formal test of L1 syntactic knowledge and assessment of L1 syntactic knowledge based on context-embedded communication.

A third implication is that validation studies (and theories of communicative competence) should be conceptualized developmentally, since very different relationships might be found between, for example, grammatical and sociolinguistic competence (in Canale and Swain's 1980a, terms) among beginning L2 learners as compared with advanced L2 learners.

Viewed from this perspective, current efforts to validate theories of communicative competence are relatively limited in scope insofar as most studies have been conducted only with adult L2 learners and the relationships among hypothesized components of proficiency have not been conceptualized developmentally. These concerns are all related to the perspective of the present chapter that the development of 'language proficiency' in an L2 can be understood only in the context of a theory of L1 'language proficiency'. This in turn necessitates consideration of the developmental relationships between language proficiency, cognitive functioning, and academic achievement.

Language pedagogy

Clearly, a major aim of schooling is to develop students' abilities to manipulate and interpret cognitively demanding context-reduced text. However, there is considerable agreement among theorists (e.g. Smith 1978a) that the more initial reading and writing instruction can be embedded in a meaningful communicative context (i.e. related to the child's previous experience), the more successful it is likely to be. The same principle holds for L2 instruction. The more context-embedded the initial L2 input, the more comprehensible it is likely to be, and paradoxically, the more successful in ultimately developing L2 skills in context-reduced situations. A major reason why language minority students have often failed to develop high levels of L2 academic skills is that their initial instruction has emphasized context-reduced communication insofar as instruction has been through English and unrelated to their prior out-of-school experiences.

In summary, a major pedagogical principle for both L1 and L2 teaching is that language skills in context-reduced situations can be most successfully developed on the basis of initial instruction which maximizes the degree of context-embeddedness, i.e. the range of cues to meaning.

SES, language and achievement

Wells (1981), in a ten-year longitudinal study, has identified two broad types of communicative activities in the home which strongly predict the acquisition of reading skills in school. One is the extent to which there is 'negotiation of meaning' (i.e. quality and quantity of communication) between adults and children; the other is the extent to which literacy-related activities are promoted in the home (e.g. reading to children). There is no clear-cut relationship between SES and the former, but a strong relationship between SES and the latter.

These results have two clear implications in terms of the present framework. First, the strong relationship observed between both literacy activities and negotiation of meaning in the home and the later acquisition of reading in school supports the principle proposed above that context-reduced communicative proficiency can be most successfully developed on the basis of prior context-embedded communication; or, to put it another way, the more opportunity the child has to process comprehensible linguistic input (Krashen 1980) and negotiate meaning, the greater the range of input which will become comprehensible.

The second implication of Wells' findings is that many low SES students experience initial difficulties in school in comparison with middle-class students because they come to school less prepared to handle context-reduced academic tasks as a result of less exposure to literacy-related activities prior to school. Clearly, schools have often contributed to students' academic difficulties by failing to ensure that initial literacy instruction is sufficiently context-embedded and culturally appropriate to students' backgrounds.

If we return to the controversial question of the extent to which 'language proficiency' is implicated in the relatively poor academic performance of low SES children, the answer will clearly depend upon how the construct of 'language proficiency' is conceptualized.

As mentioned earlier, Labov and most sociolinguists would probably deny any involvement of 'language proficiency', whereas Oller's (1979) conceptualization of 'language proficiency' would seem to imply an affirmative answer. Within the context of the present framework, Wells' results suggest that there are SES differences in students' knowledge about and interest in literacy on entry to school, such that differential performance is found on context-reduced language tasks. These differences are, of course, not surprising given the differential exposure to literacy activities in the home. However, these initial performance differences become *deficits* in academic achievement (and in context-reduced language proficiency) only when they are reinforced by inappropriate forms of educational treatment (see Cummins 1979b). Given appropriate instruction, there is no long-term linguistic or cognitive impediment to the academic achievement of low SES students.

In conclusion, the present framework is intended to facilitate discussion of a variety of issues related to the development of language proficiency in educational contexts. The context-embedded/context-reduced and cognitively undemanding/cognitively demanding continua highlighted in the present framework are clearly not the only dimensions that would require consideration in a theoretical framework designed to incorporate all aspects of language proficiency or communicative competence. However, it is suggested that these dimensions are directly relevant to the relationships between language proficiency and educational achievement. The extent to which other dimensions, not emphasized in the present framework, are also relevant is an empirical and theoretical issue which we hope will be addressed in future research.

Notes

1. The term 'context-reduced' is used rather than 'disembedded' (Donaldson 1978) or 'decontextualized' because a large variety of contextual cues are available to carry out tasks even at the context-reduced end of the continuum. The difference, however, is that these cues are exclusively *linguistic* in nature. In other words, it is the *range* of cues to meaning that is reduced rather than the context itself.

2. In describing the framework, the term 'communicative proficiency' is used interchangeably with 'language proficiency' even though it is recognized that language can be used for purposes which are not overtly communicative (as expressed, for example, in Bruner's

concept of analytic competence). This type of 'analytic' language use would be located in quadrant D and, empirically, is likely to be indistinguishable from more 'communicative' aspects of cognitively demanding context-reduced language uses (e.g. reading a difficult text, writing an essay). An advantage to the term 'communicative' is that it reinforces the point that the language proficiencies described develop as a result of various types of communicative interactions in the home and school (see, e.g. Wells 1981). Thus, in the context of relating language proficiency to academic achievement, the distinction between interpersonal and intrapersonal language proficiency or use is not seen as of major consequence. It is also likely to be difficult to disentangle these two dimensions in practice. For example, in reading, what is 'communicative' and what 'analytic', to use Bruner's (1975) terminology?

3. It should be noted that the letters A, B, C, and D are used solely for labelling purposes and do not imply an overall developmental sequence or order of difficulty. Thus, as far as *cognitive* demands are concerned, by definition, tasks in quadrants A and C will have become cognitively undemanding more rapidly than those that remain in quadrants B and D; however, nothing is implied about the comparative difficulty of tasks in quadrants A and B versus those in quadrants C and D.

Section 5
The assessment of language proficiency

The theory of language proficiency one holds will invariably influence the way one goes about assessing it. In Chapters 7 and 8 of the previous section, two different conceptualizations of language proficiency were presented. In Chapters 9 and 10, the implications of each perspective for language and academic assessment respectively are explored.

Chapter 9 describes in some detail one test of communicative proficiency that we have developed. The test is meant to assess aspects of the communicative abilities of the learners, *not* their academic linguistic potential. The description of the test is embedded in a set of four proposals which should be equally applicable in the development of other tests of communicative performance. The four proposals are 'start from somewhere', 'concentrate on content', 'bias for best' and 'work for washback'.

'Start from somewhere' essentially advises one to examine what others have done in test development both theoretically and practically before beginning one's own test development. Doing so will not only prevent reinventing the wheel, but it will allow for theoretical advances to be made. 'Concentrate on content' refers to both the content of the material used as the basis of communicative language activities and the tasks used to elicit communicative language behaviours. The content, it is argued, should be motivating, substantive, integrated and interactive. 'Bias for best' advises that the test procedures should do everything possible to elicit the learners' best performance. 'Work for washback' is a proposal which reflects the natural tendency of teachers to teach to a test. It suggests, therefore, that communicative test materials should reflect language teaching practices that one would observe in any good communicatively oriented classroom.

In Chapter 10, the use of tests to judge the academic linguistic potential of children in schools is discussed. The chapter focuses on the misuse of tests with minority students, giving examples of how scores have been misinterpreted by psychologists, and how appropriate interpretations might cautiously be made. Appropriate use of psychological tests for assessing academic and linguistic problems rests on an understanding of the theoretical and research literature. For example, research discussed in Part One of this book has indicated that it takes, on the average, five to seven years for children to reach age-appropriate levels on cognitive academic linguistic tasks in their second language. This was equally the case for early immersion children and minority children in their second language. The implication is that it is inappropriate to use test scores from linguistic academic (contextually-reduced) tasks as an accurate assessment of these skills in a child's second language for at least several years of schooling. The theoretical principle that certain aspects of language proficiency are cross-lingual – that there is a common underlying proficiency – leads to the proposal that assessment of academic potential in the initial years of schooling in a second language might best be done in the child's first language. Without the support of a bilingual programme, however, testing in the first language after this period is likely to be of suspect validity for a minority child because of possible regression of first language abilities (subtractive bilingualism) due to lack of exposure to conceptually demanding language in the first language.

Thus, it is seen that both Chapters 9 and 10 in this section illustrate the intimate link between theory (in the form of a particular conceptualization of language proficiency) and practice (in guiding the development and interpretation of assessment instruments). Research acts here as an interface, informing both theory and practice.

9 Large-scale communicative language testing: a case study*

Introduction

In Canada we are experiencing an increasing demand from English-speaking communities for schooling that will produce bilingual individuals. The motivations for this demand are varied, but minimally they include both social and economic reasons. Recent political events in Canada have heightened awareness of the needs and demands of Canada's French-speaking peoples. As a result, a genuine desire has developed on the part of some English-Canadians to learn French in order to be able to interact with French-Canadians in their own language. These same political events have also resulted in establishing bilingual proficiency in French and English as a highly desirable or, in some cases, a required qualification for employment. Clearly, then, what was needed in these circumstances were school programmes that could provide students not only with a formal knowledge of the second language, characteristic of traditional second language teaching programmes, but also with the ability to *use* the second language as a communicative tool.

Over the last decade in Canada a variety of programmes have been initiated aimed at turning out English–French bilingual students. Although these programmes differ with respect to the grade level at which they begin, the length of the programme, and the proportion of the school day taught in each of the two languages, they all have in common the exclusive use of the second language, French, as a

---

* An earlier version of this chapter was published by John Wiley and Sons as an article of the same title by M. Swain in *Language Learning and Communication* 2[2]: 133–147, by Addison-Wesley Publishing Co. in S. Savignon and M. Berns (eds.) *Initiatives in Communicative Language Teaching: A Book of Readings*, 1984: 185–199 and by Pergamon Press in A. Fok and G. Low (eds.) *New Directions in Language Testing*, 1985. Permission to reprint has been granted by John Wiley and Sons, Addison-Wesley Publishing Co. and Pergamon Press.

medium of instruction for all or most of the school day for several years. These programmes referred to in Canada as immersion programmes and considered as experiments in bilingual education, have been monitored to evaluate the students' first and second language development, as well as their academic achievements in content subjects taught to them through the medium of the second language (see Lambert and Tucker 1972; Swain and Lapkin 1982; see also this volume, pp. 37–79).

Assessments of the immersion students' second language proficiency have included the use of French achievement tests standardized on native speakers of French, word association tests, cloze tests, tests of general listening and reading comprehension, as well as oral and written production tests. However, with the exception of several isolated and small-scale studies (Genesee, Tucker and Lambert 1975; Harley 1982; Harley and Swain 1977; Szamosi, Swain and Lapkin 1979), little attempt has been made to assess the immersion students' ability to use French as a communicative tool through directly engaging them in communicative activities. With the intent of filling this gap, several of us[1] in the Modern Language Centre of the Ontario Institute for Studies in Education have undertaken the development of 'testing units' to be used in provincial-wide assessments of the communicative performance of immersion students.

The purpose of this chapter, then, is to describe the testing unit we have developed for students at the secondary school level – that is, for students who are fifteen years of age or older. I intend to describe the testing unit in the following way: first, by outlining several general proposals for communicative language testing that guided our test development; secondly, by discussing briefly the process we followed in developing scoring procedures for the test's large-scale administration, and thirdly, by discussing briefly the test results. Overall, this chapter describes aspects of the development of valid and viable communicative language tests, using one specific example of a test that we have developed to assess the communicative performance of immersion students at the grade 9 level in order to illustrate this process. My intent is to provide an educational/pedagogical viewpoint to the development of communicative language tests rather than a measurement point of view. Having said this, I would add that I see no necessary long-run incompatibility of the two approaches.

Before turning to a discussion of the general proposals for communicative language testing that guided our test construction, it will be useful to describe briefly the actual components of our testing unit. The central component is a twelve-page student booklet titled

A Vous la Parole, which can be roughly translated as 'the floor is yours'. The booklet presents information about two summer employment possibilities for youth. Included in the booklet is information about job qualifications, the nature of each job, the location of each job, remuneration, working and leisure time, and living conditions. The student booklet also contains a list of government offices that offer, or organize, special programmes for the summer employment of youth, and it encourages interested students to write for more information.

The second component consists of a series of six communicative tasks commonly required of a native speaker of the language; four involving writing, two involving speaking. The four writing tasks consist of writing a letter, a note, a composition and a technical exercise. The two speaking tasks consist of an informal discussion among three or four students at a time and a formal job interview with an adult. More details about the nature of these tasks will be given later.

The third component consists of a *Teacher's Guide*, which outlines the objectives of the testing programme, explains how to organize and administer the test unit and instructs on scoring procedures appropriate to each communicative task.

General proposals for communicative language testing

A considerable literature now exists on communicative language teaching and on communicative language testing. I have no intention of reviewing that literature here. Rather, I would like to highlight four general proposals that we found highly relevant when faced with the practical problems of developing a communicative test of speaking and writing that could be administered on a large scale, and that could be sensitive to a wide range of proficiency levels. The four proposals are:

1. Start from somewhere
2. Concentrate on content
3. Bias for best
4. Work for washback

Start from somewhere

The first proposal, start from somewhere, is intended to suggest that from both a theoretical and practical viewpoint, test development should *build from* existing knowledge and examples. Practically, of course, starting from somewhere saves reinventing the wheel. But much more is at stake in this proposal than the somewhat superficial interpretation of simply saving time and energy – namely, the gradual and systematic growth in our understanding of the nature of communicative competence.

Several years ago, Michael Canale and I had the opportunity of reading much of the then existing literature on communicative language teaching and testing. We found that the literature contained quite different conceptions of communicative language teaching (Canale and Swain 1980a). We attempted to bring together the various viewpoints into a coherent, linguistically-oriented and pedagogically useful framework, arguing that communicative competence minimally includes four areas of knowledge and skills: grammatical competence, sociolinguistic competence, discourse competence and strategic competence (Canale and Swain 1980b). The assumption is that learners may develop competence in any of these areas relatively independently, that learners and native speakers will differ in their relative mastery of these skills and that the skills are involved in different degrees in specific language tasks.

Grammatical competence is understood to reflect knowledge of the language code itself. It includes knowledge of vocabulary and rules of word formation, pronunciation/spelling and sentence formation. Such competence focuses directly on the knowledge and skills required to understand and express accurately the literal meaning of utterances.

Sociolinguistic competence addresses the extent to which utterances are produced and understood appropriately in different sociolinguistic contexts, depending on contextual factors such as topic, status of participants and purposes of the interaction. Appropriateness of utterances refers to both appropriateness of meaning and appropriateness of form.

Discourse competence involves mastery of how to combine grammatical forms and meanings to achieve a unified spoken or written text in different genres such as narrative, argumentative essay, scientific report or business letter. Unity of a text is achieved through cohesion in form and coherence in meaning. Cohesion deals with how utterances are linked structurally to facilitate interpretation of a text. For example, the use of cohesion devices such as pronouns, synonyms, ellipsis, conjunctions and parallel structures serves to relate individual utterances and to indicate how a group of utterances is to be understood logically or chronologically as a text. Coherence refers to the relationships among the different meanings in a text where these meanings may be literal meanings, communicative functions, or social meanings.

Strategic competence refers to the mastery of communication strategies that may be called into action either to enhance the effectiveness of communication or to compensate for breakdowns in communication due to limiting factors in actual communication or to insufficient competence in one or more of the other components of communicative competence. (For further discussion of the nature of these components, see Savignon 1983).

The point of briefly reviewing these four proposed components of communicative competence is not to argue for or against them, but rather to indicate our starting point for the development of the *A Vous la Parole* testing unit. Other theoretical frameworks might have equally well provided a starting point for our test development.

Having a theoretical framework to start from is crucial. In a practical sense, its constructs guide the development of the stimulus material, the tasks to which the test-taker must respond, the scoring procedures and the subsequent analyses and interpretation of the data. However, even more is at stake. Regarding accomplishments in standardized testing from 1927 to 1977, Buros states: 'Except for the tremendous advances in electronic scoring, analysis, and reporting of test results, we don't have a great deal to show for fifty years of work' (1977, p. 10). Shoemaker (1980, pp. 38–39) argues that:

> improvements will not be brought about by further refinements of what
> generally has been done in achievement testing to date, nor in the
> development of more elaborate statistical procedures for analyzing data,
> nor in the expanded use of computer systems ... advances in the state
> of the art of achievement testing are directly related to advances in the
> conceptualization of the skill domains on which student achievement is
> assessed.

We think there is merit to Shoemaker's claim in the area of communicative language testing, and that only through the specification of a theoretical framework will, as Michael Canale (1983) has stated, 'the current disarray in conceptualization, research, and application in the area of communicative language pedagogy' disappear. Competing claims about the efficacy of communicative language teaching programmes, for example, cannot be verified unless we can agree upon what is meant by communicative competence and performance. In proposing the constituent components of communicative competence (Canale and Swain 1980a) and a general outline of communicative skills involved within each component (Canale and

Swain 1980b), we were proposing a starting point. What has been proposed are constructs that need to be validated. In fact, in a separate study on the development of bilingual proficiency being undertaken at the Ontario Institute for Studies in Education,[2] we are specifically testing the model using a multi-method, multi-trait design. (See Bachman and Palmer 1981, 1982 for discussions of this approach to language test validation.) Although the data from *A Vous la Parole* will not be sufficient for a complete trait-method analysis, they can, however, provide a separate, albeit limited, validation of the theoretical constructs. Starting from somewhere assumes that a 'scientific' rather than an 'evaluation' model underlies test design and implementation. Starting from somewhere allows one to build and refine one's concepts; starting from nowhere may mean another fifty years of little progress.

Concentrate on content

The second proposal, concentrate on content, refers to both the content of the material used as the basis of communicative language activities and the tasks used to elicit communicative language behaviours. The content of the material used as the basis for generating communicative activities – the *A Vous la Parole* booklet in our case – must be sufficient to generate each component of communicative performance. Similarly, the specific tasks – the composition, letter, note, technical exercise, informal peer discussion and formal interview – must in their entirety provide the opportunity to use each component of communicative language behaviour. The necessity of the first proposal, start from somewhere, becomes all the more obvious in this context: the 'somewhere' provides the framework that guides material and task development.

To ensure that our materials and tasks are capable of generating language that includes sociolinguistic, discourse, grammatical and strategic performance, we considered that the content needed to reflect at least four characteristics: it needed to be motivating, substantive, integrated and interactive in nature. These are essential characteristics from the learners' point of view; that is, the materials need to be motivating, substantive, integrated and interactive for the testee. For example, what is motivating in content for the learner may not be for the test-maker.

I would like now to illustrate how these characteristics are reflected in our testing unit of *A Vous la Parole*.

Motivating in content

In order to provide content that would be motivating for the target student population, we could have carried out a needs assessment-type survey. But we had neither the time nor the resources to do so. Instead we contacted several high school students from immersion and francophone programmes for input into the topic of the materials. In informal sessions with these students, which took place both within and beyond the school walls (over lunch in a restaurant, in fact), project staff explored topics of greatest personal relevance and interest to these students. Recurrent themes in these discussions included travel, summer employment, care of animals, camping, bicycle riding and music. Such topics as roller-skating and student exchange programmes were considered too boring, too old hat.

After these consultations with students, the project staff went to work on a booklet that would incorporate as many of these themes of interest as was feasible. Development of the materials focused on two possible summer employment opportunities: one was to work on a rock-concert series to be organized in one francophone locale, Sudbury, in the province of Ontario; and the other was to tend vegetable gardens and farm animals in the historic francophone park of Fort Louisbourg in the province of Nova Scotia.

Early drafts of the *A Vous la Parole* booklet and tasks were pretested in classes containing some of the same students who had provided input in the design stages. Most students were thrilled to see their opinions in print. Since then the materials have been pilot-tested with a number of students who had not provided input to the content of the materials, and their feedback has been overwhelmingly positive. Thus, while we cannot claim to have hit on two topics of interest to all young people of this age, it is clear that the themes are interesting and relevant to the large majority of the students we have tested.

A second aspect to the provision of content that would motivate the students is in the actual presentation of the materials. We therefore tried to present the material in as attractive a format as possible, subject to budgetary restrictions. As a result, the *A Vous la Parole* booklet includes a comic strip, cartoons, drawings, maps, photos, and the use of bright, cheerful colours.

A third aspect to the provision of motivating content is in the nature of the communicative tasks the students are required to undertake based on the stimulus material. We felt the tasks should reflect contexts for writing and speaking that do not end with the end of education – that is, activities that would represent real uses of French by those who may or may not be continuing their studies. For this reason, the tasks of writing a letter, a note for a bulletin board, a factual paragraph, an opinion composition and of conversing with peers and participating in an interview were used. Thus, although the tasks were not truly authentic in the sense that they were performed in school rather than in the actual setting, they represented tests of the students' ability to use their second language in situations reflecting real situations of interest to them.

Substantive in content

A second characteristic of the content is that it be substantive. By this is meant not only that information be presented to the students, but that some of it be new to them. There are several reasons for presenting substantive content, some of which is new to the learner. In part, the presentation of new information should contribute to the motivation of the learner to read the materials carefully. Already known content can be boring and provide little incentive to consider the content thoughtfully. Additionally, the presentation of new information ensures that 'real' communication can occur. That is to say, real communication frequently occurs as a function of an *information gap*.

For this reason, the *A Vous la Parole* booklet contains information about the two locales of the job opportunities being proposed. In the case of Sudbury, the students are informed that approximately a third of the population speak French; that a bilingual university is situated there where some courses taught are unique in Canada; that there is a rich and dynamic cultural life with theatres, orchestras, choirs, festivals, museums and an art gallery; that Sudbury is in the northeast part of Ontario close to a lake offering exceptional facilities for swimming and water skiing; and so on.

In the case of Louisbourg, the students are given a brief history of it as a French fort set up to protect French possessions, which later became an important fishing port and active commercial centre. The fort was later destroyed by the British and the town was abandoned. In 1961 the Canadian government decided to reconstruct Louisbourg, and in so doing relieved some of the hardships of unemployment caused by the closing of the coal mines in Cape Breton. Today the fort stands as a monument to the life and times of the eighteenth century; during the summer approximately 200 people are employed to live as the colonists did, growing and preserving their own food, making their own clothes, etc. In the case of both Sudbury and Louisbourg, maps, photos and illustrations support the text.

This information, much of which will be new to many students, provides the context of the tasks they will be required to carry out. In order that the students consider this new information without feeling anxious or threatened by the test situation, we begin *A Vous la Parole* by indicating to the students that 'the authors of this booklet have tried to propose some new ideas to you in a form that pleases you and will encourage you to learn and think about them'.

From our point of view, then, presenting content that is substantive fulfils three criteria for communicative language tests. First, it provides a context for the tasks the students will be required to carry out. Secondly, it is potentially one of the few means by which the students' attention can be focused on content rather than form, which represents one way of approximating real communication in a test situation. Thirdly, to the extent that some of the content is new for the learner, the test material fulfils a genuine communicative function by responding to an information gap between the learner and the materials.

Additionally, and perhaps more an issue of pedagogy or ethics than of communicative language testing, by presenting substantive content, some of which is new, the test-taker will not go away empty-handed – or should I say, empty-headed. He or she should have gained some new ideas or knowledge, or even some new linguistic insight by having taken the test. To put it another way, in taking a communicatively-oriented test, the testee should have the experience of being communicated to, and of being able to communicate. The 'meta-test' of this is that the testee has learned something from the experience of being tested.

We have discovered that translating these criteria into practice means being prepared to spend considerable time collecting relevant and accurate information, and translating this information into age-appropriate textual material. In fact, this phase of test development was equivalent to the development of curriculum materials for use in schools by our target population. I will return to this point below in the discussion of the proposal of work for washback.

Integrated in content

Neither the characteristic of being motivating in content nor of being substantive in content implies that the content be integrated – integrated, that is, in the sense of dealing with one theme around which *all* information and activities are centred. In the case of *A Vous la Parole*, the central theme is summer employment for youth. This theme provides the focus for all the tasks the students are asked to do. As the criterion for substance in content implies, the test resembles a lesson the students might encounter in class.

Although integrated content may not seem particularly radical for those who have been working on communicative language test development, when one compares the text and tasks of *A Vous la Parole* to a typical language test, the differences are profound in this respect. Even in the communicative test items that we developed several years ago as part of an item bank for the Ontario Ministry of Education to test French-as-a-second-language communicative skills (Ontario Ministry of Education 1980), the contexts established were minimal – limited to sentences or short paragraphs. And to a large extent, each test item involved a new context. In traditional discrete-point tests of language proficiency, little attention was paid to context, let alone to integrated situational contexts.

Integrated content is essential to communicative language testing because it gives clues to meaning – the more context, the more clues. When a test item can be responded to correctly on the basis of the immediate linguistic environment alone, to that extent the task is unlikely to be reflective of the communicative aspects of language behaviour.

Interactive in content

The fourth characteristic of the content of a communicative test is that it should foster interaction. This can be accomplished in part by providing new substantive content so that the learners may be stimulated to ask questions. Perhaps more important, though, in fostering interaction is the provision of content that includes opinions or controversial ideas. This offers the possibility of an exchange of opinions, or of the expression of one's own ideas and opinions on the topic.

For example, to start the students thinking about the topic of *A Vous la Parole*, we reproduced a letter written by Eric Martin, a Montreal student of the same age as the students tested. The letter reads roughly as follows:

Dear Friends,

I would like to give you my point of view on the subject of the life of today's adolescents. I am 15 years old and I am shocked to see the ignorance and the lack of respect that is shown us by adults. For adults, we are inferior beings and of little importance. For example, in stores and restaurants, adults are served before us even if we were there long before them.

What I find the most annoying is that adults also have priority over adolescents in the work world. It's always difficult for students between the ages of 15 and 17 to find a summer job, or a full-time job after graduation, and this will be even more serious this year. Contrary to what most adults think, adolescents are more conscientious and open than those of the same age in the 1960s and '70s. We have a big contribution to make to the work world.

The preoccupations of the adolescent of the '80s are not only the threat of nuclear war, the depletion of our energy sources, and the political divisions in our country. There is also a problem we don't talk much about at school: unemployment. It turns out that we are not well- - prepared for the labor market. What a shame! So much money and time wasted.

Adults judge our situation and make decisions for us without asking our advice. Then, when these decisions don't meet our needs, they ask why! Since they don't want to consult us . . . let's speak for ourselves . . . à nous la parole!

Eric Martin

In the associated task, the learners are asked to write a letter to Eric, giving their opinions about what Eric said. The students are specifically asked to say whether they agree or disagree and why, giving examples from their own experiences or those of their friends. In order to indicate the tone and style in which their letter is to be written, they are reminded that Eric is also a student of their age.

Similarly, the *A Vous la Parole* booklet describes, among other aspects of the summer jobs, the living conditions for the students: seven to ten students will live together in a large house along with two adults. Each one will have his or her own bedroom, but will share bathroom, kitchen, and living room. In the associated task, the students, in groups of three or four, are asked to discuss such questions as: What difficulties might occur when living together like this with others they don't know? What solutions might be sought in face of these difficulties? What would they do if two people in the house didn't get along at all? and so on.

Thus the content of the stimulus material can set the stage for some form of interaction, and the tasks provide the opportunity for the interaction to occur. Together they help the student to determine the tone, the style and even the format of the interaction. This is important if one is to be able to judge the learners' sociolinguistic competence.

Bias for best

The third proposal we used in guiding our communicative test development is bias for best. This means do everything possible to elicit the learners' best performance. There is a good reason for this from the point of view of test interpretation: if the testee does well, then it can be said with some confidence that the learner can do what is expected of him or her when given the opportunity. However, if the testee does not do well, then it is not clear whether this occurs because the testee cannot do what is expected, or is prevented from doing it because of distracting factors, or whatever. In other words, it is important to minimize the effect of the measurement technique on the test-taker's performance.

In *A Vous la Parole*, we introduced several procedures into the testing situation to bias performance positively. Recognizing that individuals work at varying paces, the testees are given more than adequate time to complete the task assigned for the day. In addition to being allowed to work at their own speed on the written tasks, they are given an opportunity each day to review the work they have previously completed and are encouraged to make any changes they wish (Odell 1977). Furthermore, they are given access to such reference materials as dictionaries, and are explicitly encouraged to use them. While the task is being done, the test administrator is expected to check that everyone is following the task instructions correctly.

In addition to these procedures, we decided that we could bias results for best performance by, in some cases, informing the students of what was being tested. Thus, in the introduction to *A Vous la Parole*, the students read that 'this short booklet serves as a basis for a series of exercises in order to evaluate your written and spoken French'. In the technical exercise, where the students are required to take the point form description of the tasks to be performed in the summer jobs and write them up in a paragraph in the same style as the rest of the text, it is explicitly stated that 'the goal of this exercise is to be able to evaluate your ability to produce complete sentences'.

In a similar vein, students are given suggestions about how to proceed with the task as, for example, in writing the composition, where they are advised 'to express their ideas clearly'. In some cases the students are given suggestions of points to include in their written work or discussion, and are explicitly told who their audience is and therefore the style, or level of formality, they should adopt. For example, in the note-writing task of *A Vous la Parole*, the students who choose the Louisbourg project are given the following instructions:

> In this exercise, we are asking you to write a note to other young people your age. *The style should therefore be informal.*
> In order to do this exercise, you must imagine that you are already a participant in the Louisbourg project.

Imagine the following situation: you have been in Louisbourg for several weeks now and you would like to visit Halifax next weekend. You decide to post a note in French in the cafeteria in order to find someone who can drive you to Halifax at that time. In your note, mention that you will share expenses for the trip and that you have a driver's license. Leave your telephone number or indicate where you can be easily met. Don't forget that you are writing to *someone your own age.*

Thus, to bias for best is to provide the test-takers with useful suggestions as to what and how to respond, to provide adequate time to complete the task, and in the case of written work, to have access to dictionaries or other reference material as well as to have the opportunity to review and revise their work.

Work for washback

The fourth and final proposal guiding our test construction is to work for washback. Washback refers to the effect a test has on teaching practices. It has frequently been noted that teachers will teach to a test; that is, if they know the content of a test and/or the format of a test, they will teach their students accordingly. This is not particularly surprising, given the frequency with which educational administrators use tests, legitimately or not, to judge teacher effectiveness.

Recognizing that neither teacher nor administrative behaviour is likely to change in this regard, and believing that teaching practices, especially in the higher grade levels of immersion programmes, could profit from some changes, we have tried to build teacher involvement into the development of the test, into its administration, and into its scoring. Before discussing how we have done this, I would like to digress briefly to comment on the suggestion that some changes in teaching practices might be appropriate in the higher grades of immersion education.

Immersion education has two goals – to foster the development of high levels of second language proficiency; and to do this at no expense to mother-tongue development, cognitive growth, or academic achievement. These goals are accomplished essentially through the teaching of academic content in the second language. Although at later grade levels more class time is used for the teaching of French *per se* (Swain 1981b), the emphasis is on teaching content. The result, typical of many classroom settings, is that the teacher talks and the students listen. Student responses are typically short and elliptical.

In other words, individual students are given relatively infrequent opportunities to use their second language, especially in extended discourse or in sociolinguistically variable ways. As might be expected in this situation, the students develop native-like *comprehension* skills (Swain and Lapkin 1982), but their *spoken* French has many non-native features in it (Harley and Swain 1978; Harley 1982). We think that the sorts of materials and related activities that form the *A Vous la Parole* testing unit exemplify teaching units that may help students to overcome these weaker aspects of their second language proficiency. Incidentally, no suggestion is being made that *all* teaching be activity-oriented and student centred. Rather the implication is that communicative activities form a legitimate and significant part of the teaching-learning process for both the acquisition of language and content knowledge.

To return to the main point, that of working for washback, we have for this reason involved teachers in the development of *A Vous la Parole*, first by establishing an advisory panel that includes teachers, as well as Department of Education (Saskatchewan) officials, to comment on this and other test units we are producing, while still in the development stage; secondly, by holding a workshop to explain the test and its purposes to teachers whose classes were involved in the pilot-testing of *A Vous la Parole*; thirdly, by asking these same teachers to help supervise the students being tested; and fourthly, by informally discussing with these teachers their reactions to the test unit and their perceptions of the students' reactions to it. In general, their reactions have been both positive and thoughtful, and many excellent suggestions have been made for revisions, which have been incorporated in the present version of the testing unit.

For practical reasons, in order to administer a test like *A Vous la Parole* on a large scale, teachers must be involved in its administration and scoring. It is simply too time-consuming and therefore too expensive to hire the additional personnel necessary for its administration. Moreover, for the very reason of working for washback, we consider it advantageous that teachers be involved in test administration and scoring. To this end, we have written a *Teacher's Guide* which explains the purposes of the testing unit, a step-by-step guide of how to administer the test, including the specific wording of the information and instructions that the teachers will give to the students, and a description of how to score the exercises, including a brief theoretical and empirical rationale for the scoring criteria as well as many illustrative examples.

Through these means of involving teachers in the development and/or administration and scoring of the test, we hope not only to change aspects of what is taught, but also to suggest alternative teaching-learning strategies.

Scoring

Although *A Vous la Parole* was developed for use in a large-scale, summative evaluation of immersion education, it could also be used for formative programme evaluation or for evaluating individual student performance. The scoring procedures developed should reflect the use or uses for which the test is intended and the theoretical framework that initially guided the test's construction.

We began the development of scoring criteria with the view that each task would reveal aspects of communicative language performance; that is, each task could be scored for grammatical, sociolinguistic, discourse, and strategic aspects of communicative language performance. We did not, however, attempt to predetermine the specific aspects of each component that would be scored. Rather, we worked from the data gathered during the pilot-testing phase to determine what specifically would be scored in each task and what scoring criteria would be used. By proceeding in this way, the scoring scheme was able to reflect the most salient aspects of each task response, and the full range of responses observed for any specific aspect. Neither could have been fully known before the data were examined.

Our approach in developing scoring procedures has been to begin comprehensively, using a mixture of objective counts and subjective judgements. Scoring the note to be posted on the bulletin board, for example, included counting the number of word order errors, anaphora errors and omissions, homophonous and non-homophonous morphological errors, and the points of information provided. Additionally, judgements were made on a three-point scale about the use of attention-getting devices, the overall appropriateness of lexical register used, the persuasiveness of the note, and the physical organization and appearance of the note as a note. For purposes of large-scale testing, we reduced the number of aspects scored based on analyses carried out with the pilot data. Several factors determined the final set of features scored.

One factor was the way the data clustered in correlational analyses (there were insufficient data to run factor analyses). At least one variable was selected from each cluster of scores that approximated a theoretically posited component of communicative competence. Which variable(s) were selected depended in part on their face validity. Additionally, several variables were selected because of systematic and interesting differences. For example, the pilot data suggested systematic differences between early immersion students (those starting an immersion programme at the age of five or six) and late immersion students (those starting an immersion programme around the age of thirteen) in their ability to write homophonous morphology correctly. Early immersion students tended to make more homophonous morphological errors in their writing (e.g. tu *a* dit; les enfants *pense*) than late immersion students, reflecting perhaps the stronger oral base of the early immersion students' language learning experiences.

Thus the steps we pursued in developing scoring procedures for large-scale testing involved the selection of variables from a much larger set, the larger set being determined by the nature of the responses to each task. By proceeding in this way, the criteria for each variable reflect the range of possible responses, and the original task responses have been exploited to their fullest in contributing to theory and practice.

Test results

A Vous la Parole has now been used in conjunction with other tests to evaluate immersion programmes at the grade 9 level in two Canadian provinces (Lapkin, Swain and Cummins 1983; Lapkin and Swain 1984a) and in two Ontario boards of education (Lapkin and Swain 1984b, c). In these evaluations, comparisons have been made between the results obtained by students participating in early immersion programmes, late immersion programmes and francophone schools.

Although there are some differences in results from evaluation to evaluation on individual variables, the overall pattern which emerges is similar. On aspects of grammatical performances, few differences between early and late immersion students emerge. This is in striking contrast to the results of comparisons made between immersion (early or late) students and unilingual French-speaking students: of the more than thirty comparisons made across the four studies, over 80% of them revealed a significant difference.

Similarly, on aspects of discourse and sociolinguistic performance, differences between early and late immersion students are few in number. Furthermore, less than 40% of the comparisons between immersion students and unilingual francophone students on the aspects of discourse and sociolinguistic performance measured were statistically significant.

The similarity in performance of the two immersion groups suggests that older learners are not at a disadvantage in the acquisition of at least some aspects of speaking and writing. The contrast between the frequency of differences in grammatical performance between francophone and immersion students with that of the frequency of differences in sociolinguistic and discourse performance is interesting, and suggests that there is something different about the learning of grammatical aspects of a language relative to the learning of discourse and sociolinguistic aspects.

Summary and conclusions

To sum up, four proposals useful in guiding the development of communicative language tests have been discussed using the testing unit of *A Vous la Parole* as illustrative material. The four proposals – start from somewhere, concentrate on content, bias for best and work for washback – assume a pedagogical function to language testing as well as a scientific approach to language test design and implementation. Although some may foresee inherent conflicts between these assumptions and those of measurement theory, I do not see any necessary long-run incompatibility.

The process followed in developing scoring procedures and criteria has also been discussed. The process involved moving from maximum detail and comprehensiveness to the selection of key variables that still permit comprehensiveness in the measurement of the postulated components of communicative performance. It also involved working from the testees' responses to each task. This ensured that the scoring criteria reflected the range of possible responses and that the salient component features elicited by each task are considered.

Although the administration and scoring of *A Vous la Parole* is time-consuming, it has proved possible to undertake. The results appear quite stable over similar populations. They indicate that early and late immersion students are quite alike in their communicative performance, and that early and late immersion students are more like francophone students in aspects of their discourse and sociolinguistic performance than in aspects of their grammatical performance.

The feasibility of using *A Vous la Parole* for individual student assessment on a large scale remains uncertain, primarily, because of the testing time involved. The testing unit is well-suited, however, for use by classroom teachers as a teaching unit through which communicative language performance of individual students can be assessed.

Notes

1. Actively participating in this project are Valerie Argue, Suzanne Bertrand, Jim Cummins, Daina Green, Gila Hanna, Jill Kamin, Sharon Lapkin, Laurette Levy and Merrill Swain.
2. See Chapter 7 for results of this study.

10 Minority students and learning difficulties: issues in assessment and placement*

During the first half of this century, the inappropriate use of psychological tests with linguistic and cultural minority students has served both to reinforce educators' misconceptions about the detrimental consequences of bilingualism and to justify the active eradication of students' first language (L1) in the school context (see Cummins 1983; Mercer 1973). In recent years there has been a greater awareness among educators in Western countries of the more obvious pitfalls associated with psychological testing of minority students. In the United States, for example, court litigation during the 1970s highlighted the discriminatory use of IQ tests to label disproportionate numbers of minority students as 'mentally retarded' and resulted in the adoption of assessment and placement procedures which attempt to take into account minority students' cultural and linguistic background. However, actual implementation of nondiscriminatory procedures has been slow as a result of both practical difficulties (e.g. lack of appropriate instruments and personnel) and conceptual confusion about many of the issues (e.g. what is a 'learning disability'?).

Because research on nondiscriminatory assessment for minority language students is still in its infancy, researchers are very far from getting definitive answers to many of the questions faced with increasing frequency by practitioners. Teachers and school psychologists, who have had virtually no training in issues related to minority students, are increasingly faced with the necessity to make decisions regarding the assessment and placement of minority students. This derives both from the large numbers of minority students in many

* This chapter is adapted from one that originally appeared as an article of the same title by J. Cummins in Y. Lebrun and M. Paradis (eds.) *Early Bilingualism and Child Development*. Amsterdam, Holland: Swets Publishing Service, 1984, pp. 47–68. Permission to reprint has been granted by Swets Publishing Service.

urban settings and the adoption in the United States and parts of Canada of mandatory procedures for identifying and treating exceptional students. An example of the rapid growth of the minority school population can be seen in the fact that in several Metropolitan Toronto school systems more than half of the students have learned English as a second language. Similarly, the ethnic minority student population in California is expected to become a 'majority' (i.e. more than 50% of the total) by the mid-1980s. The legal requirement to identify exceptional students' learning needs in the United States (as a result of Public Law 94–142, 1975) and in parts of Canada (e.g. as a result of Bill 82, 1979 in Ontario) means that an increasing number of minority students are being referred for educational and psychological assessment. Thus, clarification of the underlying issues concerned with the nature of academic learning processes among minority students has immediate practical significance.

In this chapter two research studies which investigated some of these underlying issues are described and the findings are related to the assumptions of many educators regarding the assessment and placement of minority students. The first study involved a re-analysis of data from a large-scale survey conducted by the Toronto Board of Education in the late 1960s (Cummins 1981c; see also this volume, Chapter 5) while in the second study the teacher referral forms and psychological assessments of 428 students from English-as-a-second language (ESL) backgrounds in a Western Canadian city were analysed (Cummins 1984). The findings of the first study are relevant to the question of how long it takes ESL students to approach grade norms in English academic skills, while the second study analyses the assumptions which educators bring to the teaching and assessment of ESL students.

Learning English as a second language: proficiency and time

There is evidence from several studies (e.g. Snow and Hoefnagel-Hohle 1978) that within about one and a half to two years of arrival in the host country most immigrant students have acquired relatively fluent and peer-appropriate face-to-face communicative skills in the second language (L2). Most teachers and psychologists would consider that immigrant students have sufficient English proficiency to be administered psychological and educational tests when they appear to have overcome obvious communicative difficulties in the L2. However, it was found in the study of ESL students' psychological assessments (Cummins 1984) that teachers and psychologists frequently commented on the fact that students' English communicative skills were considerably better developed than their academic language skills. The following examples illustrate the point:

> *PS (094)*: referred for reading and arithmetic difficulties in grade 2; Teacher commented that 'since PS attended grade 1 in Italy I think his main problem is language, although he understands and speaks English quite well'. Verbal (V)IQ 75; Performance (P)IQ 84.

> *GG (184)*: Although he had been in Canada for less than a year, in November of the grade 1 year, the teacher commented that 'he speaks Italian fluently and English as well'. However, she also referred him for psychological assessment because 'he is having a great deal of difficulty with the grade 1 program' and she wondered if he had 'special learning disabilities or if he is just a very long way behind children in his age group'.

> *DM (105)*: Arrived from Portugal at age ten and was placed in a grade 2 class; three years later, in grade 5, her teacher commented that 'her oral answering and comprehension is so much better than her written work that we feel a severe learning problem is involved, not just her non-English background'. Her PIQ (grade 5) was 101 but VIQ was below 70.

These examples illustrate the influence of the environment in developing English communicative skills. In many instances in this study immigrant students were considered to have sufficient English proficiency to take a verbal IQ test within about one year of arrival in Canada.

How valid is the IQ score derived from such a test? The findings of the re-analysis of the Toronto Board of Education data provide a clear answer to this question. The original survey (Wright and Ramsey 1970) involved 25% of the grades 5, 7, and 9 classrooms in the Toronto system. In this group of over 6,000 students there were 1,210 ESL students who had been born outside Canada. The re-analysis (Cummins 1981c) was undertaken in order to investigate the effects of age on arrival (AOA) and length of residence (LOR) on students' academic performance. The results for one of the English language measures, an adaptation of the Ammons Picture Vocabulary Test (PVT), are presented in Figure 10.1 (p. 186)[1]. Results for the other English language measures showed the same pattern.

It can be seen that it took immigrant children who arrived in Canada at the age of six or later between five and seven years (on the average) to approach grade norms in English vocabulary knowledge. The verbal skills measured on this test are very similar to those measured on verbal IQ tests such as the Wechsler Intelligence Scale

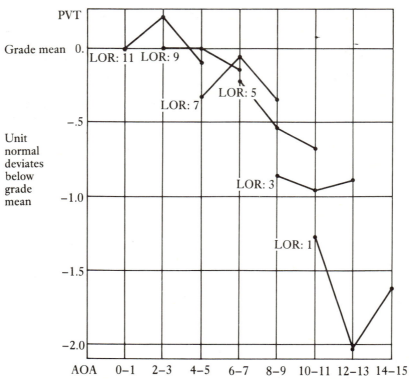

FIGURE 10.1   Age on arrival, length of residence, and PVT standard
scores

for Children – Revised (WISC-R) – where the vocabulary subtest
is typically the best predictor of overall IQ score. The developmental
pattern shown in Figure 10.1 implies that IQ scores should not be
regarded as valid indices of immigrant students' academic potential
until students have been in the host country at least five years. It can
be seen that students who had been in Canada for three years were
still about one standard deviation (i.e. fifteen IQ points) below grade
norms, but continued to progress more closely to grade norms as their
length of residence increased.

These findings carry an important theoretical implication in
addition to their obvious practical implications. Specifically, they
suggest that the language proficiency manifested in face-to-face interpersonal communicative situations differs in certain respects from the
proficiency required in many academic or test contexts. (See Chapter
8 for detailed theoretical discussion of this point.)

Language proficiency and IQ test performance among ESL students

The WISC-R is perhaps the most frequently used diagnostic tool in psychological assessments. In the present sample a WISC-R Performance IQ was calculated in 264 cases and a verbal IQ in 234. The median subtest scores on the WISC-R are represented graphically in Figure 10.2. Several things emerge clearly from the pattern of

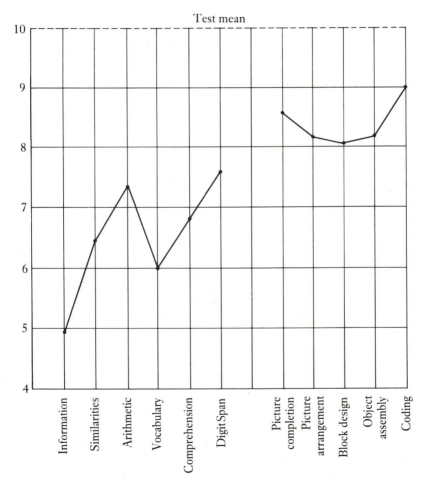

FIGURE 10.2   Median scale scores of ESL children on the WISC-R

scores. First, students perform much more closely to the average range on performance as compared to verbal subtests. There is little variation among performance subtests, although students tend to perform best on Coding where they come to within one scale point of the mean.

In contrast to the performance subtests there is considerable variation among verbal subtests. Arithmetic and Digit Span appear to be somewhat less culturally/linguistically biased against ESL students than the other verbal subtests. The worst offender in this regard is Information where the median scale score is only 4.6. This is not surprising in view of the fact that the Information subtest is the one which most obviously reflects the prior learning experiences of middle-class anglophone children and consequently excludes the learning experiences of those who have grown up in a different cultural and linguistic milieu. This can be seen from the following items from this subtest:

5. How many pennies make a nickel?
12. Who discovered America?
24. How tall is the average Canadian man?

It is ironic that the information subtest is almost invariably administered in the assessment of ESL children, whereas Digit Span, the least biased of the verbal tests is often omitted. In the present sample, Digit Span was given only to 104 students while Information was given to 242. The extent of the bias in the Information subtest can be seen from the fact that on this subtest, 70% of the ESL sample obtained a scale score of six or below and 34% obtained scores of three or below, compared to only 16% and 2.5% of the WISC-R norming sample. Yet in a large majority of cases, students' scores on the Information subtest were used in the calculation of verbal IQs.

It is worth noting that the pattern of ESL students' subtest scores shown in Figure 10.2 may have diagnostic significance. For example, when ESL children perform as poorly on Arithmetic and/or Digit Span as they do on the other verbal subtests, this may indicate specific problems in these areas which are not attributable to ESL background. Similarly, lower scores on the performance as compared to verbal subtests departs from the typical pattern and is thus diagnostically significant.

In summary, it is clear that in this sample the WISC-R is assessing ESL students' present level of functioning in English academic tasks rather than their ability, aptitude or potential. The qualitative analysis of the psychological assessments illustrates the interpretation pitfalls faced by psychologists in attempting to make sense of students' test performance.

Qualitative analysis of the psychological assessments: inferential paths and pitfalls

The approaches that psychologists take to the assessment of minority children's academic potential are categorized in Figures 10.3 and 10.4. The major distinction is whether the psychologist makes allowance for the child's ESL background in administering and interpreting the test and in inferring academic potential on the basis of test scores. The majority of assessments did make some such allowance, but a substantial minority showed little understanding of the role of the child's cultural/linguistic background in test and academic performance. The different 'inferential paths' that are involved within each of these categories will be illustrated by examples from the assessments.

A1. ESL background ignored

Because minority children often manifest no obvious deficits in English fluency, teachers and psychologists often assume that the

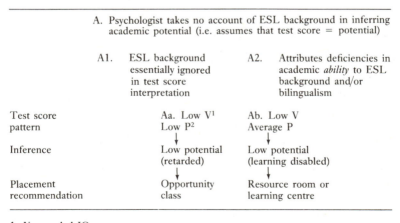

A. Psychologist takes no account of ESL background in inferring academic potential (i.e. assumes that test score = potential)

	A1. ESL background essentially ignored in test score interpretation	A2. Attributes deficiencies in academic *ability* to ESL background and/or bilingualism
Test score pattern	Aa. Low V[1] Low P[2] ↓	Ab. Low V Average P ↓
Inference	Low potential (retarded) ↓	Low potential (learning disabled) ↓
Placement recommendation	Opportunity class	Resource room or learning centre

1. V = verbal IQ
2. P = performance IQ

FIGURE 10.3 The inferential process in assessment of academic potential in ESL children

child's non-English background is not a relevant factor to take into account in interpreting test score performance. This is illustrated in the following assessment:

> *AC (005)*: AC was born in Portugal and referred for psychological assessment in grade 1 because of reading difficulties. In referring the child, the principal noted that 'AC learned English adequately while in the kindergarten but the teacher felt she would still have learning difficulties in grade 1. On the WISC-R, administered in May of the grade 1 year, the VIQ was 74, PIQ 93, and full scale (FS)IQ 82. The psychologist commented:
>
>> Psychometric rating as determined by the WISC-R places AC in the low average range of intellectual classification. There is a significant spread of 19 scale points between verbal and performance scores indicating higher aptitude for learning in the latter area of abilities . . . Overall, it is recommended that AC be considered for a resource room placement.

Comment: Logically, it is inadmissable to claim that the child's 'aptitude for learning' is greater in the performance than verbal areas since the linguistic and cultural assumptions of the test are not met. This child was reassessed on the WISC-R five months later and her scores were several points higher on both verbal and performance scales (VIQ 80; PIQ 100; FSIQ 88).

In summary, this assessment illustrates the fact that some psychologists have an extremely superficial understanding of the assumptions and consequent limitations of IQ tests. Because children's linguistic and cultural learning experiences were different from those assumed by the test, no inferences should have been drawn from the verbal score. However, the psychologist uncritically accepted the validity of WISC-R test scores, and consequently interpreted a low V, average-range P test pattern as indicative of low academic potential or learning disability. The usual recommendation under these circumstances was for resource room or learning centre placement. It is of course possible that this inference is correct, but it is equally possible that the low verbal score is a temporary function of inadequate development of English language skills.

A variation of the first pattern is where the psychologist attributes the child's low academic potential (which has been inferred on the basis of test performance) to the negative influence of the child's ESL background.

A2. Low potential attributed to ESL background

When psychologists do take note of the child's ESL background, there is a tendency to assume that the test score is nonetheless a valid indicator of academic *competence* (as opposed to performance) and to attribute deficiencies in this competence to the child's ESL or bilingual background. The assumptions that some psychologists make about the role of bilingualism in ESL children's development and about the use of the L1 at home emerge from many of these assessments. For example:

DR (110): 'A discrepancy of 20 points between the verbal and performance IQs would indicate inconsistent development, resulting in his present learning difficulties ... It is quite likely that the two spoken languages have confused the development in this area' (VIQ 94, PIQ 114; grade 1).

BC (024): 'BC, born in Italy, speaks Italian at home and this may be contributing to her problems at school ... poor verbal abilities development is most certainly influenced by her Italian background' (VIQ 65, PIQ 78; grade 1).

CG (057): 'The verbal IQ is 12 points lower than the performance IQ, although this is likely due to the effect of speaking both Italian and English ... there is *very* poor development indicated in the area of general information fund' (VIQ 74, PIQ 86; grade 4).

PE (282): 'It was noted that PE continues to have difficulty understanding and using the English language probably because the family speaks Italian at home. This seems to be a major handicap in PE's development of verbal skills' (PIQ 72; grade 2).

DA (125): 'DA came to Canada from Italy at age 5 and learned English at school. Italian is spoken in the home and this is likely to be contributing to overall below average verbal abilities development' (VIQ 80, PIQ 96; grade 7).

Comment: All of these assessments share the more or less explicit assumption that the children's experience with another language outside school exerts a detrimental effect on their verbal abilities development and on their school progress. What is wrong with this assumption? First, it assumes erroneously (see quantitative analysis) that the WISC verbal scale is a valid measure of verbal intellectual and academic *abilities* rather than indicative of present level of academic functioning in English. No attempt is made to ascertain what the child's verbal abilities might be in the mother tongue.

Second, there is no evidence that bilingualism or a home–school language switch, in themselves, have any negative effects on children's academic development (see Chapter 5). The research evidence, in fact, suggests that when continued development of minority children's L1 is promoted (either in home or school), the resulting bilingualism is educationally enriching (see Part One).

Thus, the only conclusion that is logically possible in situations such as those considered above is that the children's poorer cognitive/academic functioning in both test and school situations in comparison to middle-class monolingual Anglo-Saxon peers, *may* (or may not) be due to the fact that their cultural experiences are different from those assumed by the test and school, and that their *English language* vocabulary, information and concepts are *as yet* inadequately developed. No inference can logically be made about verbal abilities, aptitudes or potential on the basis of test scores or present academic functioning.

Conclusion

The assessments considered above reveal a lack of appreciation of the assumptions underlying IQ tests such as the WISC-R and a lack of understanding of the ways in which a bilingual or ESL background influences academic development in an all-English school programme. The psychologists and teachers, represented above, observe the fact that students from ESL backgrounds show low academic functioning in a school programme oriented towards the linguistic and cultural experiences of middle-class Anglo-Saxon monolingual children, and perform poorly on IQ tests constructed specifically to reflect these same middle-class Anglo-Saxon experiences; they ignore the relativistic perspective within which tests and schools operate and make absolute statements about ESL children's academic abilities, aptitude, competence or potential; and finally, many of them interpret the correlation between ESL background and low achievement as a causal relationship.

B. Allowance made for ESL background in test interpretation

The inferential paths that were evidenced when psychologists made allowance for children's ESL background in interpreting WISC-R scores are outlined in Figure 10.4. The first decision that the psychologist must make is whether to administer both verbal and performance batteries or only the performance battery. If both

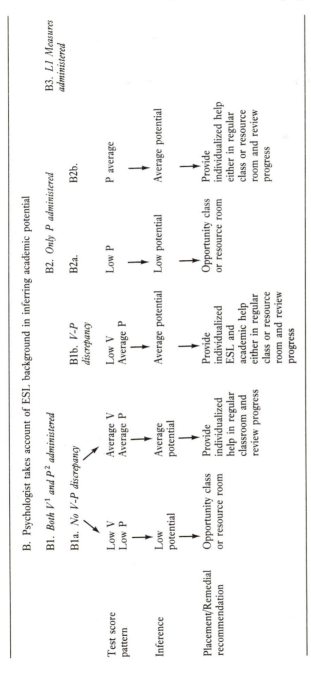

FIGURE 10.4   The inferential process in assessment of academic potential in ESL children

batteries are administered then a decision must be made as to the appropriate interpretation of the verbal score. The assessments that fall into the present category are distinguished from those considered earlier in that caution was always exercised and recommended in the interpretation of verbal scores. In some cases verbal IQs were not entered on the assessment report, in others they were entered but were clearly marked as minimal or invalid, while in the remainder, although the verbal IQ was entered in the normal way on the referral form, inferences were made only in regard to the child's present level of academic functioning rather than in regard to academic potential or aptitude.

When only the performance battery was administered, the interpretation of the test score was relatively straightforward, mainly because the screening it provided was relatively crude. There was no possibility, for example, of diagnostic interpretation of verbal-performance discrepancies.

Each of the inferential paths outlined in Figure 10.4 will be illustrated with examples from the assessment protocols.

B1. Both verbal and performance scales administered

B1a. *No verbal-performance discrepancy*

    MT (245): MT was born in Yugoslavia and arrived in the school system in grade 3. Her grade 4 teacher noted on the referral that MT 'is having difficulty with her school work, particularly written expression and comprehension. She tends to be inattentive and has poor work habits'. The teacher wanted to know whether or not MT would benefit from repeating grade 4, and whether or not language was still a barrier, and if so, to what extent. MT's VIQ was 73 (4th percentile) and PIQ was 84 (17th percentile). The psychologist placed an asterix opposite the VIQ and PIQ and indicated that 'these scores are suspect due to foreign language origin of student'. The report read as follows:

> MT appears to have low average ability – about 10–20 percentile. Verbal is of course suspect due to language but did not do much better on nonverbal tasks. Language mastery was considered more than adequate to grasp directions for nonverbal part of the test.

The psychologist suggested that language was still a barrier and made several recommendations for remedial assistance, among which was use of the resource room facility for areas such as reading and written and expressive language.

Comment: In the assessments that fall into this category the psychologists carefully consider the possible effects of cultural and linguistic background factors and interpret the performance IQ as an indicator of the child's potential. When PIQ is low, special class placement is usually recommended; when PIQ is average or high, specific remedial suggestions are usually made for helping the child within the regular classroom. Because there is not a significant discrepancy between VIQ and PIQ, difficulties in interpreting test performance are reduced. However, as is illustrated in the next section, interpretation of low VIQ, average or high PIQ test patterns is essentially a matter of intuition.

B1b. *Significant verbal-performance discrepancy*
In response to a low V, average P subtest profile, those psychologists who take account of the child's ESL background in inferring potential usually regard the PIQ as an index of academic potential and attribute the low VIQ to cultural/linguistic factors. For example:

> *BI (044)*: BI arrived from Portugal in grade 3 and was referred by her grade 5 teacher because of reading difficulties. Her WISC scores were VIQ 73, PIQ 106. The assessment report read as follows:
>> BI recently came from Portugal ($1\frac{1}{2}$ years ago). This, to a large extent, is reflected in a low overall verbal score. I believe BI to be of at least average potential as can be inferred from the 106 IQ on the performance subtests. BI requires enriched language arts experience. As with most new Canadians it is doubtful they can achieve at their grade placement. Resource room help is recommended.

> *RJ (312)*: RJ was a Chilean refugee who entered the school system in grade 3. The grade 3 teacher referred him in January noting that he is unable to work independently and finds it difficult to work for any length of time. She attempted to get him to do the grade 3 Gates McGinitie reading test but reported that 'he wasn't able to do it at all'. RJ received a VIQ of 64 and a PIQ of 100. As with the majority of VIQ assessments, Arithmetic was highest (7) and Information lowest (1). The psychologist commented:
>> It was quite evident that he has a great deal of difficulty with the English language . . . I would think that the verbal IQ of 64 obtained is *not* a true indication of ability but resulted primarily from language and cultural background. The nonverbal IQ of 100 is most probably more in line with this boy's verbal ability level.

The psychologist recommended that the itinerant ESL teacher be contacted for help.

Comment: Clearly, the conclusions drawn in these two assessments are reasonable and no other inferences can logically be drawn from the assessments. However, it is also quite possible that these children's academic difficulties derive from more than just their minority background. However, there is no way that potential long-term difficulties of this type can be detected from psychological testing administered only in English. The third example illustrates a case where it appears likely that serious learning problems were not identified by the psychological assessment.

> *UA (374)*: UA was born in South America and first referred by the grade 1 teacher who noted that she 'needs individual help in all aspects of the programme, since she's a new Canadian'. Although UA was seen by a psychologist at that time there is no record of test scores. UA was again referred in October of the grade 2 year by the resource room teacher who noted that her teacher 'says she cannot read. Has returned to grade 1 for reading period. UA also comes to me for help in resource room. She has extreme difficulty with word attack, particularly blending'. The teacher wanted to know what her IQ and potential were.
>
> UA was assessed on the WISC-R shortly after this referral. The psychologist noted that 'UA was quite friendly during the test interview. She spoke freely . . .' Her WISC-R scores were: VIQ 77; PIQ 104. The psychologist commented that
>
>> While she is progressing in English, she is still behind, resulting in a low overall verbal score. Performance (score) was within the average range and this may well be a measure of the girl's potential. It is possible that family or other problems are impeding motivation toward intellectual work. No real disability is obvious other than auditory memory and a rather impulsive manner of attacking her work.
>
> In April of the grade 2 year, UA was again referred for psychological and reading assessment. Her teacher noted that she had been in Canada for at least four years. 'We have had her taking reading with the grade 1 class and her classroom teacher has given her individual help. Her progress is minimal and she does not appear overly concerned with her lack of progress . . . She was in the resource room and it was found that her phonic attack skills, after one year of special help, did not improve at all.' The teacher wanted to know whether, in spite of the psychologist's first observation that 'there was "no real disability observed other than auditory memory" . . . UA has a sufficient degree of learning disability to warrant placement in a Learning Centre?'

Comment: The problem with attributing low VIQ performance to cultural/linguistic patterns is that many children from monolingual backgrounds who experience reading difficulties also manifest a low V, average P pattern. Thus, what is usually perceived as one of the main diagnostic clues on the WISC-R is eliminated when the VIQ is discounted, and consequently, the possibility of early detection of learning problems is reduced.

However, the data presented earlier on WISC-R patterns suggest that administration of the V scale is not necessarily useless or inappropriate under all conditions. Provided the child has been in the school system for a reasonable length of time (probably two years minimum) an exploratory use of the WISC-R V scale may be informative. In the first place, the child may score relatively high (close to P score) on the V scale, thereby suggesting that he or she is making good progress in English cognitive/academic skills. Secondly, deviations from the typical pattern of V subtest scores among ESL children (see Figure 10.2) can be very informative. The peaks at Arithmetic and Digit Span (when it is administered) are replicated in the vast majority of low V subtest profiles. Thus, a relatively low score on one of these subtests may provide a clue to a real learning problem.

The psychologists in the present sample who were sensitive to cultural/linguistic barriers to test performance often administered only the performance scale. The inferential paths which follow from this decision are considered in the next section.

B2. Only performance scale administered

When only the performance scale is administered, the PIQ is usually interpreted as indicative of the child's potential.

> *GU* (*177*): GU, whose parents were reported to speak mostly Polish, entered the system in grade 2 and was referred by her grade 3 teacher who noted that she was 'having trouble with English vocabulary and its meaning. She is very competent in other areas such as arithmetic. But she is missing a great deal, not being able to understand what she hears and sees'. The psychologist made no record of verbal scores (if administered). GU's PIQ was 73. The assessment read as follows:
>
>> GU was rather quiet during the interview and had little to say. English is a second language for her and she has difficulty expressing herself. For this reason, the verbal scores on the test should be disregarded. On performance items, GU scored consistently below

average. The scores may be somewhat lower than her actual ability level due to her lack of understanding oral instructions, however she probably would still score in the slow learner range.

Comment: Clearly, an average or high PIQ score provides useful information on students' nonverbal abilities, although a low PIQ needs to be treated somewhat more cautiously, depending upon the student's grasp of English. However, it is not necessarily valid to infer from an average or high PIQ that the student's overall academic potential is high, since reading and language arts achievement is generally more related to verbal ability than to performance. Possible visual perceptual difficulties may be noticed, but generally an assessment in which the P subtests alone are administered is usually capable of providing only limited answers to teachers' questions regarding academic potential or learning disability.

An obvious means of attempting to obtain more information on academic potential is to administer tests in the child's L1. A handful of assessments in the present sample employed this strategy.

B3. Assessment of L1 abilities

Assessment of L1 cognitive/academic abilities seems especially appropriate for the child who manifests a low VIQ, average PIQ WISC-R test profile and who has been in school in the host country for a relatively short time (less than two years). Testing L1 after this period is likely to be of suspect validity because of possible regression of L1 abilities due to lack of exposure to conceptually demanding input in L1. The assumption underlying the assessment of L1 abilities is that cognitive/academic abilities are cross-lingual or interdependent in L1 and L2 (see Chapter 5). In other words, an immigrant child's L1 cognitive/academic ability on entry to the school system will be an important factor determining the level of L2 cognitive/academic achievement. Thus, if L1 ability is well-developed it is likely that low VIQ and academic difficulties in English are a temporary function of ESL background. On the other hand, poorly-developed L1 and L2 cognitive/academic abilities would suggest that academic difficulties are likely to be more long-term.

The greater confidence which can result from assessing the child's abilities in his or her stronger language is evident in the following assessment.

SS (363): SS was referred by her kindergarten teacher who noted that she was immature and used baby talk. The speech and language assessment revealed that

SS was operating at a 2.5 to 3.0 age level for comprehension of English as compared to her chronological age of 5.3 ... Expressive language consisted mainly of one or two word utterances, or gestures ... In summary, SS exhibited a severe receptive and expressive language delay.

The psychological assessment showed SS's VIQ to be 51 and PIQ 70. The psychologist noted that during testing SS was quite chatty, but difficult to understand. One of the psychologists in the system who spoke Italian (as an L1) contacted the parents after these assessments and arranged to give SS an informal assessment in Italian in order to ascertain whether language development in Italian was normal; in other words, to ascertain whether the language delay was 'real' or a temporary function of ESL background. This informal assessment revealed that although the mother felt SS's Italian was good, SS could not name many common objects in Italian, she tended to respond inappropriately to questions given in Italian and used segments or sentence fragments. Thus, the assessment team felt reasonably confident in their diagnosis because of the congruence of symptoms in the two languages.

Comment: One must presume in this instance that the psychologist who spoke Italian was sensitive to dialectal variations. Also, it is to be hoped that advice was given to the mother about how the family could help the child's speech and language development *in Italian* in order to complement the English speech therapy the child would receive within the school system.

In general, assessment of the children's L1 proficiency can play an extremely important role in helping psychologists understand the nature of their academic difficulty. However, L1 assessment is not a panacea. Problems may exist in regard to the cultural and linguistic appropriacy of the L1 measure (e.g. dialectal variation) and no less caution in interpreting performance is called for than in an L2 assessment.

Summary and conclusions
The psychological assessments analysed in the present study illustrate the problems associated with applying assessment and placement procedures developed primarily to serve the needs of middle-class English-speaking students to students from linguistically and culturally diverse backgrounds. It is clear that there are many gaps in psychologists' and teachers' knowledge both about the limitations of psychological tests and about the development of academic skills in minority language children. Some of these gaps are due to the fact

that the knowledge base has not existed; others are due to the fact that the data which are available have not been adequately communicated to teachers and psychologists, either in university or in-service courses. Some of the information which many psychologists, teachers, administrators, policy-makers and academics concerned with special education and/or ESL students may not know about these issues is summarized below.

A. Test-related knowledge gaps

1. Psychological tests assess minority language students' present academic functioning, not potential.
Because IQ tests purport to assess academic potential, and because teachers explicitly request information about students' potential, many psychologists in the present study made inferences about minority students' potential, abilities or aptitudes which are logically inadmissible given the assumptions of the test. These inferences about low abilities can result in over-inclusion of minority students in special education classes, as documented by Mercer (1973). Contributing to psychologists' tendency to make logically invalid inferences is the apparent fluency of many minority students in English and the fact that psychologists and teachers have no information on how long it takes minority students to approach grade norms in English cognitive/academic skills. It is clearly not an easy task for a psychologist to admit that a psychological assessment has revealed little or nothing about a student's academic potential when the teacher has referred a student precisely in order to discover his or her academic potential so that realistic expectations can be established for the student.

2. The WISC-R subtest pattern of minority students may provide diagnostic clues.
The quantitative analysis suggested that, in general, performance subtests were more valid than verbal subtests. Thus, provided the student clearly understands the task demands, it is reasonable to make cautious and tentative inferences regarding nonverbal intellectual abilities based on performance scores. However, nonverbal abilities are usually less related to academic progress than are verbal abilities and thus are of limited usefulness as indicators of academic potential.

A large majority of low VIQ, higher PIQ, WISC-R profiles showed a characteristic pattern of peaks on Arithmetic and Digit Span and extremely low scores on Information. This implies that English language deficits interfere less with Arithmetic and Digit Span than with the other verbal subtests. Thus, deviations from the typical pattern for ESL students may be diagnostically important. For example, relatively low Digit Span may indicate auditory sequential processing difficulties rather than English language deficits; no such inferences (however tentative) about abilities or verbal aptitude are warranted on the basis of relatively low scores on Information, Similarities, Vocabulary or Comprehension.

Thus, it appears justifiable to administer the WISC-R Arithmetic and Digit Span subtests, as well as one of the other verbal subtests (not Information) for comparison purposes, to minority students who have been in the country for a reasonable amount of time (i.e. who have developed fluency or have been here about two years). However, obviously no IQ should be calculated on the basis of these scores and inferences should be tentative.

The present data suggest that there is very little justification for administering the Information subtest to minority students; however, if it is administered and a student's score is lower than on the other verbal subtests it should not be included in the calculation of an IQ score. For minority students Digit Span rather than Information should be the optional verbal subtest.

B. Student-related knowledge gaps

3. ESL immigrant students take five to seven years, on the average, to approach grade norms in English cognitive/academic skills.
There are many examples in the protocols where teachers refer for psychological assessment ESL students who have been in Canada for a relatively short amount of time (e.g. one to two years). Because the child's academic achievement is still poor, despite apparently good progress in English communicative skills, they wonder if some form of learning disability is involved or if the child has a low IQ. This is not surprising in view of the lack of any empirical data showing how long it takes immigrant students to approach grade norms in academic skills. The implicit assumption among teachers, psychologists, and policy-makers has been that English language deficits can no longer be invoked as a factor impeding school or test performance once the child has acquired relatively fluent English communicative skills. Normally, immigrant children can speak and understand English very well within about two years of arrival.

The re-analysis of the Toronto Board of Education data (Figure

10.1) shows that these assumptions are fallacious. Despite the fact that ESL students may be fluent in English within about two years of arrival, it takes between five and seven years, *on the average*, for students who arrive after the age of six, to approach grade norms in English cognitive/academic skills, i.e. the skills required on a verbal IQ test or on a standardized reading test (see also Chapter 5). The fact that students continue to approach grade norms with increasing length of residence suggests that inferences about students' academic potential based on a one-shot administration of the WISC-R within students' first five years in the host country are likely to underestimate potential.

4. Interpersonal communicative skills are very different from cognitive/ academic language proficiency

The difference between these two types of language proficiency is clearly shown in the numerous referrals which noted that students spoke and understood English well but were experiencing considerable difficulties in reading and academic aspects of English. The data considered in the previous section show that it can take up to seven years for immigrant students to approach grade norms in cognitive/academic skills despite the fact that their basic interpersonal communicative skills approach acceptable native-like norms much sooner.

The phenomenon is essentially the same as with pre-school children learning their first language, where, as Donaldson (1978) points out, children's understanding and production can give a misleading impression of skill with language *per se*. Thus, ESL children's rapid acquisition of facility in understanding and producing appropriate language in meaningful interpersonal contexts is not surprising. Add to this facility a near-native accent and the use of stock peer-group expressions and the surface manifestations of the ESL background have disappeared.

However, functioning in a typical academic context (e.g. learning to read by phonically based methods or performing verbal IQ tasks) often involves processing language which is stripped of its situational and interpersonal supports. Just as in a monolingual context, children's facility in basic interpersonal communicative skills provides little or no information about their academic language skills, no inferences are warranted about ESL students' cognitive/academic language proficiency or the validity of verbal IQ scores based on their interpersonal communicative skills.

5. ESL children's academic difficulties are not caused by the use of a non-English language in the home.

There were many instances in the protocols where children's low verbal IQ scores were interpreted as a valid reflection of verbal ability and attributed to the child's exposure to two languages. There were also several cases where the teacher or psychologist assumed that parents' lack of facility in English precluded them from helping their child academically at home and that the more exposure the child had to the mother tongue the greater the interference with the acquisition of English.

There is considerable research data available to refute these assumptions (see Section 2). A home–school language switch, in itself, does not cause academic problems. In fact, the research data suggest that the development of proficiency in two languages can be academically and cognitively enriching. However, in a minority language context a high level of bilingualism can usually be attained only when there is a strong emphasis, either in school or home, on the development of L1 skills. One of the reasons why this emphasis has been lacking in many cases is because minority parents and educators have assumed that an emphasis on L1 would be detrimental to English. Contrary to this assumption, the data suggest that a strong emphasis on developing L1 skills in the home may make an important contribution to the development of English academic skills.

Several studies have shown that the ways in which adults communicate with children is important for children's future academic success. For example, in a longitudinal study recently conducted in England, Wells (1981) has shown that children's rate of linguistic development is significantly related to the quality of the conversation they experience with adults and also that children's knowledge about literacy on entry to school is strongly related to the level of reading skills they attain in school.

Given the importance of the *quality* of parent-child communication in the home and the fact that concepts developed in L1 can easily be transferred to L2, it is clear that teachers' or psychologists' advice to parents to use English in the home can have potentially disastrous results. In many cases, parents will use broken English or a mixture of L1 and English and spend less time interacting with their children because they are not comfortable in using English. If minority language parents desire their children to become bilingual then they should expose them to as much L1 as possible in the pre-school years. Activities such as singing, playing, telling stories and reading aloud to children are extremely important not only in developing a high level of L1 proficiency but also in establishing a solid foundation for the acquisition of English skills and future academic success.

A clear policy implication of the present findings is that adequate interpretation of scores on a test like the WISC-R requires knowledge of more than just the characteristics of the test; it also depends upon familiarity with research findings on issues related to bilingualism and L2 acquisition among minority students. Given the increasing numbers of such students in many North American school systems, and the fact that a disproportionate number appear to experience academic difficulties (see Cummins 1981b), there is an urgent need for more than just token consideration of these issues in the training of school psychologists.

Notes

1. These data are the same as those discussed in Chapter 5 and illustrated in Figure 5.4 except that they are expressed in terms of progression towards grade means (standardized scores) on the PVT rather than in absolute PVT scores.

Section 6
A synthesis

In Part One it was suggested that the development of cognitive academic, literacy-related aspects of second language proficiency were primarily dependent on attributes of the learner, whereas the development of other aspects of language proficiency were relatively more dependent on the opportunities for input and use that the learners had in their second language. The proposal that the development of some aspects of language proficiency was relatively more dependent on learner attributes while other aspects were relatively more dependent on L2 input placed the interdependence hypothesis into a broader framework. That is, the hypothesis now proposes that those aspects of language which are interdependent across languages are those aspects which are relatively more dependent on attributes of the learner than on second language input and use for their development.

In Part Two, two different conceptions of language proficiency were discussed. One view of proficiency presented was that derived from an analysis of the requirements of language tasks with respect to two dimensions: the degree to which the language task is supported by non-linguistic contextual cues, and the degree of cognitive effort involved in task performance. The two dimensions combine to describe types of language proficiency. Literacy-related tasks, for example, would typically fall at the contextually-reduced and cognitively demanding ends of these dimensions. The claim is that academic performance and ability to perform more cognitively demanding, context-reduced language tasks are positively related.

A second view of language proficiency presented relates to the concept of communicative competence. This view is more embedded in linguistic theory as compared to the first view, which is more closely allied to psychological theory. It was proposed that a conceptual framework of communicative competence would minimally include grammatical competence, sociolinguistic competence and discourse competence. In other words, communicative performance involves drawing on all three types of knowledge. Thus far, no relationship between this view of communicative performance and academic success has been postulated.

In this concluding section, we attempt to pull together the attribute/input hypothesis and the two views of language proficiency which have been presented. The synthesis is firmly rooted in the data we have presented in the preceding chapters, and in data we are currently analysing from Portuguese background children. Essentially the argument is made that within cognitively demanding, context-reduced situations, grammatical, discourse and sociolinguistic proficiency are as much dependent on learner attributes as on L2 input and use for their development. Within cognitively undemanding, context-embedded situations, on the other hand, the development of grammatical skills is relatively more dependent on L2 input and use than are discourse and sociolinguistic skills.

The general implication which follows from this proposal is that L1-based education can promote the development of many aspects of L2 proficiency. L2-based education is particularly important, however, for the development of context-embedded grammatical proficiency, and will be most successful where the environment is rich with opportunities for interaction in the second language in purposeful, meaningful activities.

11 Towards a theory of bilingual proficiency development

The research studies reviewed in the previous chapters use a variety of methodological and analytical procedures to focus on the development of bilingual proficiency under different social and educational conditions. The initial chapters focused on the cognitive and linguistic consequences of different patterns of bilingual proficiency. This research suggested that access to two languages in early childhood can promote children's metalinguistic awareness and possibly also broader aspects of cognitive development. The conclusion that positive metalinguistic and cognitive consequences can result from the interaction between L1 and L2 is consistent with the notion of a 'common underlying proficiency' that emerges from the findings of bilingual education programmes for minority and majority language children. The interdependence of L1 and L2 development is further supported by studies of age and L2 acquisition and by investigations of bilingual language use at home.

These studies also allowed us to conclude that a distinction must be made between using language in a richly contextualized situation and using language where cues to meaning come primarily from the text itself. For young second language learners who are surrounded by native-speaking children of the target language, peer-appropriate levels of context-embedded L2 skills are attained more rapidly than is the case for academically-related aspects of proficiency. The frequent misuses of standardized tests with minority students and common misconceptions regarding the consequences of bilingual education can be traced to a failure to take account of the distinction between context-embedded and context-reduced language skills and the fact that academic skills in L1 and L2 are manifestations of the same underlying dimension.

A somewhat different perspective on these issues is provided by the research that focuses on the components of communicative competence. Several studies have used factor analytic methods to investigate the validity of various proposed components of communicative competence. Bachman and Palmer (1982), for example, examined the extent to which grammatical, sociolinguistic and pragmatic competence (discourse competence in the Canale and Swain (1980a) framework, subsequently elaborated in Canale (1983)) were separate traits. Although fairly clear conceptual distinctions can be made between these three components, studies using confirmatory factor analysis have produced what appear to be equivocal findings. Bachman and Palmer (1982), for example, were unable to distinguish grammatical and pragmatic competence in their study involving university level ESL students. Our own confirmatory factor analyses with grade 6 French immersion students (see Chapter 7) appeared to produce little evidence for the proposed distinctions.[1]

It has been assumed by many researchers that the way to assess the structure of language proficiency is to use factor analytic methods. Obviously the emergence of discrete factors would constitute evidence for the validity of distinguishing specific dimensions. On the other hand, it became clear to us as we worked with our data that failure of the hypothesized factors to emerge did not preclude the possibility of their being distinguishable using other analytical techniques or in other groups of learners with different language learning experiences. This is because factor analysis does not take into account the determinants of proficiency (as does, for example, regression analysis). Thus, the central empirical focus for future factor analytical studies should move from an attempt to test *absolute* models of communicative competence to an attempt to predict and test which components of communicative competence will become differentiated from each other for particular groups of language learners in specific acquisition contexts.

Furthermore, if in a factor analysis, predicted factors do not emerge, this does not mean that other analytical methods might not reveal distinct components. Indeed, further analyses of the grade 6 French immersion data suggested that the factor analytic procedures were providing a somewhat restricted perspective on the nature of second language proficiency. In particular, comparisons with native French speakers showed that differences between immersion and native French-speaking students were minimal on those discourse and sociolinguistic indices where grammatical knowledge plays an insignificant role in achieving correct performance. Differences between native speakers and immersion students, however, were highly significant on most grammatical measures and on those discourse and sociolinguistic measures where grammatical knowledge was essential for the production of correct linguistic forms. Additionally, it has been found that early immersion students approach native-speaker levels of proficiency in French reading and listening measures by the end of elementary school but significant differences remain with respect to oral and written grammatical skills (see Chapter 3). What seems to emerge from this is a distinction between grammatical competence, on the one hand, and sociolinguistic and discourse competence, on the other. Specifically, grammatical competence (and aspects of sociolinguistic and discourse competence that depend on grammatical knowledge) is acquired in different ways and determined by different factors than is the case with most aspects of discourse and sociolinguistic competence.

These findings raise the issue of what it is about discourse and sociolinguistic competence (abstracted from grammatical competence) that permits L2 learners in a French immersion programme to achieve close to native-speaker proficiency while grammatical competence remains far from native-like.

It is in considering what it is that permits immersion students to achieve native-speaker proficiency in non-grammatical aspects of discourse and sociolinguistic competence but not in grammatical competence that the two strands of research begin to come together and point towards a theoretical synthesis. Two questions are useful in synthesizing the research data: first, within context-embedded and context-reduced modes, to what extent is the development of grammatical, discourse, and sociolinguistic proficiency a function of exposure to the L2? Second, within context-embedded and context-reduced modes, to what extent are L2 grammatical, discourse and sociolinguistic proficiency related to cognitive or personal attributes of the individual?

Based on the data from both majority and minority situations that we have reviewed, the answers that we propose to these questions are as follows: first, in both context-embedded and context-reduced modes, the development of L2 grammatical proficiency is more dependent on exposure to L2 than is the development of L2 discourse and sociolinguistic proficiency. Second, within the context-embedded mode, the development of *grammatical* proficiency is not significantly related either to cognitive attributes of the individual or to L1 grammatical proficiency; within the context-reduced mode, on the other hand, cognitive and personal attributes of the individual play a significant determining role in the development of discourse, sociolinguistic and grammatical proficiency.

The Japanese minority student data reported in Chapter 5 provide a means of testing this hypothesis. First, it can be noted that variables concerned with morphology and syntax loaded on one factor which was distinct from the factors on which the cohesion measure loaded. Secondly, of all the variables derived from the interview with students in their second language, only the index of cohesion in describing a sequence of pictures loaded above .5 on the academic factor. Thirdly, indices of students' background and personal attributes were more strongly related to both English academic proficiency and measures of interactional style than they were to grammatical proficiency. The converse was true for indices of students' exposure to and use of English which related strongly to grammatical proficiency but much less to academic proficiency and interactional style. Examination of the determinants of academic proficiency and interactional style showed that cognitive variables accounted for the former relationships while personality variables accounted for the latter.

In another study involving grade 7 Portuguese background students in Toronto, we have also been examining the nature and determinants of different aspects of bilingual proficiency. We assessed students' grammatical, discourse and sociolinguistic competencies in both English and Portuguese and in both oral and written modalities. Three subgroups of students were assessed: one received oral grammar, discourse and sociolinguistic tests and written discourse tests in each language; the other two received either written sociolinguistic or grammar tests in each language. Of the written measures, only the written sociolinguistic test involved productive use of the language while the grammar and discourse tests involved multiple choice responses. A complete description of the measures is provided in Cummins, Harley and Swain (in press).

Our analyses revealed that grammatical proficiency in the oral (context-embedded) mode was unrelated across languages but there was evidence of some cross-lingual relationship for both oral discourse and sociolinguistic proficiency. In the written (context-reduced) mode, strong cross-lingual relationships were observed for grammatical, discourse and sociolinguistic proficiencies. Students' oral grammatical competence in Portuguese (their L1 but weaker language) was more strongly related to exposure to and opportunities to use the language than was the case for discourse and sociolinguistic competence.

These results are consistent with other research. Saville-Troike (1984), for example, studied a group of ESL learners to determine what second language learning variables best predicted academic achievement. She found that measures of L2 morphology and syntax did not correlate with academic achievement (as measured by the reading subtest of the CTBS), a finding in keeping with our results. She also found that although there was a low correlation between school achievement and time spent using English in interaction with peers or adults, there was a positive and significant correlation between learners' time spent using English and measures of their grammatical knowledge. Her findings suggest, as do our results, that grammatical proficiency is more dependent on exposure to and use of the L2 than is L2 academic proficiency. Saville-Troike concludes her study by noting that 'we need to recognize that there is a qualitative difference between the communicative tactics and skills that children find effective for meeting their social needs and goals and those that are necessary for successful *academic* achievement in the classroom' (1984, p. 216).

Thus, what emerges from these studies is support for the hypothesis that context-embedded grammatical L2 skills develop primarily as a function of exposure to and use of the L2 in the environment whereas L2 academic skills are relatively more dependent on cognitive attributes of the individual. The fact that French immersion students tend not to develop native-like patterns of French grammatical skills in either written or oral modalities can be accounted for by their limited opportunity to interact with native French speakers. The native-like proficiency attained by immersion students in reading and discourse skills can be explained by the fact that the development of these skills is determined by cognitive attributes of the individual, at least as much as they are by exposure to and use of the language in the environment.

Why do immigrant students attain proficient L2 grammatical skills within a relatively short time whereas French immersion students continue to experience difficulty in these areas? The same hypotheses appear relevant to this phenomenon. Immigrant students tend to gain peer-appropriate grammatical skills, at least in the oral modality, considerably more rapidly than is the case for immersion students precisely because their contact with and use of the L2 is far greater. The relatively greater influence of cognitive as compared to exposure/use variables on L2 academic skills development is consistent with the fact that for both immigrant and immersion groups, acquisition of age-appropriate L2 academic skills tends to take about the same time, roughly between five and seven years of exposure to L2.

The distinction between two broad types of L2 proficiency, namely, attribute-based and input-based proficiency allows the interdependence hypothesis to be placed into a broader framework insofar as all attribute-based aspects of proficiency will be interdependent across languages. This would not be the case for input-based aspects of proficiency. The model of attribute-based proficiency suggested by the present findings proposes that, for example, L1 and L2 interactional style (in the Japanese student data) are interdependent as a result of the fact that both are, to a significant extent, manifestations of personality attributes of the individual. Similarly, L1 and L2 cognitive/academic proficiency are interdependent as a result of the fact that both are, to a significant extent, manifestations of the same underlying cognitive proficiency.[2]

A synthesis of the two theoretical perspectives which oriented the data collection and analyses of studies reported in several chapters of this book has thus been suggested from the research evidence. In brief, L2 grammatical proficiency in both context-embedded and context-reduced modes is strongly dependent on the amount and type of input received by the individual. Development of context-reduced L2 grammatical proficiency also depends significantly on attributes of the individual whereas this is not the case, to the same extent, for L2 context-embedded grammatical proficiency. Discourse and sociolinguistic proficiency, on the other hand, appear less dependent on exposure to the L2 in the environment and, in the context-reduced mode, are attribute-based in that strong cross-lingual and cognitive relationships are observed.

Just as we might expect these relationships and the structure of language proficiency to vary according to learner attributes and the nature of the learning environment, so we might expect them to vary with the stage of acquisition. For example, if grammar is taught in the initial stages of L2 learning, then a relationship between cognitive attributes and context-embedded grammatical competence might emerge and grammatical and discourse competence might not show up as separate components of proficiency. Our hypothesis would be, however, that it would be L2 exposure/use variables that would primarily predict context-embedded grammatical proficiency in the long run. By the same token, L2 exposure/use variables may be strongly related to discourse proficiency in the early stages of second language learning, but cognitive variables, we would predict, would primarily explain the long-term individual differences.

In this concluding chapter we have attempted to sketch directions towards which a theory of L2 communicative proficiency might be oriented. A considerable amount of research is required, however, in order to fill in the specifics of such a theory. It is insufficient merely to examine relationships between hypothesized components of proficiency in just one language learning situation, for one group of learners who are at a particular stage of proficiency and cognitive development. Rather, specific hypotheses must be generated regarding the interactions between different components of proficiency (e.g. grammatical, discourse and sociolinguistic in both context-embedded and context-reduced modes) for learners at different developmental levels (e.g. adults, adolescents, young children) from different cultural and linguistic backgrounds (e.g. Chinese L1 compared to Portuguese L1), who are experiencing different patterns both of L2 exposure in the environment and formal teaching at school. Additionally, it is necessary to take account of the likelihood that very different relations may be observed in the early stages of acquisition than at later stages.

While this clearly represents a formidable research agenda, the importance for policy and practice of a coherent understanding of the nature and development of language proficiency is strongly suggested by the studies discussed in this volume.

Notes

1. Cziko (1984) suggests the factor analytic structure may have been masked due to statistical properties of correlational analyses (which standardize scores) and the use of standardized rather than criterion-referenced measures, both of which have the effect of reducing between-test variance.

2. In response to the input/attribute distinction, Richard Kidd asks (personal communication, 1985) 'Isn't this phenomenon at least partially explainable by the fact that languages are relatively incongruent grammatically, whereas sociolinguistic and discourse rules and procedures are somewhat more congruent? Obviously greater input is required for the acquisition of grammatical competence: the system is alien, and much more information is required for rule internalization. On the other hand, students are able to transfer discourse and sociolinguistic skills from L1 to L2 because there are so many similarities. You seem to place the causes of the interdependence phenomenon "within the learner". What I am suggesting is that the causes are perhaps more appropriately found in the subject matter learned.' If one considers that the subject matter learned interacts with attributes of the learner, then Kidd's suggestion, it seems to us, is not incompatible with our proposal.

Bibliography

Adiv, E 1980 *A comparative evaluation of three French immersion programs: grades 10 and 11*. Paper presented at the Fourth Annual Convention of the Canadian Association of Immersion Teachers (mimeo)

Adiv, E 1981 *An analysis of oral discourse in two types of French immersion programs*. Protestant School Board of Greater Montreal (mimeo)

Adiv, E and Morcos, C 1979 *A comparison of three alternative French immersion programs at the grade 9 level*. Protestant School Board of Greater Montreal (mimeo)

Allen, J P B, Bialystok, E, Cummins, J, Mougeon, R and Swain, M 1982 *The development of bilingual proficiency: interim report on the first year of research*. Ontario Institute for Studies in Education, Toronto

Allen, J P B, Cummins, J, Mougeon, R and Swain, M 1983 *The development of bilingual proficiency: second year report*. Ontario Institute for Studies in Education, Toronto

Andrew, C M, Lapkin, S and Swain, M 1979a *Report on the 1978 evaluation of the Ottawa and Carleton French immersion programs, grades 5–7*. Ontario Institute for Studies in Education, Toronto (mimeo)

Andrew, C M, Lapkin, S and Swain, M 1979b *Report on the 1978 evaluation of the French immersion program at Allenby Public School in Toronto, grades 4–6*. Ontario Institute for Studies in Education, Toronto (mimeo)

Andrew, C M, Lapkin, S and Swain, M 1979c *Report to the Elgin County Board of Education on the 1978 evaluation of the partial French immersion programs in grades 3, 6, 7 and 8*. Ontario Institute for Studies in Education, Toronto (mimeo)

Andrew, C M, Lapkin, S and Swain, M 1980 *Report on the 1979 evaluation of the French immersion program at Allenby and Glenview Public Schools in Toronto, Grades 5, 6 and 7*. Ontario Institute for Studies in Education, Toronto (mimeo)

Bachman, L and Palmer, A 1981 Basic concerns in test validation. In Read, J (ed.) *Directions in language testing*. Singapore University Press

Bachman, L and Palmer, A 1982 The construct validation of some components of communicative proficiency. *TESOL Quarterly* 16: 449–65

Bain, B 1975 Toward an integration of Piaget and Vygotsky: bilingual considerations. *Linguistics* 160: 5–20

Bain, B and Yu, A 1978 Toward an integration of Piaget and Vygotsky: a cross-cultural replication (France, Germany, Canada) concerning cognitive consequences of biliguality. In Paradis, M (ed.) *Aspects of bilingualism*. Hornbeam Press, Columbia, S. C.

216   *Bibliography*

Bain, B and Yu, A 1980 Cognitive consequences of raising children bilingually: 'one parent, one language'. *Canadian Journal of Psychology* **34**: 304 –13

Baker, K A and de Kanter, A A 1981 *Effectiveness of bilingual education: a review of the literature.* Office of Planning and Budget, US Department of Education, Washington, D.C.

Balkan, L 1970 *Les effets du bilinguisme Français-Anglais sur les aptitudes intellectuelles.* AIMAV, Brussels

Barik, H C and Swain, M 1975 Three-year evaluation of a large scale early grade French immersion program: the Ottawa study. *Language Learning* **25**: 1–30

Barik, H C and Swain, M 1976a A longitudinal study of bilingual and cognitive development. *International Journal of Psychology* **11**: 251–63

Barik, H C and Swain, M 1976b English-French bilingual education in the early grades: the Elgin study through grade four. *Modern Language Journal* **60**: 3–17

Barik, H C and Swain, M 1977a *Report to the Elgin County Board of Education re: evaluation of the 1976–77 partial French immersion program in grades 5–7.* Ontario Institute for Studies in Education, Toronto (mimeo)

Barik, H C and Swain, M 1977b French immersion in Canada: the Ottawa study through grade four. *ITL, A Review of Applied Linguistics* **36**: 45–70

Barik, H C and Swain, M 1978a Evaluation of a French immersion program: the Ottawa study through grade five. *Canadian Journal of Behavioural Science* **10**: 192–201

Barik, H C and Swain M 1978b Evaluation of a bilingual education program in Canada: the Elgin study through grade six. *Bulletin CILA* **27**: 31–58

Barik, H C and Swain, M 1978c *Report to the Toronto Board of Education re: evaluation of the 1976–77 French immersion program in grades 3–5 at Allenby Public School.* Ontario Institute for Studies in Education, Toronto (mimeo)

Barik, H C, Swain, M and Gaudino, V 1976 A Canadian experiment in bilingual education in the senior grades: the Peel study through grade 10. *International Review of Applied Psychology* **25**: 99–113

Barik, H C, Swain, M and Nwanunobi, E 1977 English-French bilingual education: the Elgin study through grade five. *Canadian Modern Language Review* **33**: 459–75

Ben-Zeev, S 1977a The influence of bilingualism on cognitive development and cognitive strategy. *Child Development* **48**: 1009–18

Ben-Zeev, S 1977b The effect of Spanish-English bilingualism in children from less privileged neighborhoods on cognitive development and cognitive strategy. *Working Papers on Bilingualism* **14**: 83–122

Bereiter, C, Engelmann, S, Osborn, J and Reidford, P A 1966 An academically-oriented preschool for culturally deprived children. In Hechinger, F (ed.) *Preschool education today*: 105–37. Doubleday, New York

Bereiter, C and Scardamalia, M 1982 From conversation to composition: the role of instruction in a developmental process. In Glasser, R (ed.) *Advances in instructional psychology. Volume 2.* Lawrence Erlbaum Associates, Hillsdale, New Jersey

Bereiter, C and Scardamalia, M 1983 Does learning to write have to be so difficult? In Freedman, A, Pringle, I, and Yalden, J (eds.) *Learning to write: first language/second language*: 20–33. Longman

Bhatnagar, J 1980 Linguistic behaviour and adjustment of immigrant children in French and English schools in Montreal. *International Review of Applied Psychology* 29: 141–58

Bialystok, E and Ryan, E In press. Towards a definition of metalinguistic skill. *Merrill-Palmer Quarterly*

Bloomfield, L 1933 *Language*. Holt, Rinehart and Winston, New York

Bruck, M 1978 The suitability of early French immersion programs for the language disabled child. *Canadian Modern Language Review* 34: 884–7

Bruck, M 1979 Problems in early French immersion programs. In Mlacak, B and Isabelle, E (eds.) *So you want your child to learn French!*: 42–7. Canadian Parents for French, Ottawa

Bruck, M, Jakimik, H and Tucker, G R 1976 Are French programs suitable for working class children? In Engel, W (ed.) *Prospects in child language*. Royal Vangorcum, Amsterdam

Bruck, M, Lambert, W E and Tucker, G R 1976 Cognitive and attitudinal consequences of bilingual schooling: the St Lambert project through grade six. *International Journal of Psycholinguistics* 6: 13–33

Bruner, J S 1975 Language as an instrument of thought. In Davies, A (ed.) *Problems of Language and Learning*. Heinemann

Bullock, A 1975 *A Language for Life*. HMSO

Burnaby, B 1976 Language in native education. In Swain, M (ed.) *Bilingualism in Canadian education: issues and research*: 62–85. Yearbook of the Canadian Society for the Study of Education, Volume 3. Western Industrial Research Centre, Edmonton, Alberta

Burnaby, B 1980 *Languages and their roles in educating native children*. OISE Press, Toronto

Burns, G E and Olson, P 1981 *Implementation and politics in French immersion*. Ontario Institute for Studies in Education, Toronto

Buros, O K 1977 Fifty years in testing: some reminiscences, criticisms, and suggestions. *Educational Researcher* 6: 9–15

Burt, M K and Dulay, H C 1978 Some guidelines for the assessment of oral language proficiency and dominance. *TESOL Quarterly* 12: 177–92

California State Department of Education. 1981 *Schooling and language minority students: a theoretical framework*. Evaluation, Dissemination and Assessment Center, California State University, Los Angeles

Campbell, R N and Gray, T C 1981 *Critique of the US Department of Education report on effectiveness of bilingual education: a review of literature*. Center for Applied Linguistics, Washington, D. C. (mimeo)

Canale, M 1983 From communicative competence to communicative language pedagogy. In Richards, J and Schmidt, R (eds.) *Language and communication*: 2–25. Longman

Canale, M and Swain, M 1980a Theoretical bases of communicative approaches to second language teaching and testing. *Applied Linguistics* 1: 1–47

Canale, M and Swain, M 1980b A domain description for core FSL: communication skills. In Ontario Ministry of Education, *The Ontario assessment instrument pool: French as a second language, junior and intermediate divisions*: 27–39. Ontario Ministry of Education, Toronto

Carey, S T and Cummins, J 1983 Achievement, behavioral correlates and teachers' perceptions of Francophone and Anglophone immersion students. *Alberta Journal of Educational Research* **29**: 159–67

Carringer, D C 1974 Creative thinking abilities of Mexican youth: the relationship of bilingualism. *Journal of Cross-Cultural Psychology* **5**: 492–504

Carroll, J B 1975 *The teaching of French as a foreign language in eight countries.* John Wiley and Sons, New York

Chesarek, S 1981 *Cognitive consequences of home or school education in a limited second language: a case study in the Crow Indian bilingual community.* Paper presented at Language Proficiency Assessment Symposium, Airlie House, Virginia

Chomsky, N 1965 *Aspects of the theory of syntax.* MIT, Cambridge, Massachusetts

Chomsky, N 1972 *Language and mind.* Harcourt Brace, New York

Clark, H H and Clark, E V 1977 *Psychology and language: an introduction to psycholinguistics.* Harcourt Brace Jovanovich, New York

Cohen, A D and Swain, M 1976 Bilingual education: the immersion model in the North American context. *TESOL Quarterly* **10**: 45–53. Reprinted in Alatis, J E and Twaddell, K (eds.) *English as a second language in bilingual education*: 55–63. TESOL, Washington, D.C.

Cohen, B 1980 *Language assessment umpire.* Santillana, New York

Cole, M and Griffin, P 1980 Cultural amplifiers reconsidered. In Olson, D R (ed.) *The social foundations of language and thought*: 343–64. Norton, New York

Cross, T G 1978 Mothers' speech and its association with rate of linguistic development in young children. In Waterson, N and Snow, C (eds.) *The development of communication*: 199–216. John Wiley, New York

Cummins, J 1976 The influence of bilingualism on cognitive growth: a synthesis of research findings and explanatory hypotheses. *Working Papers on Bilingualism* **9**: 1–43

Cummins, J 1977a Cognitive factors associated with the attainment of intermediate levels of bilingual skills. *Modern Language Journal* **61**: 3–12

Cummins, J 1977b Immersion education in Ireland: a critical review of Macnamara's findings. *Working Papers on Bilingualism* **13**: 121–7

Cummins, J 1977c A comparison of reading achievement in Irish and English medium schools. In Greaney, V (ed.) *Studies in reading.* Educational Company of Ireland, Dublin

Cummins, J 1978a Educational implications of mother tongue maintenance in minority-language groups. *The Canadian Modern Language Review* **34**: 395–416

Cummins, J 1978b Bilingualism and the development of metalinguistic awareness. *Journal of Cross-Cultural Psychology* **9**: 131–49 (see also this volume, Chapter 2)

Cummins, J 1978c Language and children's ability to evaluate contradictions and tautologies: a critique of Osherson and Markman's findings. *Child Development* **49**: 895–7

Cummins, J 1979a Linguistic interdependence and the educational development of bilingual children. *Review of Educational Research* **49**: 222–51

Cummins, J 1979b Cognitive academic language proficiency, linguistic interdependence, the optimum age question and some other matters. *Working Papers on Bilingualism* **19**: 197–205

Cummins, J 1979/80 The language and culture issue in the education of minority language children. *Interchange* **10**: 72–88

Cummins, J 1980a The cross-lingual dimensions of language proficiency: implications for bilingual education and the optimal age issue. *TESOL Quarterly* **14**: 175–87

Cummins, J 1980b The entry and exit fallacy in bilingual education. *NABE Journal* **4**: 25–60

Cummins, J 1980c Psychological assessment of immigrant children: logic or intuition. *Journal of Multilingual and Multicultural Development* **1**: 97–111

Cummins, J 1981a *Bilingualism and minority language children*. Language and Literacy Series. OISE Press, Toronto

Cummins, J 1981b The role of primary language development in promoting educational success for language minority students. In California State Department of Education, *Schooling and language minority students: a theoretical framework*: 3–49, Evaluation, Dissemination and Assessment Center, California State University, Los Angeles

Cummins, J 1981c Age on arrival and immigrant second language learning in Canada: a reassessment. *Applied Linguistics* **2**: 132–49

Cummins, J 1982 Interdependence and bicultural ambivalence: regarding the pedagogical rationale for bilingual education. National Clearinghouse for Bilingual Education, Rosslyn, Virginia

Cummins, J 1983 *Heritage language education: a literature review*. Ontario Ministry of Education, Toronto

Cummins, J 1984 *Bilingualism and special education: issues in assessment and pedagogy*. Multilingual Matters, Clevedon, Avon

Cummins, J and Gulutsan, M 1974 Some effects of bilingualism on cognitive functioning, In Carey, S T (ed.) *Bilingualism, biculturalism and education*: 129–36. University of Alberta Press, Edmonton

Cummins, J, Harley, B and Swain, M In press *The development of bilingual proficiency among Portuguese-background students in Toronto*. National Heritage Language Resource Unit, Toronto

Cummins, J 1982 *Language and literacy: let's get back to the real basics!* Ontario Institute for Studies in Education, Toronto (mimeo)

Cummins, J and Mulcahy, R 1978a Orientation to language in Ukrainian-English bilingual children *Child Development* **49**: 1239–42

Cummins, J and Mulcahy, R 1978b *Orientation to language among children in the Ukrainian-English bilingual program*. Report submitted to the Edmonton Public School Board

Cummins, J, Swain, M, Nakajima, K, Handscombe, J, Green, D and Tran, C 1984 Linguistic interdependence among Japanese and Vietnamese immigrant students. In Rivera, C (ed.) *Communicative competence approaches to language proficiency assessment: research and application*: 60–81. Multilingual Matters, Clevedon, Avon

Cziko, G A 1976 The effects of language sequencing on the development of bilingual reading skills. *Canadian Modern Language Review* **32**: 534–39

Cziko, G A 1984 Some problems with empirically-based models of communicative competence. *Applied Linguistics* **5**: 23–38

Cziko, G A, Lambert, W E and Gutter, R 1979 French immersion programs and students' social attitudes: a multidimensional investigation. *Working Papers on Bilingualism* **19**: 13–28

Cziko, G A, Lambert, W E, Sidoti, N and Tucker, G R 1978 *Graduates of early immersion: retrospective views of grade 11 students and their parents.* McGill University, Montreal (mimeo)

Darcy, N 1953 A review of the literature on the effects of bilingualism upon the measurement of intelligence. *Journal of Genetic Psychology* 82: 21–57

Diaz, R In press. Bilingual cognitive development: assessing three gaps in current research. *Child Development*

Dietrich, T G, Freeman, C and Crandall, J A 1979 A linguistic analysis of some English proficiency tests. *TESOL Quarterly* 13: 535–50

Dolson, D 1984 *The influence of various home bilingual environments on the academic achievement, language development, and psychosocial adjustment of fifth and sixth grade Hispanic students.* Unpublished doctoral dissertation. University of San Francisco

Donaldson, M 1978 *Children's minds.* Collins

Doyle, A, Champagne, M and Segalowitz, N 1977 Some issues in the assessment of linguistic consequences of early bilingualism. *Working Papers on Bilingualism* 14: 21–30

Dubé, N C and Hébert, G 1975 *St John Valley bilingual education project: five-year evaluation report 1970–1975.* Report submitted to the U.S. Department of Health, Education and Welfare

Duncan, S E and DeAvila, E A 1979 Bilingualism and cognition: some recent findings. *NABE Journal* 4: 15–50

Edmonton Public Schools 1980a *Summary of the evaluation of the bilingual English-Ukrainian and bilingual English-French program.* Edmonton Public School Board

Edmonton Public Schools 1980b *Implementation of bilingual (English-French) programs' third year 1979–80.* Edmonton Public School Board (mimeo)

Edwards, H P and Casserly, M C 1976 *Research and evaluation of second language (French) programs in the schools of the Ottawa Roman Catholic Separate School Board: annual reports 1971–72 and 1972–73.* Ontario Ministry of Education, Toronto

Edwards, H P, Colletta, S, Fu, L and McCarrey, H A 1979 *Evaluation of the federally and provincially funded extension of the second language programs in the schools of the Ottawa Roman Catholic Separate School Board: annual report 1978–79.* University of Ottawa

Edwards, H P, McCarrey, H A and Fu, L 1980 *Evaluation of second language program extensions offered in grades 3, 4, and 5: final report, 1979–80.* Ottawa Roman Catholic Separate School Board, Ottawa (mimeo)

Egan, L A and Goldsmith, R 1981 Bilingual-bicultural education: the Colorado success story. *NABE News* (January)

Ekstrand, L H 1978 *Bilingual and bicultural adaptation.* Unpublished dissertation. University of Stockholm

Epstein, N 1977 *Language, ethnicity and the schools.* Institute for Educational Leadership, Washington, D. C.

Feldman, C and Shen, M 1971 Some language-related cognitive advantages of bilingual five-year-olds. *Journal of Genetic Psychology* 118: 235–44

Fillion, B 1979 Language across the curriculum. *McGill Journal of Education* **14**: 47–60.

Fillmore, C J 1968 The case for case. In Bach E and Harmes, R (eds.) *Universals in linguistic theory*. Holt, Rinehart and Winston, New York

Fishman, J A 1968 Sociolinguistic perspective on the study of bilingualism. *Linguistics* **39**: 21–50

Fishman, J A 1976 *Bilingual education: an international sociological perspective.* Newbury House, Rowley, Massachusetts

Gardner, R C and Lambert, W E 1972 *Attitudes and motivation in second-language learning.* Newbury House, Rowley, Massachusetts:

Genesee, F 1974 *An evaluation of the English writing skills of students in French immersion programs.* Protestant School Board of Greater Montreal (mimeo)

Genesee, F 1976a *Addendum to the evaluation of the 1975–76 Grade 11 French immersion class.* Protestant School Board of Greater Montreal (mimeo)

Genesee, F 1976b The role of intelligence in second language learning. *Language Learning* **26**: 267–80

Genesee, F 1978a A longitudinal evaluation of an early immersion school program. *Canadian Journal of Education* **3**: 31–50

Genesee, F 1978b Second language learning and language attitudes. *Working Papers on Bilingualism* **16**: 19–42

Genesee, F 1978c Is there an optimal age for starting second language instruction? *McGill Journal of Education* **13**: 145–54

Genesee, F 1979 Scholastic effects of French immersion: An overview after ten years. *Interchange* **9**: 20–29

Genesee, F 1981 A comparison of early and late second language learning. *Canadian Journal of Behavioral Sciences* **13**: 115–28

Genesee, F and Lambert, W E 1983 Trilingual education for majority language children. *Child Development* **54**: 105–14

Genesee, F, Polich, E and Stanley, M H 1977 An experimental French immersion program at the secondary school level: 1969–1974. *Canadian Modern Language Review* **33**: 318–32.

Genesee, F, Tucker, G R and Lambert, W E 1975 Communication skills of bilingual children. *Child Development* **46**: 1010–14

Genesee, F, Tucker, G R and Lambert, W E 1978 An experiment in trilingual education: Report 3. *Canadian Modern Language Review* **34**: 621–43

Globe and Mail 1982 (January 9) *A dispute flares within suburb on the trend to French classes*

Goodman, K S 1967 Reading: a psycholinguistic guessing game. *Journal of the Reading Specialist* **6**: 126–35

Hakuta, K and Diaz, R 1984 The relationship between degree of bilingualism and cognitive ability: a critical discussion and some new longitudinal data. In Nelson, K E (ed.) *Children's language. Volume 5*: 319–44. Lawrence Erlbaum Associates, Hillsdale, New Jersey

Harley, B 1979 French gender rules in the speech of English-dominant, French-dominant and monolingual French-speaking children. *Working Papers on Bilingualism* **19**: 129–56

Harley, B 1982 *Age-related differences in the acquisition of the French verb system by Anglophone students in French immersion programs.* Unpublished Ph.D. dissertation. University of Toronto

Harley, B and Lapkin, S 1984 *The effects of early bilingual schooling on first language development.* Ontario Institute for Studies in Education, Toronto (mimeo)

Harley, B and Swain, M 1977 An analysis of verb form and function in the speech of French immersion pupils. *Working Papers on Bilingualism* 14: 31–46

Harley, B and Swain, M 1978 An analysis of the verb system used by young learners of French. *Interlanguage Studies Bulletin* 3: 35–79

Haugen, E 1953 *The Norwegian language in America: a study in bilingual behavior.* University of Pennsylvania Press, Philadelphia

Hébert, R *et al.* 1976 *Rendement académique et langue d'enseignement chez les élèves Franco-Manitobains.* Centre de Recherches du Collège Universitaire de Saint-Boniface, Manitoba

Hernandez-Chavez, E, Burt, M K and Dulay, H C 1978 Language dominance and proficiency testing: some general considerations. *NABE Journal* 3: 41–54

Ianco-Worrall, A 1972 Bilingualism and cognitive development. *Child Development* 43: 1390–1400

Imedadze, N V 1960 K Psikhologichoskoy priorade rannego dvuyazyehiya (On the psychological nature of early bilingualism). *Voprosy Psikhologii* 6: 60–8

Jones, R L 1977 Testing: a vital connection. In Phillips, J K (ed.) *The language connection: from the classroom to the world.* National Textbook Co, Skokie, Illinois

Krashen, S D 1980 The practical and theoretical significance of simple codes in second language acquisition and learning. In Scarcella, R and Krashen, S D (eds.) *Research in second language acquisition*: 7–18. Newbury House, Rowley, Massachusetts

Krashen, S D 1981 The 'fundamental pedagogical principle' in second language teaching. *Studia Linguistica* 35: 50–70

Krashen, S D 1982 *Principles and practice in second language acquisition.* Pergamon Press

Krashen, S D, Long, M A and Scarcella, R C 1979 Age, rate and eventual attainment in second language acquisition. *TESOL Quarterly* 13: 573–82

Labov, W 1970 *The study of nonstandard English.* National Council of Teachers of English, Champaign, Illinois

Labov, W 1973 The logic of nonstandard English. In Keddie, N (ed.) *Tinker, tailor, the myth of cultural deprivation.* Penguin

Lambert, W E 1977 The effects of bilingualism on the individual: cognitive and sociocultural consequences. In Hornby, P A (ed.) *Bilingualism: psychological, social and educational implications*: 15–27. Academic Press, New York

Lambert, W E and Tucker, G R 1972 *Bilingual education of children: the St Lambert experiment.* Newbury House, Rowley, Massachusetts

Landry, R G 1974 A comparison of second language learners and monolinguals on divergent thinking tasks at the elementary school level. *Modern Language Journal* **58**: 10–15

Lapkin, S 1982 The English writing skills of French immersion pupils at grade five. *Canadian Modern Language Review* **39**: 24–33

Lapkin, S, Andrew, C M, Harley, B, Swain, M and Kamin, J 1981 The immersion centre and the dual-track school: a study of the relationship between school environment and achievement in a French immersion program. *Canadian Journal of Education* **6**: 68–90

Lapkin, S and Swain, M 1977 The use of English and French cloze tests in a bilingual education program evaluation: validity and error analysis. *Language Learning* **27**: 279–314

Lapkin, S, Swain, M and Cummins, J 1983 *Final report on the development of French language evaluation units for Saskatchewan.* Ontario Institute for Studies in Education, Toronto (mimeo)

Lapkin, S and Swain, M 1984a *Final report on the evaluation of French immersion programs at grades 3, 6 and 9 in New Brunswick.* Ontario Institute for Studies in Education, Toronto (mimeo)

Lapkin, S and Swain, M 1984b *Second language maintenance at the secondary school level: final report to the Carleton Board of Education.* Ontario Institute for Studies in Education, Toronto (mimeo)

Lapkin, S and Swain, M 1984c *Second language maintenance at the secondary school level: final report to the Toronto Board of Education.* Ontario Institute for Studies in Education, Toronto (mimeo)

Lapkin, S, Swain, M, Kamin, J and Hanna, G 1983 Late immersion in perspective: the Peel study. *Canadian Modern Language Review* **39**: 182–206

Legaretta, D 1979 The effects of program models on language acquisition by Spanish-speaking children. *TESOL Quarterly* **13**: 521–34

Legaretta-Marcaida, D 1981 Effective use of the primary language in the classroom. In *California state schooling and language minority students: a theoretical framework*: 83–116. Evaluation, Dissemination and Assessment Center, State University of California, Los Angeles

Lenneberg, E H 1967 *Biological foundations of language.* John Wiley, New York

Leopold, W F 1949 *Speech development of a bilingual child. Volume 3.* Northwestern University Press, Evanston

Lepicq, D 1980 *Aspects théoriques et empiriques de l'acceptabilité linguistique: le cas du français des élèves des classes d'immersion.* Unpublished Ph.D. dissertation. University of Toronto

Lewis, E G 1976 Bilingualism and bilingual education: the Ancient World to the Renaissance. In Fishman, J A 1976: 150–200

Liedke, W W and Nelson L D 1968 Concept formation and bilingualism. *Alberta Journal of Educational Research* **14**: 225–32

Long, M H 1983 Native speaker/non-native speaker conversation in the second language classroom. In Clarke, M A and Handscombe, J (eds.) *On TESOL '82: Pacific perspectives on language learning and teaching*: 207–25. TESOL, Washington, D.C.

Luria, A R 1961 *The role of speech in the regulation of normal and abnormal behaviour.* Liveright, New York

MacNab, G L 1979 Cognition and bilingualism: a reanalysis of studies. *Linguistics* **17**: 231–55
Macnamara, J 1966 *Bilingualism and primary education.* Edinburgh University Press
Macnamara, J (ed.) 1967 Problems of bilingualism. *Journal of Social Issues. Special Issue* **23**: No. 2
Macnamara, J 1970 Bilingualism and thought. In Alatis, J E (ed.) *Bilingualism and language contact: anthropological, linguistic, psychological and sociological aspects: the twenty-first annual Georgetown University Round Table on Languages and Linguistics.* Georgetown University, Washington, D.C.
Mazzone, F J 1980 Current trends in Massachusetts in the assessment of language minority students. In Alatis, J E (ed.) *Current issues in bilingual education: the thirty-first annual Georgetown University Round Table on Languages and Linguistics*: 226–33. Georgetown University, Washington, D.C.
McEachern, W 1980 Parental decision for French immersion: a look at some influencing factors. *Canadian Modern Language Review* **38**: 238–46
McLaughlin, B 1978 *Second-language acquisition in childhood.* Lawrence Erlbaum Associates, Hillsdale, New Jersey
McLaughlin, B 1984 *Second-language acquisition in childhood. Volume 1: Preschool children.* Second edition. Lawrence Erlbaum Associates, Hillsdale, New Jersey
Mercer, J 1973 *Labelling the mentally retarded.* University of California, Berkeley
Modiano, N 1968 National or mother tongue language in beginning reading: a comparative study. *Research in the Teaching of English* **2**: 32–43
Morris, P 1974 *Self concept and ethnic group mixture among Hispanic students in elementary schools.* Unpublished Ph.D. dissertation. University of California, Berkeley
Morrison, F 1979 *French proficiency status of Ottawa and Carleton students in alternative programs: evaluation of the second language learning (French) programs in the schools of the Ottawa and Carleton Board of Education: sixth annual report.* Ontario Ministry of Education, Toronto

National Assessment of Educational Progress 1983a *Students from homes in which English is not the dominant language: who are they and how well do they read? No. 11-R-50.* Education Commission of the States, Denver
National Assessment of Educational Progress 1983b *Newsletter* **16**: Winter
Neisser, U 1967 *Cognitive psychology.* Appleton-Century-Crofts, New York
Neisser, U 1976 *Cognition and reality: principles and implications of cognitive psychology.* Freeman, San Francisco

Odell, L 1977 Measuring changes in intellectual processes as one dimension of growth in writing. In Cooper, C R and Odell, L (eds.) *Evaluating writing.* NCTE, Urbana, Illinois
Oeistreicher, J P 1974 The early teaching of a modern language. *Review of the Council for Cultural Cooperation of the Council of Europe* **24**: 9–16

Oksaar, E 1971 Sprakpolitiken och Minoriteterna. In Schwartz, D (ed.) *Identitet och Minoritet*: 164–75. Almqvist and Wiksell, Stockholm

Oller, J W Jr 1978 The language factor in the evaluation of bilingual education. In Alatis, J E (ed.) *Georgetown University Round Table on Languages and Linguistics* 1978: 410–22. Georgetown University Press, Washington, D.C.

Oller, J W Jr 1979 *Language tests at school: a pragmatic approach.* Longman

Oller, J W Jr 1981 Language testing research 1979–1980. In Kaplan, R, Jones, R L and Tucker, G R (eds.) *Annual Review of Applied Linguistics. Volume 1*: 124–50. Newbury House, Rowley, Massachusetts

Oller, J W Jr and Perkins, K 1980 *Research in language testing.* Newbury House, Rowley, Massachusetts

Olson, D R 1977 From utterance to text: the bias of language in speech and writing. *Harvard Educational Review* 47: 257–281

Olson, D R 1980 Social aspects of meaning in oral and written language. In Olson, D R (ed.) *The social foundations of language and thought*: 90–108. Norton, New York

Ontario Ministry of Education 1980 *The Ontario assessment instrument pool: French as a second language, junior and intermediate divisions.* Ontario Ministry of Education, Toronto

Osgood, C and Sebeok, T (eds.) 1965 *Psycholinguistics: a survey of theory and research problems.* Indiana University Press Bloomington (First published in 1954 by Indiana University Publications in Anthropology and Linguistics, Mem. 10.)

Osherson, D E and Markman, E 1975 Language and the ability to evaluate contradictions and tautologies. *Cognition* 3: 213–26

Paulston, C B 1975 Ethnic relations and bilingual education: accounting for contradictory data. *Working Papers on Bilingualism* 6: 1–44. Reprinted in Alatis, J and Waddell, K T (eds.) 1976 *English as a second language in bilingual education.* TESOL, Washington, D.C.

Peal, E and Lambert, W E 1962 The relation of bilingualism to intelligence. *Psychological Monographs* 76: 1–23

Pohl, J 1965 Bilinguismes. *Revue Roumaine de Linguistique* 10: 343–9

Posner, M I 1973 *Cognition: an introduction.* Scott Foresman, Chicago

Protestant School Board of Greater Montreal. *1972 report on the 1971–72 Roslyn French immersion results.* PSBGM, Montreal (mimeo)

Ramsey, C A and Wright, E N 1970 *Language backgrounds and achievement in Toronto schools.* Board of Education for the City of Toronto

Ramsey, C A and Wright, E N 1974 Age and second language learning. *Journal of Social Psychology* 94: 115–21

Rees, O 1981 Mother tongue and English project. In Commission for Racial Equality (ed.) *Mother tongue teaching conference report.* Bradford College

Rivera, E 1973 *Academic achievement, bicultural attitudes and self-concepts of pupils in bilingual and non-bilingual programs.* Unpublished Ph.D. dissertation. Fordham University, New York

Rosier, P and Holm, W 1980 *The Rock Point experience: a longitudinal study of a Navajo school program.* Center for Applied Linguistics, Washington, D.C.

San Diego City Schools 1982 *An exemplary approach to bilingual education: a comprehensive handbook for implementing an elementary-level Spanish-English language immersion program.* San Diego City Schools

Savignon, S 1983 *Communicative competence: theory and classroom practice.* Addison-Wesley, Reading, Massachusetts

Saville-Troike, M 1984 What *really* matters in second language learning for academic achievement? *TESOL Quarterly* **18**: 199–219

Schachter, J 1984 A universal input condition. In Rutherford W (ed.) *Universals and second language acquisition*: 167–83. John Benjamins, Amsterdam

Scott, S 1973 *The relation of divergent thinking to bilingualism: cause or effect.* McGill University, Montreal (mimeo)

Shoemaker, D M 1980 Improving achievement testing. *Educational Evaluation and Policy Analysis* **2**: 37–49

Shuy, R 1977 How misconceptions about language affect judgments about intelligence. In Wanat, S F (ed.) *Issues in evaluating reading*: 1–9. Center for Applied Linguistics, Arlington, Virginia

Skoczylas, V 1972 *An evaluation of some cognitive and affective aspects of a Spanish-English bilingual education program.* Unpublished Ph.D. dissertation. University of New Mexico

Skutnabb-Kangas, T 1984 *Bilingualism or not: the education of minorities.* Multilingual Matters, Clevedon, Avon

Skutnabb-Kangas, T and Toukomaa, T 1976 *Teaching migrant children's mother tongue and learning the language of the host country in the context of the sociocultural situation of the migrant family.* The Finnish National Commission for UNESCO, Helsinki

Siegel, S 1956 *Nonparametric statistics for the behavioral sciences.* McGraw-Hill, New York

Singer, H 1977 IQ is and is not related to reading. In Wanat, S F (ed.) *Issues in evaluating reading*: 43–55. Center for Applied Linguistics, Arlington, Virginia

Smith, F 1978a *Understanding reading.* Second edition. Holt, Rinehart and Winston, New York (First edition published in 1971.)

Smith, F 1978b *Reading without nonsense.* Teachers' College Press, New York

Smith, F 1982 *Writing and the writer.* Holt, Rinehart and Winston, New York

Snow, C E and Hoefnagel-Hohle, M 1978 The critical period for language acquisition: evidence from second language learning. *Child Development* **49**: 1113–28

Spence, A G, Mishra, S P and Ghozeil, S 1971 Home language and performance on standardized tests. *Elementary School Journal* **71**: 309–13

Spilka, I V 1976 Assessment of second language performance in immersion programs. *Canadian Modern Language Review* **32**: 543–61

Starck, R, Genesee, F, Lambert, W E and Seitz, M 1977 Multiple language experience and the development of cerebral dominance. In Segalowitz, S J and Gruber, F A (eds.) *Language development and neurological theory.* Academic Press. New York

Stern, H H 1973 *Report on bilingual education. Study E7 of studies prepared for the commission of inquiry on the position of the French language and on language rights in Quebec.* The Quebec Official Publisher

Stern, H H, Swain, M, McLean, L D, Friedman, R J, Harley, B and Lapkin,

S 1976 *Three approaches to teaching French*. The Ontario Ministry of Education, Toronto

Swain, M 1974 French immersion programs across Canada: research findings. *Canadian Modern Language Review* 31: 117–29

Swain, M 1975a Writing skills of grade three French immersion pupils. *Working Papers on Bilingualism* 7: 1–38

Swain, M 1975b More about primary French immersion classes. *Orbit* 27: 13 –15

Swain, M 1978a French immersion: early, late or partial? *Canadian Modern Language Review* 34: 577–85

Swain, M 1978b Bilingual education for the English-Canadian. In Alatis, J E (ed.) *Georgetown University Round Table on Languages and Linguistics 1978*: 141–54. Georgetown University Press, Washington, D.C.

Swain, M 1978c Home-school language switching. In Richards, J C (ed.) *Understanding second language learning: issues and approaches*: 238–51. Newbury House. Reprinted in Oller, J W and Richard-Amato, P A (eds.) 1983 *Methods that work*: 383–92. Newbury House, Rowley, Massachusetts

Swain, M 1978d School reform through bilingual education: problems and some solutions in evaluating programs. *Comparative Education Review* 22: 420–33

Swain, M 1979 Bilingual education: research and its implications. In Yorio, C A, Perkins, K and Schachter, J (eds.) *On TESOL '79: The learner in focus*: 23–33. TESOL, Washington, D.C.

Swain, M 1980 French immersion programs in Canada. *Multiculturalism* 4: 3–6

Swain, M 1981a Time and timing in bilingual education. *Language Learning* 30: 1–15

Swain, M 1981b Immersion education: applicability for non-vernacular teaching to vernacular speakers. *Studies in second language acquisition* 4: 1–17. Reprinted in Hartford, B, Valdman, A and Foster, C (eds.) 1982 *Issues in international bilingual education: the role of the vernacular*: 81–97. Plenum Press, New York

Swain, M 1981c Bilingual education for majority and minority language children. *Studia Linguistica* 35: 15–32

Swain, M 1983 Bilingualism without tears. In Clarke, M A and Handscombe, J (eds.) *On TESOL '82: Pacific perspectives on language learning and teaching*: 35–46. TESOL, Washington, D.C. (see also this volume, Chapter 6)

Swain, M and Barik, H C 1976a A large scale program in French immersion: the Ottawa study through grade three. *ITL, A Review of Applied Linguistics* 33: 1–25.

Swain, M and Barik, H C 1976b *Five years of primary French immersion: annual reports of the bilingual education project to the Carleton Board of Education and the Ottawa Board of Education up to 1975*. Ontario Institute for Studies in Education, Toronto

Swain, M and Barik, H C 1977 *Report to the Ottawa Board of Education and Carleton Board of Education re: evaluation of the 1976–77 French immersion program in grades 4–6*. Ontario Institute for Studies in Education, Toronto (mimeo)

Swain, M and Bruck, M (eds.) 1976 Immersion education for the majority child. *Canadian Modern Language Review* 32: entire no. 5

Swain, M and Burnaby, B 1976 Personality characteristics and second language learning in young children: a pilot study. *Working Papers on Bilingualism* **11**: 115–28

Swain, M and Cummins, J 1979 Bilingualism, cognitive functioning and education. *Language Teaching and Linguistics: Abstracts*, **4–18**. Reprinted in Kinsella, V (ed.) 1982 *Surveys 1: Eight state-of-the-art articles on key areas in language teaching*: 23–37. Cambridge University Press (see also this volume, Chapter 1)

Swain, M and Lapkin, S 1977 Beginning French immersion at grade 8. *Orbit* **39**: 10–13

Swain, M and Lapkin, S 1981 *Bilingual education in Ontario: a decade of research*. The Ontario Ministry of Education, Toronto

Swain, M and Lapkin, S 1982 *Evaluating bilingual education: a Canadian case study*. Multilingual Matters, Clevedon, Avon

Swain, M and Lapkin, S In press. Aspects of the sociolinguistic performance of early and late French immersion students. In Scarcella, R, Andersen, E and Krashen, S (eds.) *On the development of communicative competence in a second language*. Newbury House, Rowley, Massachusetts

Swain, M, Lapkin, S and Andrew, C M 1981 Early French immersion later on. *Journal of Multilingual and Multicultural Development* 1: 1–23 (see also this volume, Chapter 4)

Szamosi, M, Swain, M and Lapkin, S 1979 Do early immersion pupils 'know' French? *Orbit* **49**: 20–3

Tannen, D 1979 What's in a frame? Surface evidence for underlying expectations. In Freedle, R D (ed.) *New directions in discourse processing. Advances in discourse processing, Volume 2*: 137–81. Ablex, Norwood, New Jersey

Tannen, D 1980 Implications of the oral/literate continuum for cross-cultural communication. In Alatis, J E (ed.) *Current issues in bilingual education: the thirty-first annual Georgetown Round Table on Languages and Linguistics*: 326–47. Georgetown University, Washington, D.C.

Test de compréhension auditive, niveaux A and B. 1978 and 1979. Ontario Institute for Studies in Education, Toronto

Test de compréhension de l'écrit, niveaux A and B. 1978 and 1979 Ontario Institute for Studies in Education, Toronto

Torrance, E P, Gowan, J C, Wu, J M and Aliotti, N C 1970 Creative functioning of monolingual and bilingual children in Singapore. *Journal of Educational Psychology* **61**: 72–5

Toukomaa, P and Skutnabb-Kangas, T 1977 *The intensive teaching of the mother tongue to migrant children of pre-school age and children in the lower level of comprehensive school*. The Finnish National Commission for UNESCO, Helsinki

Tremaine, R V 1975 *Syntax and Piagetian operational thought*. Georgetown University Press, Washington, D.C.

Troike, R 1978 Research evidence for the effectiveness of bilingual education. *NABE Journal* **3**: 13–24

Troike, R 1984 SCALP: Social and cultural aspects of language proficiency. In Rivera, C (ed.) *Language proficiency and academic achievement*: 44–54. Multilingual Matters, Clevedon, Avon

Tsushima, W T and Hogan, T P 1975 Verbal ability and school achievement of bilingual and monolingual children of different ages. *Journal of Educational Research* **68**: 349–53

Tucker, G R 1975 The acquisition of knowledge by children educated bilingually. *Georgetown Monograph Series on Languages and Linguistics*: 267–77

Tucker, G R 1977 The linguistic perspective. In *Bilingual education: current perspective: Linguistics, Volume 2*: 1–40. Center for Applied Linguistics, Arlington, Virginia

Tucker, G R, Hamayan, E and Genesee, F 1976 Affective, cognitive and social factors in second language acquisition. *Canadian Modern Language Review* **32**: 214–26

van Dijk, T A and Kintsch, W 1983 *Strategies of discourse comprehension*. Academic Press, New York

Varonis, E M and Gass, S 1985 Non-native/non-native conversations: a model for negotiation of meaning. *Applied Linguistics* **6**: 71–90

Vellutino, F R 1979 *Dyslexia: theory and research*. MIT Press, Cambridge, Massachusetts

Vygotsky, L S 1962 *Thought and language*. MIT Press, Cambridge, Massachusetts

Wald, B 1984 *The development of writing skills among Hispanic high school students*. Paper presented at AERA, New Orleans

Warren, R M and Warren, R P 1966 A comparison of speech perception in childhood, maturity and old age by means of the verbal transformation effect. *Journal of Verbal Learning and Verbal Behavior* **5**: 142–6

Weinreich, M 1953 *Languages in contact*. Mouton, The Hague

Wells, C G 1981 *Learning through interaction: the study of language development*. Cambridge University Press

Wong Fillmore, L 1980a *Language learning through bilingual instruction*. University of California, Berkeley

Wong Fillmore, L 1980b Learning a second language: Chinese children in American classroom. In Alatis, J E (ed.) *Current issues in bilingual education: the thirty-first annual Georgetown University Round Table on Languages and Linguistics*: 309–25. Georgetown University, Washington, D.C.

Wright, E N and Ramsey, C A 1970 *Students of non-Canadian origin: age on arrival, academic achievement and ability*. Research report No. 88. Toronto Board of Education

Yee, L Y and Laforge, R 1974 Relationship between mental abilities, social class and exposure to English in Chinese fourth graders. *Journal of Educational Psychology* **66**: 826–34

Index

academic achievement 211
acculturation 94
'additive' bilingualism 18, 33, 94, 110
Adiv, E 45, 46, 47
Aliotti, N C 10, 16
Allen, J P B 118, 136
analytic orientation 13, 17
Andersen, R 136
Andrew, C M 41, 45, 46, 57, 58, 61, 62, 63, 72, 73, 78
Argue, V 182
assessment 139–141, 156–157, 166, 183ff

Bachman, L 157, 158, 170, 208
Bain, B 5, 14, 15, 16, 20
Baker, K A 82
'balanced bilinguals' 4
Balkan, L 13, 20
Barik, H C 4, 6, 10, 15, 39, 41, 44, 46, 47, 58, 59, 61, 62, 63, 73, 104, 110
Ben-Zeev, S 10, 12, 14, 20, 21, 31
Bereiter, C 144, 149, 150, 151, 156
Berns, M 165
Bertrand, S 182
Bhatnagar, J 93
Bialystok, E 4, 118
bicultural ambivalence 101
bilingual education
    core FSL programmes 49, 53
    early partial immersion programmes 39, 41, 47
    French immersion programmes 33, 34, 78
    immersion programmes 36, 37, 38, 42, 43, 54

late immersion programmes 39
minority immersion programmes 34
principles of successful 100, 101, 105
Bilingual Education Project 44, 58, 62, 67, 79
bilingualism
    as a bonus 98, 109–110
    cognitive consequences of 6
    cognitive development and 3
    cognitive flexibility and 6
    definition of 7
    degree of 5
    dependent variables of 4
    early 99
    levels of 8
    measurement of 4
    metalinguistic development and 3
    through monolingualism 97, 105–109
Bloomfield, L 7
Bruck, M 13, 17, 19, 51, 58
Bruner, J S 146, 147, 150,152, 156, 160, 161
Bullock, A 143
Burnaby, B 17, 33, 49
Burns, G E 54
Buros, O K 169
Burt, M K 113, 142, 145

Canale, M 113, 117, 138, 151, 154, 157, 158, 168, 169, 208
Carey, S T 86, 92
Carleton Board of Education 58
Carringer, D C 16
Carroll, J B 46
Casserly, M C 41, 44

Champagne, M 10
Chesarek, S 93
Chomsky, N 141, 143, 146
Clark, F V 136
Clark, H H 136
Clarke, M 99
cognitive flexibility 6, 19
cognitive functioning 8, 18
cognitive processes
  embedded 148
  disembedded 149
Cohen, B 17, 33, 58, 89
Cole, M 147, 156
Colletta, S 74
communicative
  abilities 163
  competence 113ff, 151, 157,
    169, 205
  language testing 166ff
  use of language 143
  language performance 179–181,
    206
competence
  analytic 146–147
  discourse 168, 209
  grammatical 168, 209ff
  pragmatic 208
  sociolinguistic 168, 209
  species minimum 146
  strategic 169
Comprehensible input 117, 128–
  133, 135
comprehensible output 133
conceptual development 3
Crandall, J A 145
Cross, T G 131
Cummins, J 7, 9, 12, 14, 15, 16, 17,
  18, 20, 32, 39, 42, 45, 48, 57,
  73, 82, 84, 86, 87, 88, 89, 92,
  101, 103, 104, 109, 118, 128,
  136, 138, 139, 152, 155, 156,
  157, 160, 180, 182, 183, 184,
  185, 186, 204, 210
Cziko, G A 41, 52, 54, 136, 137,
  213

Darcy, N 8
De Kanter, A A 82
Diaz, R 4, 6
Dieterich, T G 145

divergent thinking 16
Dolson, D 92, 94
Donaldson, M 148, 149, 150, 152,
  156, 160, 202
Doyle, A 10
'dual-track schools' 62
Dubé, N C 11, 17
Dulay, H C 113, 142, 145

early bilingualism, 20
Edmonton Public School Board
  39, 82, 84
Edwards, H P 41, 44, 46, 74
Egan, L A ix
Ekstrand, L H 11
Engelmann, S 144
ESL, 139ff, 184ff

feedback cues 10, 14, 17
Feldman, C 11, 16, 20, 21
Fillion, B 143
Fillmore, C J 146
first language
  development 101, 110
  maintenance 97, 110
Fishman, J A 7, 17
Fok, A 165
'fossilization' 154
Freeman, C 145
Friedman, R J 39, 57
Fu, L 46, 74

Gardner, R C 101
Gass, S 116, 117, 130
Gaudino, V 39
Genesee, F 11, 13, 14, 39, 41, 42,
  43, 45, 47, 48, 49, 50, 79, 87,
  166
Ghoziel, S 93
Goldsmith, R ix
Goodman, K S 142
Gowan, J C 10, 16
grammatical proficiency 209
Green, D 88, 89, 103, 155, 157,
  182
Griffin, P 147, 156
Gulutsan, M 15, 16
Gutter, R 52

Hakuta, K 4, 6

Hamayan, E 49
Handscombe, J 88, 89, 99, 103, 155, 157
Hanna, G 41, 47, 54, 182
Harley, B 4, 6, 39, 45, 46, 57, 63, 166, 178, 210
Haugen, E 7
'head start' children 11, 20
Hébert, R 11, 17, 86
Hernandez-Chavez, E 113, 142
Hoefnagel-Hohle, M 184
Hogan, T P 9
Holm, W ix

Ianco-Worrall, A 11, 12, 20, 21, 23, 31
Imedadze, N V 20
'immersion' 8, 10, 11, 14
'immersion centres' 62
immersion
    early 39, 43, 45
    education 37, 38
    late 39
    programmes 75, 104
    total 39–40, 43
immersion student (personal communication) 132
'incipient contrastive linguistics' 13
'interdependence principle' 34, 35, 86, 87, 89, 90, 205, 212
interlingual interference 12, 20
IQ 8, 9, 10, 11, 12, 15, 17, 21, 50, 51, 52, 59, 68, 71, 75–76, 110, 140, 145, 150, 183ff

Jakimik, H 17
Jensen, A R 144, 145

Kamin, J 41, 47, 54, 63, 182
Kidd, R 213
Kinsella, V 7
Kintsch, W 136
Krashen, S D 48, 87, 117, 128, 130, 131, 132, 159

Labov, W 138, 141, 144, 145, 146, 156, 160
Laforge, R 93, 94
Lambert, W E 8, 11, 13, 14, 15, 16, 17, 18, 20, 33, 41, 43, 45, 52, 53, 54, 57, 58, 73, 101, 166
Landry, R G 16
language learning disabilities 51, 138, 140
language proficiency
    and academic performance 152
    assumptions about 141
    cognitive deficit 144
    context-embedded 154ff
    context-reduced 155ff
    factor 113
    first language 34, 46
    global 146
    measures of 113
    nature of 113, 140
    second language 34, 39
    threshold level of 55
    traits 116ff
Lapkin, S 4, 6, 37, 38, 39, 41, 42, 45, 46, 47, 48, 54, 57, 58, 61, 62, 63, 67, 72, 73, 78, 104, 110, 128, 129, 166, 178, 180, 182
Lebrun, Y 183
Legaretta-Marcaida, D 102, 106, 107, 108
Lenneberg, E H 141, 143
Leopold, W F 20
Lepicq, D 46
Levy, L 182
Lewis, E G ix
Liedke, W W 15, 20
linguistic advantage 3
linguistic 'double standard' 43, 46
Long, M H 48, 87, 117, 130
Low, G 165
Luria, A R 5

MacNab, G L 4, 5
Macnamara, J 4, 7, 8, 9, 17, 95
Madden, C 116
majority language groups 17
Markman, E 22, 23, 24, 25, 29, 31
Martin, E 174, 175
'maximum exposure' hypothesis 80, 94
Mazzone, F J 140
McCarrey, H A 46, 74

McEachern, W 42
McLaughlin, B 3, 105
McLean, L D 39, 57
Mercer, J 183, 200
metalinguistic awareness 21, 32,
  207
minority language
  children 104
  groups 12, 15, 17
Mishra, S P 93
model
  common underlying
    proficiency (CUP) 82, 86, 87,
    94, 97
  separate underlying
    proficiency (SUP) 81, 95
Morcos, C 47
Morris, P 102
Morrison, F 47
Mougeon, R 118, 136
Mulcahy, R 12, 14, 84, 92

Nakajima, K 88, 89, 103, 155, 157
National Assessment of
  Educational Progress 93
Neisser, U 142
Nelson, L D 15, 20
New York Times 80
Nwanunobi, E 39, 41

Odell, L 176
Oestreicher, J P 7
Oksaar, E 7
Oller, J W Jr. 113, 138, 141, 142,
  143, 145, 156, 157, 160
Olson, D R 54, 147, 148, 150,
  152, 156
Ontario Ministry of Education 174
Osborn, J 144
Osgood, C 7
Osherson, D E 22, 23, 24, 25, 29,
  31
Ottawa Board of Education 58

Palmer, A 157, 158, 170, 208
Paradis, M 183
Paulston, C B 17
Peal, E 8, 15, 16, 20
Perkins, K 141, 142
Piaget, J 149

Pohl, J 7
Polich, E 39
Posner, M I 150
Protestant School Board of
  Greater Montreal 41

Ramsey, C A 88, 89, 186
Rees, O 85
Reidford, P A 144
Rivera, E 102
Rosier, P ix
Ryan, E 4

San Diego City Schools 86
Savignon, S 165, 169
Saville-Troike, M 210, 211
Scarcella, R C 48, 87
Scardamalia, M 149, 150, 151, 156
Schachter, J 128, 132
Scott, S 16
Sebeok, T 7
Segalowitz, N 10
Seitz, M 13
Shen, M 11, 16, 20, 21
Shoemaker, D M 169
Shuy, R 144, 145
Sidoti, N 54
Siegel, S 27
Singer, H 150
Skoczylas, V 102
Skutnabb-Kangas, T 9, 18, 93
Smith, F 132, 142, 150, 158
Snow, C E 184
socio-economic status (SES) 17,
  138, 156
Spence, A G 93
Spilka, I V 45
Stanley, M H 39
Starck, R 13
Stern, H H 7, 39, 57
'submersion' 8
'subtractive' bilingualism 18, 33,
  94
Swain, M 4, 6, 7, 8, 10, 15, 17, 18,
  19, 33, 36, 37, 38, 39, 41, 42,
  44, 45, 46, 47, 48, 49, 51, 53,
  54, 57, 58, 59, 61, 62, 63, 67,
  72, 73, 74, 78, 88, 89, 99,
  103, 104, 109, 110, 113, 116,
  117, 118, 128, 129, 136, 138,

143, 151, 154, 155, 157, 158, 165, 166, 168, 169, 170, 178, 180, 182, 208, 210
Szamosi, M 46, 104, 166

Tannen, D 142, 146
teaching
   language skills and 159, 178
'threshold hypothesis' 6, 18
Toronto Board of Education 184, 186, 201
Toronto *Globe and Mail* 54
Torrance, E P 10, 16
Toukomaa, P 9, 18
Tran, C 88, 89, 103, 155, 157
transfer 103
Tremaine, R V 11
Troike, R ix, 94
Tsushima, W T 9
Tucker, G R 11, 13, 14, 17, 19, 39, 43, 45, 49, 52, 53, 54, 57, 58, 73, 166

van Dijk, T A 136
Varonis, E M 117, 130
Vellutino, F R 138
verbal originality measure 16
verbal transformation illusion 14
Vygotsky, L S 5, 13, 20, 31

Wald, B viii
Warren, R M 14, 21
Warren, R P 14, 21
Weinreich, M 7
Wells, C G 138, 155, 159, 160, 161, 203
Wong Fillmore, L 106, 155, 157
Wright, E N 88, 89, 186
Wu, J M 10, 16

Yee, L Y 93, 94
Yu, A 5, 14, 15, 16